"WHAT ... THAT?"

The stories behind the greatest
(and most interesting) things ever said!

By the **"What Made Them Say That?"** Research Team

 Homecourt Publishers ■ Greenville, SC

"What Made Them Say That?"
The stories behind the greatest
(and most interesting) things ever said!

Copyright © 2003 by **Homecourt Publishers**

All rights reserved. No part of this book may be used or reproduced in any manner whatsoever without written permission, except in the case of brief quotations in articles or reviews.

Every effort has been made to make this book as complete and accurate as possible. However, *there may be mistakes*, both typographical and in content. Therefore, this text should be used only as a guide and not as an ultimate source of research. Homecourt Publishers shall have neither the liabilty nor responsibility to any person or entity with respect to any loss or damage caused by the information contained in this book.

For information or comments, write to:
Homecourt Publishers
2435 East North St., Box #245
Greenville, SC 29615-1442
info@homecourtpublishers.com
www.homecourtpublishers.com

(discounts available for educators)

Cover design by Carol Tornatore

Publisher's Cataloging-in-Publication Data

"What made them say that?": the stories behind the greatest (and most interesting) things ever said! / by the "What made them say that?" research team. — 1st ed. — Greenville, SC: Homecourt Publishers, 2003.

   p. ; cm.
   Includes index
   ISBN: 0-9741017-0-2

   1. Quotations. 2. Anecdotes.

PN6080.W43 2003	2003105904
080 – dc21	0307

Table of Contents

CHAPTER 1	**Familiar Expressions**	5
CHAPTER 2	**Sports & Athletics**	25
CHAPTER 3	**Arts & Entertainment**	43
CHAPTER 4	**Philosophy**	67
CHAPTER 5	**Religion**	85
CHAPTER 6	**Business & Economics**	105
CHAPTER 7	**Science & Technology**	119
CHAPTER 8	**Exploration**	141
CHAPTER 9	**Equal Rights**	151
CHAPTER 10	**American History**	163
CHAPTER 11	**American Wars**	203
CHAPTER 12	**World History**	231
CHAPTER 13	**World Wars**	257
	REFERENCES & ACKNOWLEDGEMENTS	274
	INDEX	278

"Grasp the subject, the words will follow."
— Cato the Elder
Roman Censor (234 BC-149 BC)

Chapter 1

Familiar Expressions

6—"What Made Them Say That?"

Edward Teach—the infamous "Blackbeard"

"Shiver me timbers!"

Ahoy mate! This phrase is usually connected with the infamous pirates of the late 1700's. That's a list that includes notorious men like Captain Kidd, Edward Teach (AKA Blackbeard), and Henry Morgan. These pirates commanded vessels that robbed and looted merchant ships, striking terror in the high seas.

The term *"Shiver me timbers"* comes from the type of ships that the pirates navigated. These ships consisted of large masts made of wood, or timbers. When the vessels unexpectedly ran aground, or if they were struck by a cannon, the masts shook violently. Thus, *"shiver me timbers"* became a saying to express the unanticipated surprise.

Because the saying is connected to pirates, it has also become part of an inaccurate myth. This misconception is usually one where a scruffy, uneducated man wearing an eye patch forces a prisoner to walk the plank and yells, in his poor English, *"Shiver me timbers!"* In truth, pirates were often educated and certainly capable. Captain Kidd was originally a shipowner employed by the British government, and Henry Morgan was even knighted by King Charles II. As for Blackbeard, his demise came only after the governor of Virginia was forced to employ two British ships to hunt him down off the coast of North Carolina.

7—Familiar Expressions

"When in Rome, do as the Romans do."

Around 390 AD, Saint Augustine approached his mentor, Saint Ambrose, with a serious question—Ambrose responded with the most honored advice in history. At the time, Augustine and his mother, Monica, were living in Milan. On a visit to Rome, Monica realized that the Romans obeyed different fasting laws on the holy days than she was accustomed to. She wanted to follow her normal traditions, but didn't want to be offensive. To play it safe, Monica asked Augustine to go to Saint Ambrose, the leading bishop in Milan at the time, and ask about the proper etiquette. His answer— *"When in Rome, do as the Romans do."*

And they did. As a result, the two were openly accepted by the Romans. In fact, before the incident, Saint Augustine was a little reluctant to follow in his mother's Christian beliefs. But apparently he changed his mind, becoming one of the most influential Fathers of the Church. It was Saint Ambrose who baptized him as an adult on Easter Eve in 387.

With all of the names and dates aside, it is really the phrase, *"When in Rome..."* that has lived on. It remains today a solid reminder to appreciate the customs of the host.

"You'd better mind your P's and Q's..."

If somebody ever tells you this, you're probably doing something that you shouldn't be doing. Today, the phrase *"mind your P's and Q's"* is a reminder to be cautious of inappropriate behavior and actions. For example, a friend might tell you, "You'd better mind your P's and Q's, and stop insulting that professional boxer." In actuality, this use of this phrase is not far from its original meaning.

It was in old England that the idea of *"mind your P's and Q's"* originated. In the pubs of the time, ale was ordered by pints and quarts. When a customer became rowdy and drunk, the bartender warned him to *"mind his P's and Q's"*—meaning mind his Pints and Quarts. The phrase caught on and expanded into everyday language. And, though it is no longer used as a literal expression in an English pub, the sentiment behind the phrase has remained very much the same— *don't get carried away!*

"Balls to the wall!"

This is not an allusion to any part of the male anatomy as it might first appear. The expression *"Balls to the wall!"* simply means to give an all-out effort, and it became commonplace in the English language during the second half of the 20th century. Today, a young runner might declare, "If I want a chance of winning the big race, I need to train balls to the wall from here on out." In other words, nothing is going to be held back.

The origin of the phrase comes from aviation during the Korean War, in the early 1950's. The controls on a fighter plane consisted of a throttle regulator—this was just a metal stick with a ball on the top for gripping purposes. Not too surprisingly, the pilots referred to these controls as "balls". In order to increase the plane's throttle, or speed, the pilot would push the throttle sticks towards the edge of the cockpit. Or, as it became known, he would push the *"balls to the wall!"*

But, the idea may have been around even earlier. Before airplanes, steam engines on railroad locomotives had speed governors that consisted of two steel balls connected to a vertical shaft. As the train sped up, the balls would spin, and the centrifugal force caused them to rise. Since the entire speed governor was encased in a metal housing, the balls would be near the wall of the housing when the train hit top speed. While the phrase wasn't absolutely known to exist during this time, it certainly would have been another appropriate origin of *"Balls to the wall,"* and the meaning would still be the same.

"It passed with flying colors!"

This is another one of those sayings that everyone knows, and nobody ever gives any thought to how silly it really sounds. How exactly does a color fly? Nonetheless, to say that something *"passed with flying colors"* is to say that it exceeded all expectations. A proud student might exclaim, "The test was hard, but I passed it with flying colors."

The phrase originates from the days when wooden sailboats frequently traveled across the ocean. Occasionally, one ship would pass another en route to its destination. In order to be recognized, the crews of both vessels would wave their flags (or colors) high on the mast. The flags, of course, were always flown with a great deal of pride. As a result, the ships did not just pass, they *"passed with flying colors!"*

The concept of *"passing with flying colors"* is also common in an everyday parade. When marching bands and other organizations stride past the crowds, a flagman, whose job it is to make sure that the crowd can see the group's *"flying colors,"* usually leads them.

"I'll have a baker's dozen."

Any time you ask for a dozen of something, you probably expect to get twelve of that something—one dozen widgets equals twelve widgets. But, when you ask for a *"baker's dozen,"* you are going to get thirteen of those same widgets. So, what's so special about a baker's dozen, and where did it come from? You can trace the phrase back in two ways.

First, thousands of years ago, it just wasn't an option for a baker to shortchange his customers. In fact, because it was so easy for him to bake bread that was lighter than it should be, he was always watched with a close eye. In the times of Babylonia, operating under the heavy hand of King Hammurabi, a baker that cheated his buyers could be subject to punishment as severe as having his hands cut off. Even in the 1200's, the British government imposed heavy financial penalties on any baker that was caught selling light loaves. Afraid of being falsely accused, bakers started adding another loaf of bread when they sold a dozen. This was just extra protection to make doubly sure that there was enough in the bag. Since loaves were all of slightly different sizes and weights, adding that thirteenth loaf was the only way to guarantee that there would be no complaints.

Another reasonable origin of a "baker's dozen" can be derived from when the baker wasn't selling directly to a customer. Instead, he may have been selling to a vendor who planned to resell the loaves of bread. In order for the vendor to make a profit, he would strike a deal with the baker to buy from him regularly if there was an extra loaf thrown in with each dozen. So, when the vendor ordered one dozen, he received thirteen individual loaves—or, as it became known, he got a "baker's dozen."

A Bad Reputation

"Your name will be Mudd!"

To warn a man that his *"name will be mud"* is to tell him that his reputation is on thin ice. And, it makes sense that the comparison to mud would be chosen—mud is messy and dirty. And, let's face it, *"your name will be roses"* just wouldn't have the same effect. That's the quick and easy origin of the expression—now for the more interesting part.

Dr. Samuel Mudd

On April 14, 1865, President Lincoln was assassinated by John Wilkes Booth at Ford's theater in Washington, DC. When Booth shot the president, he quickly jumped from the private box and onto the stage, breaking his leg in the process. The assassin was able to make a getaway, but he eventually had to stop and seek medical attention for his injury. Late that night, Booth arrived at the house of Dr. Samuel Mudd, and Mudd helped set the broken leg. He also housed Booth for twelve hours.

From that point on, Dr. Samuel Mudd's name was *"mud"* in more ways than one. He was accused of helping in the conspiracy to assassinate the President, and was sentenced to a lifetime in jail. Mudd claimed to be innocent, saying that he didn't know who John Wilkes Booth was when he came to him for help. It didn't matter, though, the doctor's reputation was ruined. This popularized the expression, **"your name will be mud"** by slightly changing the concept. It was now, **"your name will be Mudd."**

Because the conviction was a little shaky, President Andrew Johnson issued a pardon for Dr. Samuel Mudd after he had served only four years in prison. Still, the damage to the doctor's reputation could never be salvaged.

11—Familiar Expressions

John Wilkes Booth's assassination of President Lincoln was not a run of the mill shooting. In fact, it was a huge conspiracy. Here's a brief rundown of the events:

- In March 1865, John Wilkes Booth and other conspirators try to kidnap Abraham Lincoln, but the President's last minute change of schedule foils their plans.

- On April 14, Lincoln attends a showing of the play *Our American Cousin* at Ford's theater in Washington, DC. Booth sneaks into the presidential box and shoots the President.

- At the same time, Booth's accomplice, Lewis Powell, tries to assassinate Secretary of State William Seward at his home. Trying to stab Seward, he is fought off by several people and runs away.

- Booth breaks his leg by jumping onto the stage at Ford's theater. He escapes out the back door, and takes off on horseback.

- At 4:00 AM, Booth and another accomplice (David Herrold) arrive at Doctor Samuel Mudd's house. Mudd treats Booth's injured leg, and provides the men shelter for nearly twelve hours.

- For the next 10 days, Booth remains on the run in the swamps of Virginia, receiving help from southern sympathizers.

- Over twenty men of a Northern Calvary unit are persistently trailing Booth as he tries to make his escape.

- Meanwhile, Mary Surratt, Lewis Powell, Samuel Mudd, Michael O'Laughlin, and George Atzerodt are all arrested for having suspicious connections with John Wilkes Booth.

- On April 26, 1865, Booth is found in a tobacco shed. He refuses to surrender, forcing the Calvary to set the shed on fire. Booth is shot and then pulled from the burning building.

- Booth dies soon after. His last words are reported to be, **"Tell my mother I did it for my country..."**

- Eight people besides Booth are arrested in the conspiracy. Of them, all but one are sentenced to death or life imprisonment.

"As mad as a hatter!"

As far as phrase origins go, it doesn't get any simpler than this. When someone accuses you of being *"as mad as a hatter,"* he is basically calling you crazy. And, it's appropriate — back in the 18th century, hatters really were mad.

The common practice for making hats back in the 1700's consisted of soaking the felt in a variety of chemicals, most namely mercury. The vapors from the mercury were extremely potent and often inflicted the hatter with tremors and hallucinations. If exposed to the mercury long enough, he would literally go insane. Therefore, there was a certain degree of truth in the concept of being *"as mad as a hatter."*

The most famous Mad Hatter is featured in Lewis Carroll's timeless book, *Alice's Adventures in Wonderland*, published in 1865. The character of Mad Hatter was friends with the March Hare (at the time, there was another popular expression — *"As mad as a March Hare")*. Lewis's depiction of the Mad Hatter helped popularize the phrase, but the idea of being "as mad as a hatter" existed well before the novel was ever written.

Because it's impossible to exactly pinpoint how a phrase worked its way into everyday language, there have been other theories behind *"as mad as a hatter."* Some argue that the word "hatter" is derivation of the word "adder." Adder is a type of highly venomous snake. In this less likely scenario, *"mad as a hatter"* is an obstruction of *"mad as an adder."* In other words, as dangerous as a snake.

"An eye for an eye, and a tooth for a tooth."

King Hammurabi didn't go easy on crime. As the ruler of ancient Babylonia in the late 1700's BC (nearly 4,000 years ago), he set up one of the most sophisticated set of laws that the world had ever seen. Carved into a column, his code of justice was actually extremely humanitarian — it dealt with personal relations, business affairs, property, and worker's rights. Still, there was one aspect of it that might stir up a little bit of controversy — the concept of *"an eye for an eye, and a tooth for a tooth."* The idea behind this was clear—what goes around comes around. If you cut off another man's hands, then your hands are cut off. If you kill another man, then it's your turn to be killed. Get the point?

The concept of "an eye for an eye" was later outlined in the Bible. In the Old Testament (Exodus 21:24) it is written *"eye for eye, tooth for tooth, hand for hand, foot for foot."* The concept is repeated in the New Testament (Matthew 5:38), only this time the harsh form of justice is somewhat disputed.

In any case, King Hammurabi and the Bible had something in common. He made an *"eye for eye"* the centerpiece of his code of ethics and, as cruel as it sounds, it actually worked—the empire of Babylonia was able to maintain a civilized sense of order that was thousands of years ahead of its time.

"Bring home the bacon!"

We all know that to *"bring home the bacon"* is to walk away with some prize or to be the breadwinner in a family. But, at some point in history, did a person ever really bring home any bacon? The answer: Yes! In fact, there's more than one instance to demonstrate what an honor it was to *"bring home the bacon".*

First, around the year 1100 AD, a strange contest began in the village of Great Dunmow, in Essex County, England. The challenge was to see if any couple could prove that they had maintained an absolutely harmonious marriage for one year and a day. Not an easy task. In fact, in over five hundred years, there were only eight winners (and they were probably even a little sketchy). The prize that the victorious couples took home was—you guessed it—a side of bacon. The reward was known as a "flitch," and it was highly coveted during the several hundred-year history of the event.

Another case of "bringing home the bacon" occurred during the 1800's. At county fairs and other outdoor events, it became a game to chase around a greased pig to try to catch it. This was undoubtedly an enjoyable spectator sport, but the prize attracted many contestants. The person who succeeded in catching the pig got to keep it. He, too, was able to *"bring home the bacon."*

"No holds barred!"

Go ahead and throw out the rule-book. In a situation where there are *"no holds barred,"* all of the usual restrictions are eliminated. Basically, anything goes. The phrase comes from the sport of wrestling. The popular sport is known for being aggressive and demanding, but there are a number of different techniques and holds that are illegal for the safety of the competitors. A wrestling match where these rules don't apply would be downright brutal.

In fact, the sport of wrestling today, as physically demanding as it is, is probably too tame for its first participants 15,000 years ago. Even in more recent history, when Greek athletes wrestled in the first Olympic games, there wasn't much that the competitors weren't allowed to do. The wrestlers battled until someone finally gave in. It was the society of ancient Rome that took the brutality out of the sport, resulting in rules very similar to the ones used today.

"Bury the hatchet."

While it's good that people often forgive each other after senseless fighting, it's unusual to see any of them literally go out back and bury a hatchet. So, where did the expression *"bury the hatchet"* come from? Well, conveniently, it comes from the days when people *did* bury hatchets. The American Indians had a custom of meeting with their opposition after a war to show that they truly meant for the fighting to end. The tribes would bury hatchets and other weapons that were used during the battles. From this, the phrase stuck.

Another common practice came from this same idea. Have you ever heard someone say, *"Why don't you just shake hands and make up?"* The act of shaking with your right hand after a disagreement shows that you aren't carrying any weapons. After all, swords and knives are usually held with the right hand. In today's civilized society, it's usually assumed that the person you're arguing with doesn't intend to suddenly break out a knife and stab you (at least you hope not). Nonetheless, the sentiment behind the hand shake remains the same.

"Strike while the iron's hot."

To *"strike while the iron's hot"* is to be at the right place at the right time, and to take full advantage of it. The expression may seem a little odd. But, like so many other phrases, its origin comes from a time when people used to do exactly that. During colonial times, a blacksmith shaped metal by using a hammer and an anvil—he heated the iron until it became manageable, and then hit it until it took the form he wanted.

Obviously, if the blacksmith tried to hit the iron without it being properly heated, he could beat on it continually with little result. In order to get what he needed, he had to *"strike while the iron was hot."* This combination of action and timing fit well into other scenarios—in order to get results, you have to know when to strike. Because it was so universal, the everyday job of a blacksmith became a piece of wisdom for everyone else.

"Put a sock in it!"

When you tell someone to *"put a sock in it,"* chances are you don't really want them to do anything with a sock. You just want them to shut up. Back in the late 1800's, when a person wanted to quiet something down, that's exactly what they did—put a sock in it.

In 1877, renowned inventor Thomas Edison recorded the first human voice when he recited the words to "Mary Had a Little Lamb" into his newly invented phonograph. His new creation was groundbreaking, and the phonograph quickly gained popularity throughout the country. But, while Edison was undoubtedly a genius, he did forget one thing—there was no volume control. When it became too loud, people would take a sock and stuff it in the horn that played back the sound. It was simple, but it worked. Unfortunately, placing a sock in someone's mouth to quiet him down isn't always as easy a solution. But the sentiment is the same, and it's from the days of the phonograph where the phrase *"put a sock in it"* first came into the language.

16—"What Made Them Say That?"

Charles Darwin—Shaking up the world with evolution

"I'll be a monkey's uncle!"

That's just ridiculous! It's not particularly surprising that the outburst *"I'll be a monkey's uncle"* is used to express both disbelief and skepticism on a certain topic. After all, to declare that you are the monkey of an uncle is just silly. Isn't it?

There's one small problem with the way the phrase is sarcastically used today. In reality, we all might very well be a monkey's uncle (or aunt). Hear me out. The expression originated in the mid-1800's when British scientist Charles Darwin laid the foundation for the theory of evolution. He proclaimed that, through the process of natural selection, modern man may have come from an animal similar to an ape. In other words, our great ancestors were monkeys. In 1859, he detailed this theory in his book, *The Origin of Species*. The controversy of the work earned it the title of the "book that shook the world". Darwin later drove home his evolutionary beliefs in 1871 by writing *The Descent of Man*.

Not surprisingly, many people thought that this idea of man descending from monkeys was simply outrageous. Darwin's biggest opposition was from the Church, which argued the theory of creationism. The non-believers in evolution would mockingly remark, *"I'll be a monkey's uncle"* when they heard something absurd. Today, the argument over evolution still rages on. But, while not too many people can say that they're the uncle of one particular monkey, the statement isn't as silly as it once used to be.

17—Familiar Expressions

"Pull out all the stops!"

When your back is against the wall, it sometimes becomes necessary to focus all of your energy on one goal. That's when you *"pull out all the stops,"* and don't hold anything back. The phrase is one we're all familiar with. The term *"pull out all the stops"* refers to an organ player who makes music by releasing the "stops" on the instrument's pipes. This allows air to travel through the pipe and sound to be released.

Today's usage of the phrase *"pull out all the stops"* fits the origin—you can't successfully play the organ unless you're ready to give it your complete focus. The complicated instrument consists of a series of massive pipes and several keyboards that control the air stops. The organ player has the tricky task of using both his hands and feet, sometimes completely independent of each other. The organ was invented around the third century BC, and was originally played for the entertainment of the public. It wasn't until hundreds of years later that it became popular in churches.

"Wild goose chase."

Have you ever been sent on one of these? The phrase *"wild goose chase"* is used when a person devotes time and energy to a pursuit that is as impossible as catching a wild goose. It seems appropriate, except for the fact that no one is literally trying to catch a wild goose.

In the 16th century, people came a little closer to that concept. At the time, a certain kind of horse race was popular. In the race, there was a lead horse that had the option of running in any direction; the horses behind him had the challenge of keeping up. To the spectators, this line of horses resembled a flock of geese flying in pattern. From this, the expression *"wild goose chase"* came about, describing anyone that is being hopelessly led in different directions. Even Shakespeare caught onto it, using the phrase in his legendary play, *Romeo and Juliet.*

"Ring around the rosy..."

Do you remember that sweet little nursery rhyme from Mother Goose? You know, the one where kids would hold hands with other kids, and then they would walk in a circle as they recited a verse. At the end, everyone would fall down laughing. But they probably wouldn't be laughing if they knew the most likely origin of that innocent little game. *"Ring around the rosy"* is a tribute to the Bubonic Plague that swept through Europe in the 1600's.

It works like this. The first line of the rhyme, *"Ring around the rosy,"* refers to the first symptoms of the disease, a red rash that forms all over the body. The next line, *"Pocket full of Posy,"* tells of the tradition where a person surrounds themselves with a sweet smelling flower to cover up the smell of death.

There are actually two versions to the third line of the verse. The most common is *"Ashes, Ashes"*, which tells about the tremendous amount of dead bodies that needed to be burned when burying them became too time consuming. Older versions of the rhyme use the line, *"Atchoo, Atchoo"*, which is a reference to the coughing and sneezing associated with the disease.

The last line of the innocent nursery rhyme is *"We all fall down."* This doesn't need too much of an explanation—when Black Death comes to town, it very well might kill everyone.

"He's blown his top!"

Luckily, this is only a figure of speech. It is highly uncommon for a person to lose his temper to such an extent that his head literally blows off. So, where did the expression come from? Well, people may not actually blow their tops, but there are things that do—volcanoes. And, it's a volcano that a person is being compared to when it's said that *"he's blown his top"*.

As far as strange sayings go, this one really fits. A person who's *"blown his top"* can be dangerous, and so can a volcano. There are over 1,500 volcanoes in existence, and over 500 of them have "blown their tops" at one time or another. The result can be devastating—hot ash and molten lava spill out and destroy any surrounding areas.

Before an active volcano actually erupts, it's common for it to let out steam for a time before it blows. Sometimes, the steam is just a false alarm, or it is able to let out enough steam that an all-out eruption isn't necessary. From this occurrence, the phrase *"He's just letting off steam"* originated. This is to say that a person is just venting his frustrations, which can be a good thing. After all, if he doesn't do that, he may just *"blow his top!"*

"Never look a gift horse in the mouth."

Why would you want to? This suggestion might seem a little strange, but once you know the story, it's really pretty sound advice. When a person says, *"Never look a gift horse in the mouth,"* he is reminding you not to be ungrateful or critical when you receive a gift. And, if you know about horses, it makes complete sense.

A reliable method of telling about the age and health of a horse is by examining its teeth and gums. If you were buying a horse and knew what to look for, you would most certainly check inside the horse's mouth to make a sound judgment. But, if you receive a horse as a gift, you wouldn't want to be so critical as to carefully check the teeth and gums. After all, an old horse is better than no horse at all. The idea of *"never look a gift horse in the mouth"* is just a reminder to appreciate that bargain.

There is one instance where this advice turned out to be a disaster. According to legend, Greek soldiers used a gift horse to gain admittance into the city of Troy during the Trojan War. The soldiers hid themselves inside the large, wooden horse until it was taken into the city. Once inside, the soldiers were able to sneak out and win the war. Had the Trojans been inconsiderate enough to *"look a gift horse in the mouth,"* they may have spoiled the devious plan.

"Turn over a new leaf."

Every once in a while, it's necessary to break away from old habits and start with a new beginning. That's what it means to *"turn over a new leaf."* But, when you pick a leaf up off of the ground, it's tough to make that connection. As it turns out, that's not where the expression came from.

The phrase *"turn over a new leaf"* is really another way of saying, *"turn the page,"* which makes a little more sense. When you turn the page of a book, you allow yourself to experience something new, and you leave the pages already turned behind you. It just so happens that the first pages were made out of leaves—the leaves of the *papyrus* plant. People have been using some form of paper for nearly two thousand years. By the year 900, the Egyptians were manufacturing paper fairly extensively, and they had developed an advanced method for turning the papyrus plant into pages for writing. It's from them that the concept of *"turn over a new leaf"* was created, and it didn't have anything to do with leaves that had recently fallen off of a tree. The leaf, in the expression, is the page of a book.

"He's got a chip on his shoulder!"

When it's said that a man has a *"chip on his shoulder"*, chances are he's looking for a fight. Now, if there really was a chip of some kind on his shoulder and he couldn't get it off, you could see why he would be a little irritated. Unfortunately, that's not exactly the case.

The phrase originated in America during the 1800's. At the time it was somewhat of an odd formality for a boy who was angered to literally place a chip of wood on his shoulder. The sentiment was simple—anyone who had the nerve to knock the piece of wood off was asking for a fight. The warning was certainly straightforward, leaving little room for confusion.

Today, it's very rare to see an angry person actually take a piece of wood and place it on his shoulder. Still, the general idea remains the same. A person with a *"chip on his shoulder"* is still just walking around daring someone to give him a reason to start a fight.

"Kick the bucket."

Don't try this at home. When someone has *"kicked the bucket"* he has, of course, died. It's not a gentle way to deliver the news, and the expression's origin is equally gruesome. Back in the 1700's, pigs were hung upside down by a beam before they were slaughtered. This beam was referred to as a "bucket." When the pig's throat was cut, it would naturally kick and flail with little success. Once the pig had *"kicked the bucket,"* it was all over—the pig was dead.

There is another angle that fits the saying. A man about to commit suicide will place a noose around his neck and then stand on a bucket as he prepares to hang himself. When he has worked up the nerve, he will *"kick the bucket"* out of the way. At that point, the deed is done. This form of *"kicking the bucket"* certainly fits the phrase, but the butchering of the pig is the more likely origin.

"Not fit to hold a candle to..."

By declaring that someone is *"not fit to hold a candle to,"* you are saying that they are not worthy to even be in the presence of another. These days, it doesn't necessarily mean that the person doesn't know how to hold a candle, but that's exactly how the saying started.

Back in the days before electricity, working at night was somewhat of a hassle. That's not to say that it couldn't be done. If a craftsman had to work after hours, he would assign to his apprentice the job of holding a candle near him so he could see what he was doing. It's very similar to modern times where a lowly apprentice holds a flashlight while his boss works in hard to see places. Obviously, the task of holding the candle didn't require nearly as much skill as doing the work itself.

From that set of roles, the idea of being *"not fit to hold a candle"* became a pretty common, and appropriate, insult. If an apprentice couldn't even perform that simple task, then there was really no use in having him around.

22—"What Made Them Say That?"

"The writing is on the wall."

It's all over. When the *"writing is on the wall,"* then the end result is evident—and it's usually not pretty. But, the question remains, what exactly *is* written on the wall? If you refer back to the origin of the expression, the words on the wall don't make any sense. In fact, they're so confusing that only one person can understand what they mean.

The story behind the *"writing on the wall"* comes from the Bible. In the book of Daniel (chapter 5), King Belshazzer holds a great feast for a thousand of his lords. During the feast, a mysterious hand appears and writes a series of incomprehensible words on the wall. Unable to decipher the message, the King becomes worried and sends for the prophet Daniel. Fortunately, Daniel is able to interpret the writing. Unfortunately, it isn't good news. Daniel informs the King that God has become angry with him, and that his days are numbered. Later that night, King Belshazzar is slain. From that, the phrase came to exist. And, the same was true then as it is today—nobody ever looks forward to seeing that the *"writing is on the wall."*

"Saved by the bell!"

Of course, we've all seen it when a boxer is up against the ropes, struggling to stay on his feet. Then, just before he's about to get hit with that knock out punch, the bell rings to end the round. They say that the boxer was *"saved by the bell,"* and he gets a chance to recover for a moment before the fight continues. But, long before professional boxing was a popular sport, people were still being *"saved by the bell."*

In the late 17th century, a sentry was hired to stand guard at Windsor Castle near London, England. The sentry was accused of falling asleep on the job and was consequently court-martialed. During his defense, the guard claimed that he couldn't have been sleeping because he heard the bell at St. Paul's ring at mid-night. There were two problems with his story. First, St. Paul's was over twenty miles away. Second, the sentry claimed that, instead of the normal twelve rings, the bell rang an odd thirteen times that night.

Of course, the prosecutors thought he was crazy. But

when news of the trial hit London, several witnesses appeared to say that, on that particular night, the bell tower did strangely ring thirteen times. Apparently, the sentry was not only awake, but he was paying excellent attention. As a result, he was found innocent in his court-martial, and the phrase *"saved by the bell"* began to be used to describe anyone who is bailed out at the last moment by some odd occurrence.

"He's got a frog in his throat."

When a person is said to have a *"frog in his throat,"* it means that he is suffering from a hoarse voice or nasty cough. Of course, if a frog was actually in his throat, it could very well be the cause of those symptoms. But, few people ever really have a frog stuck in their throat, and that's not how the expression originated.

Instead, frogs were used to *cure* throat infections. Sound a little strange? During the Middle Ages frogs were placed in the mouth to cure a disease known as "thrush." Thrush is a fungal infection where the early symptoms begin in the mouth and on the tongue. People at the time believed that, when they placed the head of a live frog near the throat, the frog's breathing actually transferred the disease from the person to itself. Whether it worked or not can be left to the doctors to debate. What we do know is that, from this practice, the phrase *"he's got a frog in his throat"* began to describe not only victims of thrush, but anyone suffering from a hoarse voice.

"Don't let what you cannot do interfere with what you can do."
—John Wooden
College Basketball Coach, mid-1900's

Chapter 2

Sports & Athletics

"Honey, I forgot to duck!"
Jack Dempsey (1926)

Professional boxer Jack Dempsey had a little explaining to do after his title fight against Gene Tunney. Dempsey had successfully defended his title for seven years, but Tunney finally dethroned him in 1926. After the fight, Dempsey answered to his disappointed wife: *"Honey, I forgot to duck!"*

The fight between Dempsey and Tunney excited the public so much that a rematch was immediately scheduled for the next year. Boxing fans throughout the world loved the Dempsey/Tunney match-up. For starters, the two fighters had opposite styles and personalities. Dempsey, known as the "Manassa Mauler," fought like a fierce street fighter. Tunney, on the other hand, was a superb tactician.

Even more hyped than the original, Dempsey vs. Tunney II became one of the classic bouts of all time. Known as the "Battle of the Long Count," it seemed that Dempsey would get his revenge on Tunney when he knocked him to the canvas. But, Dempsey failed to return to his corner, and the referee didn't start the count until he did so. Many believe that these extra few seconds allowed Tunney to compose himself and avoid the knockout. Tunney went on to win by a decision.

The sentiment behind Dempsey's original logic wasn't forgotten. In 1981, when President Ronald Reagan was shot in an attempted assasinatin, he also had some explaining to do. He joked to the first lady, Nancy Reagan, *"Honey, I forgot to duck!"*

"Thanks, King."
Jim Thorpe (1912)

Jim Thorpe was a man of few words. His victories in both the decathlon and the pentathlon at the 1912 Olympic Games in Stockholm seemed to speak for themselves, and Thorpe was quickly recognized as one of finest all-around sportsmen ever. At the closing ceremonies, King Gustav V of Sweden congratulated him by saying, *"Sir, you are the greatest athlete in the world."* Thorpe answered with the famous line, *"Thanks, King."*

Remarkably, Thorpe's Olympic wins came in two events that were ordinarily dominated by Europeans. But he won easily, adding to his already exceptional athletic career. As a descendant of the Sac and Fox Indian tribe, Thorpe had attended Carlisle Indian School in Kansas and trained under renowned football coach Pop Warner. He also excelled in other sports such as track and field, football, baseball, boxing, swimming, basketball, tennis, and lacrosse. Many believe that Thorpe was the greatest athlete of the twentieth century.

Unfortunately, one year after winning his track and field events at the Stockholm Olympics, he was stripped of his gold medals. It was learned that Thorpe had previously played semi-pro baseball. He would continue to play professional baseball and football after his Olympic stardom, but would never regain the medals in his lifetime. In 1982, nearly thirty years after his death, the International Olympic Committee overturned its decision, and restored to Jim Thorpe his two Olympic victories.

"Never change a winning game."
Bill Tilden   (1920's)

This is the advice of Bill Tilden — and, he knew something about winning. Tilden was the most dominant tennis player in the world during the 1920's. He was the United States champion on six different occasions, and the first American to win Wimbledon. His powerful style of play helped elevate the level of competition among the nation's top players. The result was a winning streak of seven years for the American Davis Cup team. Tilden credited this consistency to his simple rule: *"Never change a winning game; always change a losing one."*

Even today, Tilden's recipe for winning serves as a standard in athletics. Of course, like all great philosophy, it seems almost too simplistic. Why would someone want to change a winning game? And, on that note, why *wouldn't* someone want to change a losing one? Obvious or not, when Tilden found a way to win he stuck with it. Sports fanatics argue that, for the first half of the century, he was further above the competition in his sport than any other athlete. That compliment compares him to legends like Babe Ruth in baseball and Jack Dempsey in boxing.

Junk Talkers

> *"...float like a butterfly, sting like a bee."*
> **Muhammad Ali**

Psyching out your opponent is nothing new in sports. In fact, it seems like that heated exchange just before the starting whistle is just part of the game. This is especially true in the sport of boxing, where opponents do anything they can to get under each other's skin. There is no better example of this than the great Muhammad Ali.

Ali is considered one of the most dominant fighters in the history of the boxing. In 1978, he became the first man to win the heavyweight title on three different occasions. But, despite his enormous success, Muhammad Ali was probably known just as much for his behavior outside the ring. He was notorious for his bold statements, earning the nickname "Mighty Mouth." The cocky fighter never failed to put on a show for the reporters, but he always seemed to back up his confident predictions when it came time for the actual fight. That's not an easy task, however, when you refer to yourself as "The Greatest."

Muhammad Ali

While Muhammad Ali may have been the most visible "junk talker," he certainly wasn't the first. Heavyweight prizefighter John L. Sullivan, the bare-knuckle champion in 1882, was also a relentless self-promoter. With famous boasts like, **"My name is John L. Sullivan, and I can lick any son of a bitch alive,"** he was able to stir up an enthusiasm for the sport during the late 1800's.

Sullivan's rise to stardom came when boxing still operated under the London Prize Ring rules. In this system, boxers fought with bare knuckles—wrestling, hugging, and hitting knocked-down opponents were all part of the game. Fights often had to end in knockout, regardless of the amount of time it may have taken. Sullivan was the last bare-knuckle champion. The sport began to be fought with gloves in 1882 after the more civilized Queensbury rules were instituted.

Even when wearing gloves, Sullivan remained dangerous and managed to keep a following of loyal fans across the country. He was exaggerating, though, when he said he could, *"lick any son of a bitch alive."* In New Orleans on September 7, 1892, he was knocked out by James Corbett in the 21st round, losing the heavyweight title.

But Sullivan just started the "junk talking" trend. In 1897, British boxer Bob Fitzsimmons became the heavyweight champion by defeating American James Corbett. Fitzsimmons was both shorter and lighter than his opponent, and he explained the reasons for his victory by declaring, **"The bigger they are, the harder they fall."**

Not long afterwards, Fitzsimmons may have regretted his own statement. In 1899, he was forced to defend his title against another American fighter, Jim Jeffries. Jeffries was both taller and heavier than Corbett had been, but this time the confident Fitzsimmons was wrong when he declared, *"The bigger they are, the harder they fall!"* Aside from being bigger than Corbett, Jeffries must have also hit harder. The fight, taking place in New York City, ended with Fitzsimmons being knocked out in the eleventh round.

Because of his small stature, Fitzsimmons was able to go down a weight-class and capture the light heavyweight title in 1903. He obviously didn't let those bigger guys get to him—Fitzsimmons stayed in the physical sport until 1914, finally retiring at the age of fifty-two.

Some people feel that the constant promotion and hype outside of the boxing ring deteriorates from the essence of the sport. Others don't take it quite so seriously, arguing that all of the "junk talking" is part of the entertainment package.

"I had a better year than he did."
Babe Ruth   (1931)

This is a classic response given by baseball great Babe Ruth in 1931 when it was brought to his attention that he was making more money than President Herbert Hoover. Ruth's salary for 1931 was $80,000; the President's was $75,000.

In truth, Ruth's logic — *"I had a better year than he did"* — was fairly accurate. President Hoover was serving his term during one of the low points in American history, the Great Depression. He had won the 1928 election in a landslide but, by 1931, was being condemned by the population for the loss of jobs and a terrible economy. Franklin Roosevelt took advantage of Hoover's tarnished image, and he won the next election by promising a "New Deal" to pull the country out of the depression.

Unlike Hoover, Babe Ruth had a tremendous year in 1931. For starters, he was winding down an amazing career with the New York Yankees, and the American public loved him. Ruth was also holding the record for the most home runs hit in a single season (60), a record that would stand for over thirty years. The New York Yankees were riding on the Babe's success, but they didn't win the World Series that year. Ruth would have to wait just one more season, in 1932, for that to happen.

"He shoots—he scores!"
Hewitt Foster   (mid 1900's)

If you're a sports fan, you love to hear these words — so long as it's your team doing the scoring. Sportscaster Foster Hewitt is the one responsible for the famous phrase that has now become commonplace in the world of athletics. In the early 1920's, Hewitt began doing his play-by-play announcing over the radio. He was broadcasting hockey games in Toronto, working in a small booth at ice level because it allowed him to get the best view of the game. Foster's passion for his work came through in his radio broadcasts, and he became popular across Canada by the 1930's.

Obviously, listening to a sports broadcast over the radio isn't the same as watching it on television. Hewitt Foster had to keep the listener involved in the game, usually for over two hours. And hockey is a low scoring sport, so you can imagine the excitement transferred over the radio when he yelled, *"He shoots—he scores!"* Foster continued doing his play-by-play over the radio even into the 1950's, when sporting events frequently began to appear on television.

"Don't look back, something might be gaining on you!"
Satchel Paige   (mid 1900's)

Satchel Paige had a secret for staying young. The legendary pitcher possessed unbelievable stamina, playing professional baseball for over forty years on more than twenty different teams. That's right—for over *forty* years. It's no surprise that Paige was often questioned about his ability to compete at such a high level for so long. Finally, he confessed his simple rules to live by—and they weren't what you would think. For example, Paige advised staying away from fried meat and to avoid running at all times. But, most remember his one classic rule: *"Don't look back, something might be gaining on you!"*

Paige began his career with Birmingham Black Barons in the early 1920's. He spent several years in the Negro Leagues playing with different teams, and he gained a reputation for his unorthodox, but highly effective, pitching style. His wind-up and unpredictable deliveries were enough to confuse any batter. Still, it wasn't until 1948 that he finally got a shot in the major leagues. By that time, he had already played on teams all around the United States. Paige was obviously ready, earning Rookie of the Year in his first season. While that's an impressive accomplishment in its own right, it was even more impressive considering he was already over forty years old.

Despite his late start, Satchel Paige didn't get shortchanged in the time he spent in the big leagues. He played almost twenty years as a pitcher for a variety of different teams, securing himself a place in the baseball hall of fame.

"Win one for the Gipper!"
Knute Rockne   (1928)

During halftime of a 1928 football game between Notre Dame and Army, legendary Coach Knute Rockne desperately needed to motivate his team. He did just that with one of the most memorable lines in sports history. When he urged his players to *"Win one for the Gipper,"* Rockne was referring to the best athlete he had ever coached—George Gipp. During the 1920 season, Gipp was an All-American at Notre Dame. Unfortunately, he contracted strep throat soon after the football season ended. The great athlete did not recover, dying in December of that year.

As the legend goes, Knute Rockne went to visit his star player in the hospital. Gipp knew he didn't have much longer to live, so he made his coach promise him one thing. He wanted Rockne to remember him sometime in the distant future, when the outlook for the Notre Dame football team was desperate and hopeless. At that point, Rockne should ask his team to *"Win one for the Gipper!"*

Eight years later, during the 1928 season, injuries and inexperience hampered the Notre Dame team, and they were having the worst season of Rockne's career. It didn't seem like it would get any better, either, when the team took on the powerful program at Army. But by half time of the game, neither team had managed to score. Rockne knew that his players needed the victory, so he decided to make good on Gipp's final wish. During the half time break, he relayed the emotional story of Gipp to his team, concluding with the most famous pep talk in sports. Rockne asked his players to *"Win one for the Gipper!"* They did. Notre Dame upset Army by a score of 12 to 6.

Rockne's famous speech was immortalized in the 1940 movie, *Knute Rockne—All American*, which starred future president Ronald Reagan.

33—Sports & Athletics

Wilt Chamberlain—Dominant basketball player.

"Nobody roots for Goliath."
Wilt Chamberlain   (1960's)

    Famed basketball player Wilt Chamberlain found himself in a strange predicament. Despite his obvious domination on the court during the 1960's, he wasn't a fan favorite. Standing at 7'-1", Chamberlain often towered above his opponents, and he became a powerful scoring force below the basket. But that wasn't enough. He was criticized because his teams won very few championships, and the fans constantly booed him when he played on the road. Ultimately, "Wilt the Stilt" began to understand that this ill treatment was inevitable. As he stated several times throughout his career, *"Nobody roots for Goliath."*

    Despite not being well received, Chamberlain continued to thrive on the basketball court. From 1960 to 1966, he carried on a streak of seven consecutive scoring titles in the National Basketball Association. During the 1961-62 season, he averaged an amazing 50.4 points per game. That same year, he scored 100 points in a single game, causing excited fans to rush the court.

    It's true that during his fourteen seasons, Chamberlain was often robbed of the NBA title by his greatest rival, Bill Russell, and the Boston Celtics. However, the criticism that Chamberlain was unable to win big games was unfounded. H e did win titles during the 1967 and 1972 seasons.

"He can run, but he can't hide!"
Joe Louis   (1941)

Preparing for a title fight against light-heavyweight champion Billy Conn, boxer Joe Louis taunted his opponent with this now-familiar threat. Since 1939, Louis had defended the heavyweight title fifteen times against unworthy opponents. The matches were so lopsided that the public began to refer to his challengers as the "bums of the month." In 1941, Billy Conn became the first significant challenger to face Louis since he gained his title. Conn was outweighed by thirty pounds, but he clearly outmaneuvered the champ. However, Louis caught him with a series of punches in the thirteenth round to win the fight.

Soon after, Joe Louis would leave boxing and serve in the military during World War II. But, in 1946, he decided to return to the sport. He wanted to show he was still a champion, so he called for a rematch against Conn. This time Louis was hoping to earn a more decisive victory. With a colossal amount of hype around the rematch, he boasted, *"He can run, but he can't hide!"*

Joe Louis was victorious again in the second fight, this time with a knockout in the eighth round. But, what the fans saw were two fighters who were obviously past their primes, and it was in no way the highlight of Louis's tremendous career. It didn't compare, for example, to his 1938 match-up against Max Schmeling. In that fight, Louis avenged a loss against a German fighter whom Adolf Hitler had deemed a prime example of racial supremacy. After being defeated by Schmeling two years earlier, Louis came out much more aggressively, winning the fight in the first round. With this victory, he shattered the color barrier in the sport and became an American hero.

"Nice guys finish last."
Leo Durocher   (1940's)

Feisty baseball manager Leo Durocher coined this classic motto in the 1940's. As the manager of the Brooklyn Dodgers, Durocher was so competitive that he sometimes lost his temper. Appropriately, he earned himself the nickname, "The Lip." When asked how he felt about his rowdy Dodgers defeating the more tame New York Giants, Durocher responded, *"Nice guys finish last."* Ironically, it wasn't until 1954 that Durocher was able to lead one of his ball clubs to a World Series victory. That club was the "tame" New York Giants.

Durocher earned his reputation as a fierce competitor when he was a player. He held the position of a major league shortstop for almost two decades, his best years being with the St. Louis Cardinals during the 1930's. Durocher's athletic skills opened the doors for him to become a manager, and that's how he became a baseball legend. For twenty-four years, he used his passion for winning to motivate his teams. Unfortunately, Durocher may have been a little too enthusiastic. In fact, he was suspended during the entire 1947 season for a number of incidents in which he "failed to use acceptable conduct." Afterwards, he returned to baseball and, for the most part, stayed out of trouble. Durocher retired as a manager in the 1970's, and was later elected to the Hall of Fame.

"Winning isn't everything—it's the only thing!"
Vince Lombardi   (1960's)

Vince Lombardi believed it, and so did his players. During the 1960's, Lombardi built a dynasty in the National Football League (NFL) with his Green Bay Packers. Before he became head coach in 1959, the team had come off a season with one win and eleven losses. By 1961, Lombardi had helped the Green Bay Packers become NFL champions.

But Lombardi's talent to create winning teams wasn't entirely because of his knowledge of football. What he was most known for was his ability to motivate his players and others around him. And those around him had to have the same thirst for winning as he had. In his own words, *"If you aren't fired with enthusiasm, you'll be fired with enthusiasm".*

With Vince Lombardi at its helm, the Green Bay Packers won three NFL championships and two Super Bowls during the 1960's—not a bad decade. Lombardi looked back at his success by noting, *"Winning is a habit; unfortunately, so his losing."*

Berraisms

"It ain't over till it's over!"
Yogi Berra   (mid 1900's)

This honored, and perhaps obvious, sports adage is just another piece of wisdom from baseball legend Yogi Berra. During his eighteen years in the Major Leagues, Berra became known for his ability to twist around simple phrases. He motivated his teammates with remarks like, **"It ain't over till it's over,"** and other "Berraisms." He was the one who pointed out that **"Baseball is ninety percent mental—the other half is physical,"** and **"No wonder nobody comes here, it's too crowded."**

Joining the New York Yankees in 1946, Berra played in fourteen World Series, winning ten of them. A solid catcher and batter, he earned the American League's Most Valuable Player award three times. And, when his playing days were over, Berra continued to be involved with baseball by managing the Yankees and later the New York Mets. In 1972, he was honored as a member of the National Baseball Hall of Fame.

Yogi Berra

With all of Yogi Berra's tremendous baseball success aside, he is still probably most remembered for his clever sayings and unique outlook on life. But, while he is credited with numerous quips over the years, Berra is the first to admit, **"I didn't really say everything I said!"**

37—Sports & Athletics

Here are some other thoughtful "Berraisms":

- "A nickel ain't worth a dime anymore."
- "It's déjà vu all over again!"
- "We made too many wrong mistakes."
- "When you come to a fork in the road, take it!"
- "If the world were perfect, it wouldn't be."
- "It gets late early here."
- "The future ain't what it used to be!"
- "You can observe a lot by watching."
- "I wish I had an answer to that, because I'm tired of answering that question."
- "Pair up in threes."
- "Never answer an anonymous letter."
- "If you don't know where you are going, you will wind up somewhere else."
- "I ain't in no slump! I just ain't hitting."
- "I take a two hour nap—from one o'clock to four."
- "90% of the putts that are short don't go in."
- "If the fans don't come out to the ballpark, you can't stop them."
- "You should always go to other people's funerals—otherwise, they won't come to yours."

"It ain't over till the fat lady sings."
Dan Cook   (1978)

      This less-than eloquent maxim has served as a long time reminder to those finding themselves in a tight spot. It's message is simple, "don't give up." The phrase is also a stern warning against overconfidence. Obviously, the *"fat lady"* is alluding to an opera and the stereotypical scene where a heavyset woman concludes the show with one last window-shattering number. But, the saying rarely refers to the opera in this day and age. It is usually used in the context of a sports competition, and that is how it became so recognizable.

      In 1978, the San Antonio Spurs battled the Washington Bullets in the playoffs of the National Basketball Association. Television sports commentator Dan Cook was sent to cover the games in San Antonio. The Spurs found themselves down three games to one and facing elimination. Stressing that the series was still not clinched, Cook reminded the fans, *"It ain't over till the fat lady sings."* The Spurs gathered themselves for another win, but ultimately fell short to the Bullets and lost the series.

      After hearing Cook's broadcast, Washington Bullets' Coach Dick Motta repeated the sentiment to his team. He wanted to warn them against overconfidence as they headed into the next round of the playoffs. From him, the basic wisdom caught on, and the phrase became common across the country.

"Do you believe in miracles?...YES!"
Al Michaels   (1980)

      Talk about great moments in sports history. It was during the closing seconds of the USA and Soviet Union hockey game at the 1980 Winter Olympics in Lake Placid, New York, when ABC-TV sports announcer Al Michaels posed this famous question. As the game ended, and the USA team came out as victors, Michaels didn't feel he needed to wait for an answer.

      Only one week before the Olympic games, the underdog United States team took on the Soviets in an exhibition. The Soviets, seemingly ready to repeat as Olympic champions, won the game by a score of 10 to 3. The United States team, on the other hand, entered into the Olympics seeded only seventh out of twelve teams—there were no great expectations for a medal.

The U.S. team went unbeaten through the first round, though, and they found themselves in the semi-finals facing the powerful Soviets. This game was played on February 22, almost twenty years since the last time the United States had beaten the Russians in 1960. Playing in front of an enthusiastic American crowd, the U.S. trailed 3-2 going into the third period. Midway through it, team captain Mike Eruzione scored a go-ahead goal, and goalie Jim Craig played some outstanding defense.

In the second half of the third period, the U.S. desperately held onto the one-goal lead. With only seconds left in the game, and the puck at center ice, announcer Al Michaels screamed, *"Do you believe in miracles?"* Then, as the horn sounded to secure the victory, he answered, *"YES!"* Within hours, the streets of Lake Placid were covered with excited fans waving American flags.

"Hey, look, there's John Candy!"
Joe Montana   (1989)

Joe Montana could stay cool under pressure. Take this pointless comment, for example, which he made at a completely inappropriate time. The great quarterback said it during Super Bowl XXIII, the championship game for the 1989 NFL season, when the San Francisco 49ers trailed the Cincinnati Bengals late in the fourth quarter and seemed to be running out of time.

With terrible field position, and barely enough time on the clock for one final drive, Joe Montana ran into the game to join his team in the huddle. Each player was feeling the adrenaline and nerves of an entire season on the line, but Montana just pointed into the crowd and said, *"Hey, look, there's John Candy!"* The players looked up to see that Montana was right—comedian John Candy was in the crowd watching the game. The observation eased the anxiety of his teammates, and Joe Montana proceeded to march his San Francisco 49ers 92-yards up the field and win the game with a spectacular touchdown pass.

With that kind of coolness under pressure, Montana ultimately led his team to four Super Bowl victories. He was named the Most Valuable Player in three of them.

Jim Valvano — Miracle coach of college basketball

"Don't give up. Don't ever give up!"
Jim Valvano   (1993)

     Jimmy Valvano went back to the basics when he decided to form the Jimmy V Foundation for Cancer Research in 1993. He announced the organization at ESPN's ESPY Awards Show while receiving the Arthur Ashe Award for Courage. Valvano wanted to raise money for cancer research and awareness, and he centered his foundation on the concept *"Don't give up."*

     Jim Valvano was a college basketball coach during the 1970's and 1980's, best known for his coaching at North Carolina State University. There, he led an underdog team to a national championship in 1983. After the game, the enthusiastic coach showed his true character by running onto the court looking for someone to hug.

     In 1992, Jimmy Valvano was diagnosed with terminal cancer. By the time the ESPY awards came around, he was visibly weak and in pain. Nonetheless, he remained in high spirits. While giving the acceptance speech for his award, a monitor flashed to tell him that he had thirty seconds left to speak. Valvano replied, *"I got tumors all over my body. I'm worried about some guy in the back going 30 seconds?"* The crowd exploded with applause and, as promised, Valvano continued to finish what he had to say.

He used the speech to detail the Jimmy V Foundation and its focus on battling cancer. He announced, *"Its motto is, 'Don't give up, don't ever give up.' That's what I'm going to do every minute that I have left."* And, he stayed true to his word, remaining an inspiration until his death on April 28, 1993.

"I don't want to be graded on a curve."
Mary Carillo   (1990's)

You might say that commentator Mary Carillo couldn't take a compliment. Carillo, a former professional tennis player, had become a well-known sports commentator for several major television stations by the 1990's. She covered major tennis events such as the French Open, Australian Open, and Davis Cup. Because of her complete understanding of the sport, she was told that she was *"the best woman tennis expert or anything else with the word woman in it."* Not overtaken by the flattery, Carillo responded, *"I don't want to be graded on a curve."*

Competing on the Women's Professional Tennis Tour from 1977 to 1980, Carillo was an excellent player, but she achieved only marginal success on the international level. Her highest world ranking came in 1979, when she was rated the #34 woman player in the world. Fortunately, equal to her tennis skills were her communication skills. As an articulate speaker and a clever writer, Carillo began to represent the tennis world by making appearances on television, and by writing columns in tennis magazines. Less than a decade after her career on the court had ended, Carillo was working as the leading commentator for the all sports network, ESPN.

"Creativity is allowing yourself to make mistakes. Art is knowing which ones to keep."
—Scott Adams
Creator of the comic strip, "Dilbert"

Chapter 3

Arts & Entertainment

44—"What Made Them Say That?"

Wolfgang Amadeus Mozart — Marvel composer, and child star

"Just as many, Your Majesty, as there should be."
Wolfgang Mozart (1782)

Roman Emperor Joseph II decided that he wanted to bring a German opera to the German people. And who else, the Emperor reasoned, would be more suited to take on such a task than the young and great Austrian composer Wolfgang Amadeus Mozart? Joseph II employed Mozart to compose the operetta *The Abduction from the Seraglio* in 1782. When he heard a rehearsal of the new creation, the Emperor complained that there were *"too many notes."* The twenty-six year old Mozart brushed aside the criticism by replying, *"Just as many, Your Majesty, as there should be."*

There is no doubt that the young composer was an expert on the subject. By the time he was six, Mozart had already established himself as a skilled musician. In less than a thirty-year time period, he produced over 600 works — among these were symphonies, concertos, and operas. That number would have undoubtedly grown, too, but Mozart died at the young age of thirty-five. He didn't need any longer, though, to go down in history as one of the world's foremost composers.

There's no doubt that Mozart had remarkable talent (and he wasn't about to let Emperor Joseph II forget it). But what really sets him apart from other composers, or most of history's other geniuses for that matter, is that much of his work was created while he was still a child or in his teenage years.

"There was no one to confuse or torment me, and I was forced to become original."
Franz Haydn   (mid 1700's)

Looking back on his days as the musical director for Prince Esterhazy, Austrian composer Franz Joseph Haydn didn't see any need to complain about his living conditions. Forget the fact that most of the musicians around Vienna during the 18th century were socializing with other musicians and learning from that interaction. Haydn, on the other hand, was living a relatively isolated life. He was in his late twenties when Prince Esterhazy first hired him, and his duties were to compose and perform music only at the Prince's request, with very small audiences. But Haydn was thankful for the experience— *"I was cut off from the world; there was no one to confuse or torment me, and I was forced to become original!"*

It was Haydn's originality that earned him worldwide recognition, enabling him to become one of the leading contributors to the "classical era." During his excess of twenty years with the Prince, his music was virtually unknown. In the 1780's, however, Haydn's compositions began to be heard throughout Europe, and fame soon followed.

With a career that lasted nearly seventy-years, Haydn created over 100 symphonies. That's a long time to remain an original!

"I am about to die—or I am going to—die; either expression is used."
Dominique Bouhours   (1702)

    It's never too late to use correct sentence structure. As he lay on his deathbed in 1702, French grammarian Dominique Bouhours uttered these appropriate last words. He had spent much of his life relying on the power of the written word. During the latter part of the 17th century, Bouhours had gained a reputation as both an author and a critic. In his book, *The Art of Criticism*, he established strict rules for determining the quality of poetic verses. He introduced a new school of rational criticism, and it managed to create controversy because it passed off previously popular poetry as completely unmerited.

    Bouhours didn't stop there—he also made waves as a Jesuit author. The Jesuits, sometimes known as the Society of Jesus, was an order of the Roman Catholic Church that encouraged an ongoing process of preaching and education. Bouhours offered his skills to the church by translating the New Testament of the Bible into French. Then, during the 1670's and 1680's, he used his penmanship to write the biographies of Saint Ignace and Saint Francois-Xavier. These two works quickly circulated throughout Europe, becoming extremely influential at the time.

"I awoke one morning and found myself famous."
George Byron   (1812)

    Sometimes the strangest things happen. Try, for instance, the legendary poet George Gordon Noel Byron, better known as Lord Byron, who received almost instantaneous fame throughout Europe in 1812. That year, he had just published the first two cantos of his epic poem, *Childe Harold's Pilgrimage*. It became popular immediately, leading him to declare, *"I awoke one morning and found myself famous."*

    The popular poem was the narration of a young man, Childe Harold, detailing his travels throughout Europe. Byron, who was only twenty-four when it was published, had just spent two years himself traveling throughout Europe. He created several more narrative poems in the next couple of years, all depicting a hero similar to Childe Harold—a character with strong emotions who has trouble fitting into society. The public loved it, and Byron enjoyed tremendous fame from 1812 to 1815.

Unfortunately, as is often the case with popular artists, Byron had his share of controversy as well. Caught in the midst of a sex-scandal involving his half-sister, he left England in 1816 and did not return. Settling in Venice, he continued to have success with his writing through works like *Don Juan* in 1823, which many consider his highest achievement.

"When I wrote that, God and I knew what it meant, but now only God alone knows!"
Robert Browning   (mid 1800's)

Robert Browning managed to confuse the London Society of Poetry. The members were reviewing his poem, "Sordello," originally published in 1840. The work had a simple enough theme, detailing the stormy life of the 13th century Italian poet, Sordello. Of course, Browning complicated the story by mixing in his psychological insights and perceptions of human emotion. Years later, when the readers demanded an explanation, he looked over the ambiguous verse and tried to appease them. However, after reading it over a couple of times, he shrugged and remarked, *"When I wrote that, God and I knew what it meant, but now God alone knows."*

While Browning may have gotten a little carried away when writing "Sordello," he built his reputation by commenting in his poetry on the human soul. Considered one of the greatest poets of the 19th century, his major contribution to verse was the development of dramatic dialogue, where the speaker reveals his or her own character.

Even with his unique vision, widespread fame wouldn't come for Browning until he was in his late fifties. Much of that fame was from what many consider his greatest work, *The Ring and the Book*, a multi-volumed collection of verse about an Italian murder trial.

The Greatest Show on Earth!

"There's a sucker born every minute."
David Hannum   (1869)

This popular statement is often credited to circus entrepreneur P.T. Barnum—but he's not the one who said it. Barnaum does, however, play a major part in the story. In October 1869, a twelve-foot tall piece of rock shaped like a man was "discovered" in a field in Cardiff, New York. News of this event quickly spread, though some key facts were jumbled. Instead of a rock, it was advertised that what had been found was a preserved giant.

P.T. Barnum

The "Cardiff Giant" wound up in the hands of banker David Hannum, who began to profit by displaying the amazing spectacle. Reading about the discovery, renowned showman P.T. Barnum decided that this "giant" would be perfect for his collection of freaks and exhibits. He offered to buy it from Hannum, but Hannum refused. Barnum didn't let this bother him—he simply made a replica, and advertised his version as authentic and Hannum's as an impostor. Thousands of people flocked to see Barnum's Cardiff Giant, to which Hannum could only respond, *"There's a sucker born every minute."*

Of course, neither Hannum nor Barnum had an authentic Cardiff Giant. So, when Hannum tried to sue Barnum, he really didn't have much of a case. In truth, Barnum meant no harm. He often displayed outlandish freaks, such as a 161 year old woman whom he claimed was a nurse to George Washington. His audience loved it and, even though they probably never really believed it was true, they wanted to see it anyway. In 1871, Barnum made history when he launched his traveling circus, which he publicized as "The Greatest Show on Earth."

These days, every county fair has a set of freaks (like the lobster boy or the two-headed goat) for spectators to marvel at. But, it was P.T. Barnum who started the trend with his display of unbelievable side-shows. Here are some of the "freaks" in Barnum's original circus:

- The Cardiff Giant (a twelve foot tall preserved giant)

- Joice Heth (the 161 years old former nurse of George Washington)

- The thin man (5'-4" tall, weighing 52 pounds)

- The three-legged boy

- The Fejee Mermaid (constructed using a monkey's head and a fish's body)

- General Tom Thumb (a 25 inch tall midget)

- The Bearded Lady

- The Armless Wonder

- The Alligator Boy

- The Lucasie Family (A family of albinos—husband, wife, and children)

- A few "Educated" seals

- A white, albino elephant

- Siamese twins (Two brothers named Eng and Chang from Siam. From them, the term "Siamese" twins originated.)

"The play was a great success, but the audience was a total failure!"
Oscar Wilde   (1890's)

Well, you can't have everything. In the early 1890's, playwright Oscar Wilde attended one of his premieres and was encouraged to see that, not only had his work been represented properly, but the actors had also performed brilliantly. Unfortunately, the audience wasn't too excited. Wilde, in typical egotistical fashion, reasoned that the audience must have had an off night—there certainly wasn't anything wrong with his work.

Luckily, the playwright did win over the audience with most of his presentations. Receiving minimal dramatic training, Oscar Wilde had a skill for weaving clever dialogue and ironic themes into his plays. In his successful comedy, *Lady Windermere's Fan* (1892), he introduced the recognizable maxim, *"Experience is the name everyone gives to their mistakes!"*

With his controversial lifestyle, Wilde helped lead what became known as the "Aesthetic Movement". This movement was based on the simple notion of art for art's sake. And Oscar Wilde was nothing short of a true artist; he sported unkempt long hair and never seemed to conform to the rigidity of society. His work, though, remains respected as a social commentary about life in the late 1800's.

"If it clashes, it is not art."
Marc Chagall   (1900's)

Painter Marc Chagall didn't need a complicated method for assessing his own work. The Russian-born artist did most of his painting in France, but his unique style made him recognized throughout the world. It also helped influence modern art. Chagall easily explained the secret to his success— *"When I judge art, I take my painting and put it next to a God made object like a tree or flower. If it clashes, it is not art."*

But fame didn't come all that easily. Chagall found out early on that he had one big obstacle to overcome if he was to become a successful artist—he was a Jew living in Czarist Russia.

With no support in his home country, he traveled to Paris in his early twenties to receive an art education. He remained in France for the majority of his life. Still, many of his paintings, such as *I and the Village* (1911), were influenced by his life as a Jew in Russia.

Later in his career, Chagall branched out from painting. During the 1960's, for example, he became known for his impressive stain-glass window designs. His more popular window work exists at the Hadassah-Hebrew University Medical Center in Jerusalem, as well as the United Nations headquarters in New York City.

"My God, I have shot the wrong architect!"
Harry Thaw   (early 1900's)

An honest mistake. This fiasco began when Architect Stanford White began having an affair with actress Evelyn Nesbit, the wife of Pittsburgh millionaire Harry Thaw. In 1906, the jealous Thaw committed one of the most sensational murders of the century by shooting White on the rooftop of New York City's Madison Square Garden.

Immediately, Harry Thaw was arrested for the crime, and he spent over a decade in prison. Upon his release, he visited a theater in New York where Stanford White had been the architect. Completely in awe of the magnificent interiors of the building, Thaw is said to have declared, *"My God, I have shot the wrong architect!"*

Fortunately, while he may have shortened the career of Stanford White, he certainly didn't erase it. White started out in 1879 by joining the offices of McKim, Mead, and White. The group went on to become one of the largest architectural offices in the world. As part of the firm, Thaw designed such notable structures in New York City as the Metropolitan Club, the Washington Arc, and the first Madison Square Garden.

A False Alarm

> "The report of my death was an exaggeration."
>
> Mark Twain (1897)

On June 2, 1897 an obituary announcing the death of legendary writer Samuel Clemens, better known as Mark Twain, ran in an American newspaper. Not surprisingly, the rumors of Twain's death quickly spread across the country. However, there was one small error in the report — Mark Twain was still alive. While in London, the 61 year-old Twain heard the news of his untimely passing, and responded to the rumors appropriately — *"The report of my death was an exaggeration."*

Mark Twain

While the origin of the rumor is unknown, Twain's reaction to it was consistent with the wit and humor that had made him such a popular writer. Over thirty years earlier he had published the short story, "The Celebrated Jumping Frog of Calaveres County," which gained him national recognition. And, in 1885, Twain published the legendary *The Adventures of Huckleberry Finn*, which became his masterpiece.

Although he had already secured his place as one of the most influential writers in American history, Mark Twain would still go on to live another thirteen years after the erroneous report of his death.

Here's a small sample of some of the other wit and wisdom attributed to Mark Twain:

- "Under certain circumstances, profanity provides a relief denied even to prayer."

- "It is better to deserve honors and not have them than to have them and not deserve them."

- "Let us be thankful for the fools. But for them the rest of us could not succeed."

- "Go to Heaven for the climate, Hell for the company."

- "Keep away from people who try to belittle your ambitions. Small people always do that, but the really great make you feel that you, too, can become great."

- "Part of the secret of a success in life is to eat what you like and let the food fight it out inside."

- "Suppose you were an idiot... And suppose you were a member of Congress... But I repeat myself."

- "Always do the right thing. This will gratify some people and astonish the rest."

- "Clothes make the man. Naked people have little or no influence on society."

- "If you tell the truth you don't have to remember anything."

- "It usually takes more than three weeks to prepare a good impromptu speech."

"Less is more."
Ludwig Mies van der Rohe   (1900's)

It was Ludwig Mies van der Rohe who, when describing the simple concept that would make him one of the most influential architects in history, expressed this now famous paradox. The German-American architect helped form the International style of design, creating skyscrapers with steel frames, glass walls, and strict geometric shapes. His buildings lacked the ornamentation of architecture styles in the past, but the power of his simple designs caught on rapidly from the 1930's to the 1950's.

The Seagram Building of New York City is perhaps Mies' most distinguished undertaking. The skyscraper, constructed in 1958, is truly representative of his tastes: a rectangular, 37-story building with a steel frame and bronze and glass-wall exterior. Today, most major cities in the United States boast structures that were influenced by the simplicity of Mies' designs, even buildings that were constructed after his death in 1969.

When he first moved to the United States in 1937, Mies became the director of architecture at the Illinois Institute of Technology. He held that position for twenty years, and used it as an opportunity to help educate and inspire a new generation of architects. They helped carry on his unique approach to design— *"less is more."*

"Wait a minute, you ain't heard nothing yet!"
Al Jolson   (1927)

These words, spoken by Al Jolson in 1927, began nothing short of a Cultural Revolution. Playing Jakie Rabinowitz in *The Jazz Singer*, the first feature length film to include sound, Jolson's line, *"Wait a minute, you ain't heard nothing yet,"* became the first sentence ever to be spoken in a major film.

Depicting a young man trying to make it on Broadway (despite his father's wishes for him to return to the synagogue), *The Jazz Singer* became an immediate success. The days of sound in the movies had begun. Jolson, who had already achieved some success as a Broadway star and musical comedian, used the Academy-Award winning movie as a stepping stone to several other popular films.

The Jazz Singer featured popular songs such as "Toot, Toot, Tootsie Goodbye" and "Blue Skies," and it would be remade several times throughout the years. However, none of the newer versions can match the significance of the 1927 original—it started a trend that completely changed an ordinary trip to the movies.

"I guess that'll hold the little bastards!"
Don Carney   (1930's)

Oops! As he finished telling the last story of the day on his children's show, radio announcer Don Carney leaned back in his chair and dropped the act. Unfortunately, the station had not yet switched to a commercial break, and millions of listeners across the country heard his none-too-tactful remark.

The familiar story, which has become something of a radio "urban legend," originated during the early 1930's. At the time, radio shows were at the height of their popularity, with listeners across the country tuning into an assortment of shows each night. Don Carney, known as "Uncle Don," hosted a popular juvenile variety show beginning in 1928, and it continued throughout the 1940's. His infamous blunder has been reported by several sources, and there are certainly those who claim to have been listening when he actually said it. But, in truth, Uncle Don's career continued long after the alleged incident, so there can be some doubts raised as to whether he actually made the devastating mistake of calling his loyal fans *"little bastards."*

Similar stories have also been attributed to other radio personalities of the era, mostly those hosting children's programs. Nonetheless, most of the accounts are usually tied back to the seemingly innocent Uncle Don.

Groucho Marx—Starting his career as part of the Marx Brothers

> **"Please accept my resignation. I don't want to belong to any club that will accept me as a member."**
> **Groucho Marx   (mid 1900's)**

This was the reasoning of American comedian Groucho Marx as he resigned his position at Hollywood's prestigious Friar's Club. He felt like he had to draw the line somewhere.

In actuality, Groucho was at the height of his popularity, and most clubs would have been honored to have him as a member. Thrown into show business by his mother, Groucho Marx and his siblings began a comedy act that they billed as the "Marx Brothers." They achieved a great deal of success throughout the 1930's, starring in several films. Their popularity stemmed from the fact that each of the three brothers developed a unique persona. The most unforgettable, of course, was Groucho. The comedian always appeared with his mustache and a cigar, as well as a good bit of sarcastic wit.

The gag-comedy of the Marx Brothers paved the way for the funny films of the future. After they made their last film in 1948, Groucho took his act to the small screen as the host of the successful television show "You Bet Your Life."

"I never met a man I didn't like."
Will Rogers   (early 1900's)

American humorist Will Rogers proudly lived by this impressive motto, and he even jested that he would have liked to have the phrase etched into his gravestone. Rogers declared, *"I joked about every prominent man of my time, but I never met a man I didn't like."* And he didn't act like he did, either. While Will Rogers used the celebrities of the time as the focus of his humor, his jokes were never mean-spirited or meant to tarnish anyone's reputation.

Growing up in Indian Territory in what is now the state of Oklahoma, Rogers began his career with a trick rope-throwing act that he took to New York City in 1905. He also began to include humorous monologues, and his wit earned him national attention. Eventually, he became known for his take on current events and celebrated political figures of the day, declaring in his act, *"All I know is what I read in the papers."*

Will Rogers not only made frequent public appearances, but he projected his comedy through newspaper columns, books, and radio shows. By the 1920's and into the early 1930's, he expanded his comedic career to include the movies, starring in over fifty films.

"I believe that man will not merely endure—he will prevail!"
William Faulkner   (1950)

William Faulkner wanted to say more than just thank-you to his fans. On December 10, 1950, the legendary American novelist graciously delivered an acceptance speech after being awarded the Nobel Prize in literature. But the prize came at a crucial time in American history, just after World War II and at the beginning of the Cold War. The nation seemed to be living in constant fear of atomic warfare, and Faulkner used his speech to identify these fears. He spoke specifically to young writers, urging them to stay focused on their writing despite the wavering world around them.

Having written his timeless novel *The Sound and the Fury* over twenty years earlier, Faulkner explained, *"There are no longer problems of the spirit. There is only one question: When will I be blown up?"* He remained optimistic, though— *"I believe that man will not merely endure—he will prevail!. He is immortal, not because he alone among creatures has an inexhaustible voice, but because he has a soul..."*

Throughout his career, Faulkner made a name for himself through his ability to deeply define the characters in his novels. And he had some clever ways of doing this. He used extended stream-of-consciousness, mixed narratives, and rambling sentences to help the reader become involved in the story. His complicated style frustrated many, but there were plenty of others who appreciated the unique approach.

"Youth is a wonderful thing. What a crime to waste it on children!"
George Bernard Shaw   (1930's)

George Bernard Shaw didn't think that life was completely fair. With that in mind, the popular writer made this classic observation in the 1930's. At the time, Shaw was in his seventies, and he had already enjoyed a successful career. That didn't keep him from getting frustrated at times, though, as he watched the energy and naiveté of the younger generation. In the

59—Arts & Entertainment

midst of his frustration, he declared, *"Youth is a wonderful thing. What a crime to waste it on children!"* Shaw went on to live to the age of ninety-four.

Ironically, for George Bernard Shaw, youth was not always such a *"wonderful thing"*. He grew up in a poor family that ended with the separation of his parents. Largely self-educated, he wrote five novels from 1879 to 1883, while still in his twenties. Unfortunately, only two of the novels were published. The lack of recognition didn't stop Shaw, however. He eventually gained national attention as a critical journalist and playwright.

As one of Britain's most significant playwrights since Shakespeare, George Bernard Shaw continued to write until just a few years before his death. After authoring numerous successful plays in the early 1900's, particularly *Saint Joan* (1923), he received the Nobel Prize for literature in 1925.

"There's good news tonight!"
Gabriel Heatter   (1941)

At the start of World War II, it became all-too common for families to turn on their radio and hear about another alarming tragedy for the American people. Radio broadcaster Gabriel Heatter didn't like this new trend one bit. He made it a point to begin his program every night with a little bit of optimism.

Heatter's outlook of the glass being half full began a few months into the war, when a United States warship sank a Japanese destroyer. Taking advantage of the fortunate event, Heatter started his program that night with the words, *"There's good news tonight!"* The reaction to the positive statement was immediate, and Heatter continued to use the line at the beginning of each show. It was his goal to find some silver lining in the midst of an otherwise devastating time period.

It was important for the public to have a popular figure like Gabriel Heatter to help keep their minds at ease. The radio broadcaster first became esteemed as a news announcer in 1933, when he covered the Lindbergh baby kidnapping. And with his new catch phrase throughout World War II, his popularity spread even further.

Goldwynisms

> "Any man who goes to a psychiatrist ought to have his head examined."
> Samuel Goldwyn   (early 1900's)

This statement is a classic example of what is appropriately referred to as a "Goldwynism," named for renowned film producer Samuel Goldwyn. Goldwyn arrived to the United States from Poland when he was just a teenager, and he not only earned a reputation for making successful films, but also for butchering the English language. He often made conflicting remarks like the often repeated, **"If I were in this business only for the business, I wouldn't be in this business!"** and **"If I look confused, it's because I'm thinking."**

Samuel Goldwyn

Forming his first producing company in 1913, Goldwyn had a string of success in film from the 1930's to the 1950's. His movies helped introduce several notable actors, among them being Lucille Ball and Will Rogers. In 1946, the well-respected producer won the Academy Award for best picture with *The Best Years of Our Lives*.

Without a doubt, Goldwyn was a brilliant man, but that didn't enhance his ability to form logical sentences. He once claimed, **"If I could drop dead right now, I would be the happiest man alive."** In fact, Goldwyn's constant abuse of seemingly simple phrases resulted in him becoming known for more than just his films. Luckily, his mix-ups always seemed to come out in a comical manner, making the producer an American favorite.

Here are some other "Goldwynisms" attributed to Samuel Goldwyn:

- "Give me a couple of years and I'll make that actress an overnight success."

- "I read part of it all the way through."

- "A verbal contract isn't worth the paper it's written on!"

- "In two words—im-possible."

- "A bachelor's life is no life for a single man."

- "A hospital is no place to be sick!"

- "I never liked you and I always will."

- "Never make forecasts, especially about the future."

- "I had a great idea this morning, but I didn't like it."

- "Include me out."

- "I'm willing to admit that I may not always be right, but I am never wrong."

- "When I want your opinion I will give it to you."

- "You are going to call him William? What kind of a name is that? Every Tom, Dick, and Harry is called William."

- "Put it out of your mind. In no time, it will be a forgotten memory."

"In the future, everyone will be famous for fifteen minutes."
Andy Warhol   (1960's)

When he became a leader of the pop art movement during the 1960's, Andy Warhol made a prediction. He took notice of the onslaught of television and media which, for the first time in history, brought world events into the common person's living room each night. His comment, *"In the future, everyone will be famous for fifteen minutes,"* predicted that, sooner or later, each individual would be included in this mass media, even if just for a short time.

Warhol himself had far more than fifteen minutes of fame. He attracted attention with his silk-screened paintings, which he usually created featuring objects from daily life. Perhaps his most recognizable is *Campbell's Soup Can*, painted in 1965. Warhol's ability to point out trends and fads of the period, and to show them in a new light, caused him to unintentionally become a social commentator. He also painted the people, such as Marilyn Monroe, who had an influence on pop culture.

Painting wasn't Warhol's only passion. He eventually branched out to become an unorthodox film producer. As the creator of over sixty films, he used undisciplined plot and improvised dialogue to create movies of varying qualities. Warhol did, however, manage to stir up controversy by focusing on taboo topics of the era.

"It's either easy or impossible."
Salvador Dali   (mid 1900's)

As the story goes, an admirer once asked Spanish painter Salvador Dali if it was difficult to paint a picture. Dali, the best known of the surrealist painters, understood that art was something that couldn't be forced. He therefore responded, *"It's either easy or impossible."*

Dali's ability to paint realistic and detailed objects, but in a dream-like world, made him perhaps the most impressive of the surrealist painters working in Paris during the 1930's. His best known piece, *The Persistence of Memory* (1931), portrays a variety of limp and hanging watch faces. Unlike many artists throughout history, Dali's paintings *were* popular even in his own time. He had a knack for combining his talent with self-promotion. This often made him the subject of criticism among his contemporaries, but it didn't hurt his success with the public.

In the 1950's, after achieving fame as a surrealist, Dali branched out into writing and sculpting. And when he did paint, he often focused on religious themes rather than his previous dream-like worlds.

"I don't want to achieve immortality through my work, I want to achieve it through not dying!"
Woody Allen   (1960's)

It seems like a reasonable enough request. Film director and actor Woody Allen made this remark in reference to the success that he began to achieve in the late 1960's. Often portraying the part of the neurotic underachiever living in the big city, Allen became a favorite in the United States and abroad for his offbeat charm. But not wanting to place too much emphasis on his film career, Allen made it clear, *"I don't want to achieve immortality through my work, I want to achieve it through not dying!"*

Woody Allen began his career as a television writer and a stand-up comedian during the early 1960's. Within a decade, he was writing, directing, and acting in a variety of theater productions and films. In 1977, his largest success came with the movie *Annie Hall*. The film won him Academy Awards for best picture, best director, and best screenplay. Although his goal for "immortality" was probably a little out of reach, Allen continued to direct and act in movies well into his sixties.

After a career that spanned over four decades, Woody Allen has been nominated for twenty Academy Awards and nine Golden Globe Awards.

George Burns—Popular and everlasting performer

> *"I was always taught to respect my elders and I've now reached the age when I don't have anybody to respect!"*
> **George Burns   (1980's)**

It's hard to feel sorry for someone with that problem. Comedian George Burns made this observation after an enduring career of over seventy years. Born in 1896 and entering show business as a child, Burns was still making movies in the late 1980's.

With such a long professional life, the entertainer was able to make an impact on several domains of show business. Burns began as a vaudeville dancer when he was a young child, just after the turn of the century. As he got older, he began to specialize in stand-up comedy. Then, in the early 1920's, Burns met Gracie Allen. Aside from becoming his wife, she became his comedy partner for thirty-five years. Together, the two worked on several motion pictures, starred on a popular radio show, and later brought their act to television.

After Gracie's death, Burns continued to perform in a variety of his own comedy acts. In the 1970's, he returned to motion pictures, earning an Academy Award for his supporting role in the movie *The Sunshine Boys*. Despite being in his eighties, Burns was as popular as ever, starring in several more films before his death in 1996.

> ***"If I had known I was going to live this long, I would have taken better care of myself."***
>
> **Eubie Blake** **(1983)**

Celebrated pianist Eubie Blake was a little surprised when he turned 100 years old in 1983. The ragtime musician, who performed in public almost until his death, was a lifelong smoker with poor health habits. Never imagining that he would live for over a century, he had only one regret — *"If I had known I was going to live this long, I would have taken better care of myself."*

Entering into the world of music at the age of 12, Blake played in hotels and clubs between Baltimore and Atlantic City when he was a teenager. In 1915, he met up with lyricist Noble Sissle, and the two began performing as "The Dixie Duo." Prior to World War I, they became popular when the musical style known as "ragtime" swept across the country. Ragtime, which focused mainly on the piano, required a tremendous amount of technical skill. Blake was one of the few who had the ability, and he quickly became one of the genre's top performers.

In 1921, Blake and Sissle took on another challenge, writing the successful all-black musical "Shuffle Along," which was performed on Broadway. Even when the popularity of ragtime began to fade, Blake was still able to find success through writing and performing his music.

"We can easily forgive a child who is afraid of the dark. The real tragedy of life is when men are afraid of the light."
—Plato
Greek Philosopher (429-347 BC)

Chapter 4

Philosophy

Socrates—Famed philosopher, put to death by drinking hemlock

"We owe a cock to Aesculapius; please pay it..."
Socrates (399 BC)

These are the strange last words of the philosopher Socrates in 399 BC. He had just taken a drink of the poison hemlock, and he knew that he only had a few moments left to live. Socrates felt in debt to the Greek God of Medicine, Aesculapius, for providing him with such an easy death, and he told those standing around him, *"We owe a cock to Aesculapius; please pay it and don't let it pass."* As he anticipated, he died just moments later.

Drinking the poison was not the idea of Socrates, but of the Greek court that had sentenced him to death for corrupting the minds of the young. In truth, he had simply expressed his beliefs to anyone willing to listen. With a philosophical opinion on a variety of subjects including love, justice, and ethics, Socrates had a tremendous impact on the thinking of the western world. His main focus, though, was the belief that people are inherently good—nobody would do harm or commit a crime just for the sake of doing so, but they do it out of ignorance. When people gain the knowledge of the right thing to do, then they will choose to do it.

Because of the enormous following that Socrates was gaining, the state began to become suspicious. A series of charges were trumped up against him and he was taken before the Athenian court in a controversial trial. His star pupil, Plato, later reported the events of his trial and death sentence.

"Therefore, my little sisters, beware of the sin of ingratitude."
Francis of Assisi   (early 1200's)

Italian mystic Saint Francis of Assisi was a brilliant man, and he was also a little crazy. In the early 1200's, the preacher delivered an important warning. However, he wasn't directing his warning towards a typical audience—he was speaking to a group of birds. Often referring to animals as his brothers and sisters, Assisi announced, "*My little sisters, the birds, much bounden are ye unto God, and always in every place ought ye to praise him, for that he hath given you liberty to fly....*" In other words, he was telling the birds that they were awfully lucky. He continued by saying, "*Therefore, my little sisters, beware of the sin of ingratitude, and study always to give praises unto God.*"

Despite his eccentricity, Saint Francis developed a significant following around 1205. He had grown up in a life of luxury, constantly making himself the center of the party. However, in 1202, a battle broke out between the cities of Assisi and Perugia and, in the midst of the violence, Saint Francis was captured. He was held as a prisoner for a year, and came back with a different view of the world.

Immediately, he renounced his worldly possessions, giving them to charity. Angered at the sudden change, his father disowned him, but Saint Francis was happy with his new life of poverty. He created a group known as the Franciscans, eventually numbering in the thousands. The Franciscans reached out to the outcasts of the world, striving to help the sick and poor.

"Perhaps your fear in passing judgment is greater than mine in receiving it!"
Giordano Bruno (1600)

On February 8, 1600, Italian philosopher Giordano Bruno was given one last chance by the cardinals of the Roman Inquisition to recant his beliefs. He had been imprisoned for eight years on the charge of heresy, and several times his case was brought to trial. On each occasion, Bruno was pressured by the authorities of the Inquisition to disclaim his philosophies. Each time, he refused.

Bruno was imprisoned for his freethinking, which the Roman authorities saw as a threat to the Christian church. He believed in the world and universe as an infinite body, with God as its soul. But, aside from the details of Bruno's opinions, he brought more attention to himself by his lack of fear in proclaiming them, as well as his refusal to withdraw his convictions.

Time after time, Bruno was sent back to prison, only to be brought before the cardinals again with another opportunity to disclaim his beliefs. Of course, Bruno would provide them with the same answer. Eventually, the authorities were forced to announce the inevitable sentence. Still, they gave the philosopher one final chance to recant, and a frustrated Bruno responded, *"Perhaps your fear in passing judgment is greater than mine in receiving it!"* With this, the cardinals sentenced him to death, and he was burned at the stake a week later.

"Now, my good man, this is no time for making enemies."
Voltaire (1778)

As he lay on his deathbed in 1778, notable French philosopher and writer, Voltaire, was visited by a priest. The priest asked him if he would like to take advantage of his final living moments to denounce the devil. To this, Voltaire responded, *"Now, my good man, this is no time for making enemies."*

This was a new attitude for the controversial philosopher,

who had never hesitated to make enemies in the past. Throughout the 1720's and 1730's, Voltaire placed himself in conflict with the French authorities for his attacks on the country's political systems and traditions. But his true strife came out with his views on religion. While Voltaire seemed to have his own beliefs about God, he consistently denounced the organized church. He advocated, instead, a purely rational belief system. With his stand against the clergy, Voltaire became a key defender to those who were persecuted because of their beliefs.

The controversy that surrounded Voltaire was apparent in his work. Perhaps, by refusing to denounce the devil during his priest's final visit, he saw an opportunity to make one last demonstration.

"Be ashamed to die until you have won some victory for humanity!"
Horace Mann   (1859)

As the president of Antioch College in Ohio, Horace Mann offered this advice to the graduating class of 1859. Mann had founded Antioch College in 1852, creating the first nonsectarian, coeducational institution in history. Conservative members of the Christian Church criticized him, feeling that the college only created Unitarians. But Mann's experiment was largely a success, and similar institutions soon followed. In his last address to a graduating class, Mann proclaimed, *"I beseech you to treasure up in your hearts these my parting words: Be ashamed to die until you have won some victory before humanity."* Mann gave the speech only two months before his own death.

Mann's commitment to the field of education began in the 1830's when he served as a representative in the Massachusetts state legislature. He helped to create the first state board of education in the United States, and was immediately appointed as its secretary. He used this position to address the problems with the nation's school systems, campaigning for better wages and training for teachers. Before he began his crusade for interdenominational education, Mann also served for five years in the U.S. House of Representatives.

Before He Knew it All...

> *"You are young, and have the world before you; stoop as you go through it..."*
>
> **Cotton Mather**   (early 1700's)

This sentence changed Benjamin Franklin's life. As a teenager, the great statesman went to visit the distinguished Boston minister, Cotton Mather. As he was walking through his house, Franklin failed to notice a low hanging crossbeam. Mather warned him by yelling, "Stoop! Stoop!" but Benjamin still banged his head on the beam. Seeing this, the pastor gave him some advice: *"You are young, and have the world before you; stoop as you go through it, and you will miss many hard bumps."*

Benjamin Franklin

Benjamin Franklin took the advice to heart. Even in his later years, he thought back on it as a reminder not to get too caught up in pride. He remembered not to hold his head too high—he didn't want to hit it again.

Mather, however, was a strange person to be helping out the young Franklin. The preacher had become a controversial figure when, during a smallpox epidemic in the early 1720's, he suggested that the disease be fought through vaccinations. Many experts found it hard to believe that it was possible to conquer a disease by exposing more people to it.

At the time, Benjamin Franklin was working for his older brother, James, who published a popular New England newspaper. James was among those who criticized Cotton Mather during the smallpox episode, and he had a great deal of support in his arguments against the preacher. Luckily, this didn't deter the young Franklin from visiting Mather only a couple of years after he stopped working for his brother. After all, that visit changed his life.

From 1733 to 1738, Benjamin Franklin shared an assortment of his advice through the publication, *Poor Richard's Almanac*. Written under the name Richard Saunders, here's a small sample:

- "There are no gains without pains."
- "At the working man's house, hunger looks in but dares not enter."
- "Fish and visitors stink in three days."
- "Beware of little expenses, a small leak will sink a great ship."
- "If you would have a faithful servant and one that you like—serve yourself."
- "Women and wine, game and deceit, make the wealth small and the wants great."
- "Wish not so much to live long as to live well."
- "When befriended, remember it; when you befriend, forget it."
- "He that lives upon hope will die fasting."
- "Wink at small faults; remember thou hast great ones."
- "Hear no ill of a friend, nor speak any of an enemy."
- "Many a man thinks he is buying pleasure when he is really selling himself as a slave to it."
- "What you would seem to be, be really."
- "He that lies down with dogs shall rise up with fleas."
- "Be slow in choosing a friend, slower in changing."
- "Fear to do evil and you need fear nothing else."
- "When there is marriage without love, there will be love without marriage."

"Work is the grand cure for all the maladies and miseries that ever beset mankind..."
Thomas Carlyle (1866)

While speaking at his alma mater, Edinburgh University in Scotland, essayist Thomas Carlyle took a moment to break down the meaning of "work." By 1866, Carlyle was already known as a social critic and champion of worker's rights, so he remarked, *"The most unhappy of all men is the man who cannot tell what he is going to do, who has got no work cut-out for him in the world, and does not go into it."* He continued by declaring, *"Work is the grand cure of all maladies and miseries that ever beset mankind—honest work, which you intend getting done!"*

As an expert in many fields, Carlyle was certainly qualified to make a convincing argument on the value of work. He had been educated in divinity school, but abandoned the clergy to become a mathematics teacher. He later used his broad background to contribute several articles to the *Edinburgh Encyclopedia*.

However, Thomas Carlyle is best known as a social critic and historian. In 1834, he published the satire, *Sartor Resartus*, which translates to *The Tailor Retailored*. This partly autobiographical piece immediately established him as a forerunner in social commentary, and an advocate of the British working class. His later work includes a variety of history books and essays, most importantly a ten-volume account of the Prussian King Frederick the Great.

"Men are men before they are lawyers, or physicians, or merchants, or manufacturers..."
John Stuart Mill (1867)

As one of the premier advocates of personal liberty, John Stuart Mill had an understanding of an individual's role in society. Speaking at Scotland's University of Saint Andrews in 1867, the British philosopher remarked, *"Men are men before they are lawyers, or physicians, or merchants, or manufacturers; and if you*

make them capable and sensible men, they will make themselves capable and sensible lawyers and physicians."

His address was to define the purpose of an institution of higher learning. Mill explained that any individual can learn to make shoes, or build a chair, or perform any specific task; but it is the job of a university to teach that person to think. Perhaps best known for his 1859 essay "On Liberty," Mill was extremely outspoken in areas like politics, economics, and social sciences. Even as early as the mid-1800's, he was rallying support on cutting edge issues like womens' equality and birth control.

As with any radical thinker, Mill was something of a controversial figure. He did earn himself a position in parliament for a short period, but was too much of a revolutionary to achieve higher political success.

"Who dares to teach must never cease to learn."
John Cotton Dana (1912)

This official motto of Kean College in Newark, New Jersey, was originally the declaration of librarian John Cotton Dana. In 1912, Dana, who had upgraded the library system in Newark, was asked to find a Latin quote that would be suitable as an inscription for a new building at the college. Unable to find one that he felt was appropriate, Dana created his own.

Arriving in Newark in 1902, Dana found the city to be a perfect place to experiment with his new ideas on improving the library system. Newark had several colleges, as well as a diverse population of immigrants and established businessmen. He wanted to make a library that would be useful to all of the people in the city, regardless of their particular needs.

To reach his goal, Dana helped institute the concept of open stacks, where a library user was free to browse the material on his own. He also brought in an immense amount of foreign language materials to cater to the high immigrant population. Going one-step further, Dana helped create a specialized business library branch — one of the first to be dedicated solely to one field of research.

Sigmund Freud — The father of psychoanalysis

"Sometimes a cigar is just a cigar."
Sigmund Freud   (early 1900's)

Sigmund Freud, the father of psychoanalysis, is credited with this renowned observation. As legend has it, Freud was preparing to light a cigar when a colleague asked him if there was any significance to the fact that he was holding an obvious phallic symbol in his hand. Freud, who had theorized that people are often driven by their sexuality on an unconscious level, defended himself by saying, *"Sometimes a cigar is just a cigar."*

Towards the end of the 19th century and into the beginning of the 20th century, the highly controversial doctor stirred up the medical world with his studies on human behavior. Freud gathered evidence to support new ideas such as the repression of painful memories and other defense methods unconsciously used by patients to deal with anxiety. While this was all well and good, Freud started to develop a long list of critics when he began to throw sexuality into the mix. Among his most contested theories is that of the Oedipus complex, in which he proposes that there is an erotic attachment of a child for the parent of the opposite sex. The result is hostile feelings toward the other parent.

While many of Freud's theories are certainly subject to argument, there is no doubt that he was a tremendous contributor

77—Philosophy

to the field of psychoanalysis. And even in the midst of all of the psycho-babble, give him credit for understanding that, *"Sometimes a cigar is just a cigar."*

> **"Far better it is to dare mighty things, to win glorious triumphs, even though checkered by failure, than to take rank with those poor spirits who neither enjoy much nor suffer much, because they live in the gray twilight that knows neither victory nor defeat."**
> **Theodore Roosevelt (1899)**

Theodore Roosevelt, while holding the office of governor of New York, delivered this speech on April 10, 1899. Given before a crowd in Chicago, it became known as "The Strenuous Life" speech, and it remains a true testament to Roosevelt's beliefs and lifestyle.

Growing up as a sickly child, Roosevelt became involved in the rigorous outdoors and exercise at an early age. He was a true believer that character is molded through adversity. When he delivered his "Strenuous Life" speech in 1899, Roosevelt had just recently returned from leading a volunteer regiment known as the "Rough Riders" in the battle of San Juan. He urged the audience not to shy away from a life of adversity. Instead, adversity should be attacked head on. He remarked, *"I wish to preach, not the doctrine of ignoble ease, but the doctrine of the strenuous life, the life of toil and effort, of labor and strife…"*.

This particular speech would become Roosevelt's most famous, but he repeatedly delivered the same message. In 1901, upon President McKinley's assassination, Theodore Roosevelt became the youngest president ever at age 42.

"Behold the turtle—he makes progress only when he sticks his neck out."
James Bryant Conant   (1933)

Don't underestimate the things you can learn from a turtle. This is the advice given by American educator James Bryant Conant upon becoming president of Harvard University in 1933. Conant made radical changes in the curriculum, improving the university's diversity, as well as its professional schools. By pointing out that the turtle makes *"progress only when he sticks his neck out,"* Conant was responding to the numerous critics who opposed his sudden reforms.

Just like the turtle, Conant didn't hesitate to take risks throughout his tenure at Harvard. Aside from adjusting the curriculum at the university, he served as the director for the National Defense Research Committee during World War II. This group was instrumental in making the controversial decision to drop the atomic bomb on Hiroshima, Japan.

Conant's dynamic approach to leadership paid off. During his twenty years as president of Harvard University, the institution grew both academically and physically. In 1953, only a few years after his career at Harvard had ended, Conant once again returned to academia. This time he dedicated himself to pushing curricular reforms in high schools across the country.

"Sometimes the first duty of intelligent men is the restatement of the obvious!"
George Orwell   (mid 1900's)

Things aren't always what they seem. George Orwell's two most influential novels, *Animal Farm* (1945) and *Nineteen Eighty-Four* (1949), seem to be simple and entertaining novels. But, that's only half the truth. While they are simple narratives, both are interwoven with complex social commentary.

In *Animal Farm*, the story is told through the eyes of farm animals that are forced to establish their own society. On the surface, the novel is innocent enough. Underneath, it is a powerful exposition condemning totalitarianism by demonstrating its inevitable self-destruction — quite a lot to fit into a story about farm animals!

Nineteen Eighty-Four paints an equally strong picture, though Orwell tackles a different scenario. He creates a futuristic world where people live in fear and are always under the watchful eye of "Big Brother." Again, the story itself is entertaining, though the novel contains a deeper message.

George Orwell had the ability to show how easily a society could yield to totalitarianism if it was not constantly guarded against. But, he didn't feel that he was delivering a message that was new or groundbreaking. In his own words, he was only making a *"restatement of the obvious."* During the Cold War, Orwell's novels were often utilized to highlight the faults of communist governments like the one used in the Soviet Union.

"In the long run of history, the censor and the inquisitor have always lost."
Alfred Whitney   (1950's)

As the president of Yale University, Alfred Whitney Griswold had his share of critics. He was constantly meeting opposition in his campaign to add liberal arts studies to the more traditional classes. Griswald was an idealist, and he felt that this adjustment was necessary for the university to move in the right direction. Responding to those who thought he was only going to poison young minds with his new curriculum, Griswold declared, *"Books won't stay banned. They won't burn. Ideas won't go to jail. In the long run of history, the censor and the inquisitor have always lost."*

As a teacher in the history department for nearly twenty years, Griswold understood the importance of keeping up with the times and circumstances. And when he became the college president in 1952, he feared Yale would have trouble remaining a respectable institution if it didn't update its curriculum. *"The only sure weapon against bad ideas is better ideas,"* he maintained, *"The source of better ideas is wisdom. The surest path to wisdom is a liberal education."* For over a decade, he reformed the entire agenda. As a result, the already respected Yale University became one of the most honored institutions in the country.

Silent Cal

"If you don't say anything, you can't be called upon to repeat it."
                            Calvin Coolidge   (1920's)

Timeless philosophy. As the 30th president of the United States, Calvin Coolidge earned a reputation for giving short answers and speaking only when he was spoken to. Nicknamed "Silent Cal," he offered his reasoning for being so reserved—***"If you don't say anything, you can't be called upon to repeat it."***

An example of Coolidge's tight-lipped nature occurred while at a dinner party during his presidency. A woman seated next to him joked about his reputation, saying, ***"I bet I can make you say more than three words."*** Without any change of expression, Coolidge replied, ***"You lose."***

Calvin Coolidge

Fortunately, Coolidge's desire to stay out of the spotlight served him well as president. He was highly regarded for his ability to effectively do nothing while in office—in other words, for not attempting to change things that didn't need to be changed. He came into office in 1923 with the national economy strong and the morale of the nation soaring. Instead of trying to exercise his power as president, he simply let the country continue to ride the wave it was on. Because the "Roaring Twenties" were such a positive time in the nation's history, he was well respected in office.

Calvin Coolidge was President during one of the most interesting times in American history. Here are some of the highlights of the "Roaring Twenties":

- First radio broadcast takes place (1920).
- The 19th amendment, focusing on Women's Suffrage, is ratified (1920).
- Warren G. Harding becomes president (1921). He dies two years later, and Vice-president Coolidge takes his place (1923).
- Vanzetti and Sacco trial gains worldwide attention. The trial focuses attention on the mistreatment of immigrants (1921).
- Baseball's World Series is broadcast for the first time over the radio (1921). The first radio commercial is aired (1922). The President makes his first address over the radio (1923).
- Jazz music peaks in popularity (1922).
- The Scopes-trial, known as the "Monkey Trial," stirs-up controversy by dealing with the teaching of evolution (1925).
- Gertrude Ederle becomes the first woman to swim across the English Channel (1926).
- Charles Lindbergh makes the first solo, transatlantic flight at the age of 25 (1927).
- Al Capone, known as "Scarface," gains notoriety as the top gangster in Chicago (1927).
- In *The Jazz Singer*, Al Jolson speaks the first line ever in a motion picture when he says, *"You ain't heard nothing yet..."* (1927).
- Babe Ruth hits 60 home runs in a single season. The record will stand for over thirty years (1927).
- The first talking film featuring Mickey Mouse is created (1928).
- Alexander Fleming discovers penicillin (1928).
- Women compete for the first time in the Olympics (1928).
- Construction begins on The Empire State Building, which for a time will be the tallest building in the world (1929).
- The Stock Market crashes on *Black Thursday*, rapidly bringing an end to the good times of the "Roaring Twenties" (1929).

Ayn Rand — Author of the acclaimed novel, Atlas Shrugged

> *"When men abandon reason, they find not only that their emotions cannot guide them, but that they can experience no emotions save one: terror!"*
>
> **Ayn Rand (1974)**

Controversial philosopher Ayn Rand had a stern warning for the 1974 graduating class of the United States Military Academy at West Point. The country seemed to be infected by the atmosphere of the Vietnam era, and the popularity of the military was at an all-time low. Rand cautioned the cadets to be wary of their critics. Her philosophical views centered on the basic principle that, if logic is abandoned, all direction is lost. Because those denouncing the military during the period often formed their view based on sentimental reasons rather than on fact, Rand made the point, *"When men abandon reason, they find not only that their emotions cannot guide them, but they can experience no emotions save one: terror!"*

Rand's legendary novels, *The Fountainhead* (1943) and *Atlas Shrugged* (1957), both displayed her philosophy. She was a believer in Objectivism, or, put more simply, the "virtue of selfishness." This theory encourages an individual to look out for his own interests and needs, which will ultimately help him serve the world better. In other words, if a person worries about what others think and do, they start to lose sight of the best within themselves, in turn causing pain and suffering to others.

Ayn Rand was often criticized for the lack of leniency in her viewpoints—she didn't believe in shades of gray. This inflexibility came from her own past. Born in Russia, she had experienced the Bolshevik Revolution firsthand and openly despised communism. She had seen a communist attitude form that operated under a backward principle— if everyone couldn't be rich together, then they should at least be poor together. Unfortunately, she was beginning to see that same outlook forming in America. Therefore, Ayn Rand reminded the cadets at West Point, *"You are attacked, not for any errors or flaws, but for your virtues. You are denounced, not for any weaknesses, but for your strength and your competence."*

"The only human institution which rejects progress is the cemetery."
Harold Wilson   (1967)

From the moment he was elected Prime Minister in 1964, Harold Wilson found that it was necessary to do a little reorganization to deal with the problems facing Britain. And, right from the beginning, he found out that not everyone encouraged change. On January 24, 1967, Wilson spoke to a Consultative Assemble in Europe and pleaded his case: *"He who rejects change is the architect of decay. The only human institution which rejects progress in the cemetery."*

During his term in office, Wilson would have to stand by his bold statement—he couldn't fear change. Britain was, after all, suffering from a poor economy and there were some serious foreign policy problems. The Prime Minister made some bold moves by devaluing the currency, reducing overseas trade, and moderating Britian's colonial rule in Africa. He was aggressive in his changes, with varying degrees of success.

Over all, Harold Wilson had his ups and downs in office, and he took his share of criticism as well. Still, he also had his share of loyal followers. He was victorious in three general elections, serving as Prime Minister for eight years. In 1976, however, a frustrated Wilson resigned from office.

"Aim at heaven and you will get earth thrown in. Aim at earth and you get neither."
---C.S. Lewis
Novelist and essayist (1898-1963)

Chapter 5

Religion

Martin Luther—Causing an uproar with his 95 Theses

"I cannot and will not retract anything, for it is neither safe nor salutary to act against one's conscience. God help me. Amen."

        Martin Luther (1521)

  After defending himself before the Roman Emperor at the Diet of Worms, Martin Luther concluded with these candid lines. Emperor Charles V had called for the reformer in 1521 as a result of the stir that he had created throughout Europe. The trouble started when Luther nailed his 95 Theses to the door of a church in Wittenburg, Germany, four years earlier.

  Luther's 95 Theses, originally written in Latin, laid the framework for Protestantism. Soon, they were translated into German for the public to read. The writings quickly gained widespread fame, exposing the fact that many of Luther's beliefs differed from Roman Catholicism. He was asked several times to retract his statements, and each time refused.

  Charles V, who had just become Emperor in 1519, saw that Luther's writings had the potential to cause serious conflict throughout Rome. He summoned Luther and asked him once again to retract his statements, only this time giving him one day to consider. Luther returned the next day and very calmly explained his position—he would not recant on anything he had said or written. He told Charles V, *"Here I stand, I can do no other."* This stance would begin the Reformation in Europe, leading to the rise of Protestantism.

"I make war on the living, not on the dead."
Charles V   (1546)

Make no mistake, Roman Emperor Charles V and religious leader Martin Luther were heated enemies right up until Martin Luther's natural death. Even so, when the King of Spain suggested that Charles V hang Luther's corpse for the public to see, it seemed like a little much. The Emperor decided to respect the dead body of Luther, despite their long line of differences.

In 1517, twenty-nine years before his death, Martin Luther nailed his 95 Theses to a church in Wittenburg, Germany. This began the Reformation in Europe, giving rise to Protestantism. When Charles V became Emperor two years later, he wasn't pleased that Luther was the source of tense debate in Rome. What's more, Luther defiantly refused to retract any of his statements, even after some serious threats.

In fact, Martin Luther continued to publish writings, and he translated the Bible into German, all of which added fire to the Reformation. He became Charles V's greatest obstacle in keeping control over his empire. In 1546, Luther died from sickness. At the time, Charles V was still the Emperor, and he was still struggling with the religious turmoil that Luther had created. It was no secret that he despised Martin Luther. The suggestion to hang the body in public may have been tempting, and it was supported by many of Charles V's followers, but he made his position clear: *"I make war on the living, not on the dead."*

"Oh, Holy Simplicity!"
John Huss   (1415)

Religious reformer John Huss muttered this line as he watched an old woman throw a log into the fire that was intended to burn him at the stake. He knew that the naïve woman had the best of intentions, and she didn't truly understand what she was doing. Being uneducated and misled, she had joined the mob that had come to watch him die. Civil to the end, Huss didn't see any point in holding a grudge. Instead, he empathized with the woman's innocence, saying only the words, *"Oh, Holy Simplicity!"*

After joining sides with other controversial religious leaders such as John Wycliffe in the early 1400's, Huss had spoken out against the abuses of the church by its authorities. His beliefs were that Christ and the Bible should always be regarded at the head of the church—not a corrupt official. Huss's sermons on the subject won him the support of the people. Unfortunately, those in power didn't care too much for him. Antipope Alexander V excommunicated him from Prague in 1410 despite riots and demonstrations from Huss's supporters.

In 1415, John Huss was summoned to attend the Council of Constance where he was assured that he would have an opportunity to express his views. Taking the bait, he arrived, and was immediately arrested. Found guilty of heresy after refusing to recant his beliefs, Huss died a martyr's death when he was burned at the stake shortly thereafter.

"Lord, open the king of England's eyes!"
William Tyndale   (1536)

William Tyndale had one last request when he was burned at the stake on October 6, 1536. The request was to Henry VIII, the king of England and the man who had had Tyndale arrested and put to death.

Tyndale's crime had been translating the Bible from Greek into English. This enabled the Bible to be read and understood by the common man. Unfortunately, straying from religious tradition was a dangerous game in England, and Tyndale received no backing. As a result, he traveled to Germany to meet up with Martin Luther. In 1525, the two began to translate the New Testament into English. The translation was forbidden in England, but several smuggled copies made their way into the country.

In 1535, Tyndale was seized in Antwerp, Belgium, and found guilty of heresy. His claim, *"Lord, open the king of England's eyes!"* was a plea for Henry VIII to realize that he had translated the Bible, not to destroy England, but to empower the common man.

"As we were saying yesterday..."
Luis Ponce de Leon (mid 1500's)

Have you ever forgotten what you were saying in mid-sentence? That probably never happened to Spanish poet Luis Ponce de Leon. He had been teaching theology and philosophy at the University of Salamanca when, as a result of the Spanish Inquisition, he was arrested for heresy in the mid-1500's. When released from jail, he resumed his role there. Wanting to begin right where he had left off four years earlier, de Leon began his lecture, *"As we were saying yesterday..."*

De Leon's imprisonment was a result of his disagreement with the traditional religious teachings of the Dominican monks. The Spanish Inquisition, beginning in 1478, was established to "deal" with any Christians or others who posed a threat to those traditional beliefs. As a freethinker, de Leon was in trouble from the start. In fact, he was marked as a serious threat because he was a known expert on biblical studies and philosophy. But, the danger that loomed over him didn't stop de Leon from teaching what he felt was right. Though only a few of his works survive, most prominently *The Names of Christ* published in 1583, he is regarded as one of the most important Spanish theologians in history.

"Tremble at the word of the Lord!"
George Fox   (1650)

Very rarely does a single statement result in the naming of an entire religion. That's what happened, though, when this phrase by George Fox became the namesake for the religious group known as the "Quakers". It had been just a few years earlier that Fox, an English minister, began to preach that Christ comes from within; a concept that became known as "inner light," He gained a substantial following, and because his beliefs were spreading so quickly, Fox became a controversial figure. In October of 1650, he was arrested on a bogus charge of blasphemy.

George Fox was sent before Justice Gervase Bennett to defend his followers, who were formally known as the Religious Society of Friends. In his defense, he warned the judge, *"Tremble at the word of the Lord!"* After hearing this, Bennett referred to the entire group as "Quakers," and the name would stick.

Fox found himself constantly at odds with British officials, but the Quakers continued to rise in popularity. The success of the religion was due to its simplicity. Quakers believe that people are inherently good, and, emulating Christ, the members choose a natural life of few luxuries. Therefore, they believe in plain clothes, mild mannerisms, and even simple speech.

"You have offended him infinitely more than ever a stubborn rebel did his prince..."
Jonathan Edwards   (1741)

During the rigid times of Puritan New England, these harsh words helped spark a rebirth of religious activity known as the Great Awakening. Clergyman Jonathan Edwards delivered the sermon July 8, 1741, in Enfield, Connecticut. It became appropriately entitled, "Sinners in the Hands of an Angry God."

The Calvinist preacher's sermon was based on the biblical verse Deuteronomy 32:35, which reads in part, "To me belongeth vengeance, and recompence." He told his congregation, *"The God that holds you over the pit of hell much as one holds a spider or some loathsome insect over the fire abhors you, and is dreadfully provoked!"* His warnings were intense, but he wanted his listeners to understand that the "Angry God" was all that was keeping them from damnation. Edwards explained, *"You have offended him infinitely more than ever a stubborn rebel did his prince, and yet it is nothing but his hand that holds you from falling into the fire every moment!"*

The scare tactics of the sermon were a success. The congregation rose crying from their seats, and hundreds of members converted to avoid suffering from this temperamental God. While the speeches of Jonathan Edwards helped bring a strong discipline to the church, his heavy-handed approach eventually caused his followers to turn against him. He crossed the line when he began to punish people for crimes like reading books that he felt were improper. This led to his dismissal in 1750.

"When God pleases to convert the heathen, he'll do it without consulting you or me..."
John Ryland, Sr. (1786)

In 1786, twenty-five year old William Carey stood before a group of respected Baptists and tried to persuade them of the need to go on missionary trips around the world. It was his vision to preach Christianity to people who had never before been exposed to it. A pastor of the church, John Ryland, Sr., wasn't blown away by the idea. He replied, *"Young man, sit down! You're an enthusiast. When God pleases to convert the heathen, He'll do it without consulting you or me..."* And, Ryland's viewpoint was shared by many of the older men in the church who had listened to Carey speak.

Despite the fact that others weren't prepared to follow him, William Carey didn't shy away. In 1793, he became the first Baptist missionary to travel to India. There he founded the Serampur mission in 1799 to help him spread his teachings. For forty years, Cary remained in India sharing the Bible with the local people and exposing the country to Christianity. He spent nearly thirty of those years as a professor in Calcutta, one of India's most populated cities. With the goal of exposing as many people as possible to Christianity, William Carey became one of the most influential missionaries of the 19th century.

The Battle of Morality

"My concern is not whether God is on our side, but whether we are on God's side."
        Abraham Lincoln   (1860's)

They say that there are no atheists on the battlefield. During the brutal fighting of the American Civil War, President Abraham Lincoln was asked by an aide, **"Do you think God is on our side?"** Lincoln responded, **"My concern is not whether God is on our side, but whether we are on God's side."** Given the gravity and consequences of the events that were taking place at the time, this was a reasonable concern.

Abraham Lincoln

Beginning in April 1861, the Civil War claimed over 600,000 American lives and caused nearly $5 billion in property damage. The nation was torn apart over sensitive issues like state's rights and slavery. Brothers literally found themselves facing off against each other on the battlefield. Abraham Lincoln knew that, when he was running for president in 1860, a war would be devastating to the country. But, he was prepared to stand by certain principles. He believed that the practice of slavery needed to come to an end, despite the inevitable backlash that such a proclamation would bring. He also believed that, no matter how intense the differences within the country became, the union had to be preserved.

These strong ideals sounded good in speeches but, in reality, the harsh stance meant the death of thousands of Americans. It's not surprising that people throughout the country questioned Lincoln, including many that lived in the Union states. When the nation began to battle against itself, there were moments when he undoubtedly questioned himself as well. Fortunately, Lincoln held onto the belief that the Union was on *"God's side."* The Civil war was fought to a Union victory in 1865, keeping the United States intact and putting an end to slavery.

93—Religion

God, religion, and war have always been intertwined. Here are a few more quotes about this strange interaction:

- There will be no peace as long as God remains unseated at the conference table.
  —*Unknown*

- "There is a time for all things, a time to preach and a time to pray, but those times have passed away. There is a time to fight, and that time has now come."
  —*Peter Muhlenberg*
  Lutheran Clergyman (American Revolution)

- "Is life so dear, or peace so sweet, as to be purchased at the price of chains and slavery? Forbid it, Almighty God! I know not what course others may take, but as for me, give me liberty or give me death!"
  —*Patrick Henry*
  American Patriot (American Revolution)

- "As you know, God is generally on the side of the big squadrons against the small ones."
  —*Comte De Bussy-Rabutin*
  French soldier and writer, mid 1600's

- All the Gods are dead except the God of war.
  — *Eldridge Cleaver*
  African–American leader, 1968

- "War springs from the love and loyalty which should be offered to God being applied to some God substitute, one of the most dangerous being nationalism."
  — *Robert Runcie*
  British Archbishop, 1982

- "As to the thirty-six Senators who placed themselves on record against the principle of a World Court, I am inclined to think that if they ever get to Heaven they will be doing a great deal of apologizing for a very long time—that is if God is against war—and I think He is."
  — *Franklin D. Roosevelt, 1935*
  American President (Referring to post-World War I)

"It is absurd to argue men, as to torture them, into believing."
John Henry Newman   (1831)

In 1831, just before the start of the Oxford Movement, Cardinal John Henry Newman made this self-evident observation. Trying to win support for his cause, Newman gained a following, not by bold criticism, but by simply detailing his beliefs through a series of sermons.

In September 1833, Newman and theologian John Keble printed a series of ninety pamphlets entitled *Tracts for the Times*. In them, the men expressed the need for the Church of England to return to its roots and become a more traditional Catholic Church. This was the focus of the Oxford Movement, which began to be referred to as "Tracterianism" after the influence of those pamphlets.

Knowing that his cause was building momentum, Cardinal Newman began giving weekly sermons to his supporters, and he continued to do so for eight years. The movement revived the discipline in the Church of England. It also brought a great deal of attention to Cardinal Newman, and that began to alarm church officials. As a result of growing hostility, Newman eventually left the church. He was followed by several hundred clergymen who felt that he was being treated unfairly.

"You must believe in God despite what the clergy tell you."
Benjamin Jowett   (mid 1800's)

Benjamin Jowett had some sound advice for his students at Oxford University. A clergyman for the Church of England, Jowett was fluent in Greek, and he used this skill to translate Greek works such as *Epistles of Saint Paul* into English. His translations, as well as the material in the literature, brought him enormous heat from the church officials. In fact, he was charged with heresy for his teachings. But Jowett understood the importance of faith, and he didn't back down from the church authorities. As he explained to his students, *"You must believe in God despite what the clergy tell you."*

It all started in 1855, when Jowett became a professor of the Greek language at Oxford University. Immediately, he began translating the works that would stir up so much controversy. By the early 1860's, Jowett's run-ins with the church had come to a head, and he was brought before the chancellor's court. In the end, he was acquitted of all charges, and was able to continue a long career at the university. Jowett eventually rose to the position of vice-chancellor, playing a major role in helping to improve the undergraduate curriculum at the university.

"I'm looking for loopholes!"
W.C. Fields   (1946)

Comedian and actor W.C. Fields gave this surprising answer to a friend shortly before his death in 1946. The sixty-seven year old, ill-healthed, Fields was at his home reading the Bible when an old friend visited him. But Fields was an agnostic who repeatedly downplayed the Bible, so the confused visitor asked, *"What are you looking for?"* To this, the actor responded, *"I'm looking for loopholes!"* Fields died a few days later.

While it is uncertain whether he had any luck in the afterlife, Fields was extremely successful during his lifetime. He had been involved in show business since the age of fourteen, performing in New York City as part of the legendary Ziegfeld Follies from 1915 to 1921. Most of Fields' recognition, though, would come from his movie roles during the 1930's and 1940's. Starring in films like *David Copperfield* (1935) and *The Bank Dick* (1940), he developed the comedic role as an unkempt cynic who despised authority. Working right up to the time of his death, Fields' autobiography, *Fields by Himself*, was published posthumously in 1973.

Brigham Young—Bringing the Church of Latter-day Saints to Utah

"This is a good place to make Saints..."
Bringham Young (1847)

In 1847, religious leader Brigham Young walked across the Rocky Mountains and into the isolated Great Salt Lake Valley—he knew he had found his home. Young was leading nearly 5,000 members of the Church of Jesus Christ of Latter-day Saints, commonly known as Mormons, in search of a place to settle. When he found the land, which today is the state of Utah, he remarked confidently, *"This is a good place to make Saints, and it is a good place for Saints to live."*

It was Young's belief that the Lord had brought him to the Great Salt Lake so that the Mormons could have a proper place to organize. He explained simply, *"We shall stay here, until He tells us to go somewhere else."* Apparently, he was never told to move anywhere else—today, almost 70% of Utah's population is Mormon.

Brigham Young never intended to lead the Mormons to their new home. Born a Methodist, he didn't convert until he was over thirty years old. He was persuaded by the teachings of

Joseph Smith, who had founded the Church of Jesus Christ of Latter-day Saints. Though he was new to the religion, Young quickly became an effective preacher. In 1844, after Joseph Smith was assassinated by a mob, Brigham Young became the recognized leader of the Mormons.

> **"I don't see why we can't get along just as well with a polygamist who doesn't polyg as we do with a lot of monogamists who don't monog!"**
> **Penrose Boise   (1902)**

Pennsylvania politician Penrose Boise used this argument as the senate debated whether Reid Smoot, a Mormon from Utah elected in 1902, should be allowed to take a seat in the senate. Though Smoot himself was not a polygamist, it was known that the Mormon religion advocated it. Only a few years earlier, Brigham Rogers, a polygamist elected to the House of Representatives, had been forbidden to take his seat. As Smoot's debate rolled on, the influential and conservative Penrose Boise took his surprising position.

The dispute continued for three years, but Reid Smoot was eventually allowed to retain his seat. The reasoning was that, despite being a Mormon, he wasn't a polygamist. In fact, the predominately Mormon state of Utah, which had been made a state only six years before Reid's election, didn't even support the practice. It was this stance against polygamy that enabled Utah to finally be approved for statehood after petitioning the government for nearly half a century.

Even in the 1890's, officials of the Mormon religion began to advise members not to practice polygamy. Eventually, the issue disappeared altogether, allowing Utah to gain full acceptance across the nation.

"...but this may be my last chance to see you."
Phillips Brooks   (1893)

As the popular clergyman Phillips Brooks lay on his deathbed in 1893, he had just a few words for his friend Robert Ingersoll. Ingersoll, the son of a preacher, had long since developed a strong distaste for organized religion. During the second half of the 19th century, he constantly spoke out against the church, earning himself the nickname, "The Great Agnostic."

Surprisingly, Bishop Phillips Brooks, a leader of the Protestant Episcopal Church in Boston, befriended the agnostic. When Brooks became very sick, he refused to see all visitors, but did allow Ingersoll to enter the room. His friend questioned, *"Why would you see me, when you're not receiving visitors?"* Brooks replied, *"I feel confident of seeing my other friends in the next world, but this may be my last chance to see you."*

Throughout his life, Brooks was an outstanding preacher and theologian. But he may be best remembered as the author of the Christmas hymn, "O Little Town of Bethlehem." And, despite his great concern for his friend Robert Ingersoll's afterlife, he couldn't make him change his ways. In fact, Ingersoll wrote over twenty lectures against the organized church, his most famous being "Why I Am an Agnostic" in 1896.

"I do not pretend to know where many ignorant men are sure..."
Clarence Darrow   (1925)

In the midst of one of the most controversial trials of the 20th century, distinguished defense lawyer Clarence Darrow made this confession in an effort to explain the position of his client. He was defending a high school biology teacher named John T. Scopes, who had been accused of violating the Butler Act. The law prevented the teaching of the theory of evolution in public schools over the account of creation that is presented in the Bible.

The Scopes Trial, taking place in Dayton, Tennessee, in 1925, received immediate and worldwide publicity because it dealt so closely with people's personal beliefs. Darrow himself was an outspoken agnostic, and he used his opinions to help sway the jury. He explained, *"I do not consider it an insult, but rather a compliment to be called an agnostic. I do not pretend to know where many ignorant men are sure—that is all agnosticism means."*

In the end, prosecuting attorney William Jennings Bryan, a well-known fundamentalist, defeated Darrow in the trial, and Scopes was fined $100. However, the defeat did little to tarnish the theory of evolution. Clarence Darrow did an excellent job of showing logic and proof, while William Jennings Bryan and the prosecution often seemed to be uninformed about new scientific findings.

"I would rather be a servant in the House of the Lord than to sit in the seats of the mighty."
Alben Barkley (1956)

In 1956, seventy-eight year-old Kentucky senator Alben Barkley delivered what could very well be the best exit line in American history. He was visiting Washington and Lee University in Virginia when he remarked, *"I am glad to sit in the back row, for I would rather be a servant in the House of the Lord than to sit in the seats of the mighty."* The crowd answered with applause and, seconds later, Barkley fell dead from a heart attack.

It is appropriate that the senator was attending a mock Democratic convention at the university. Barkley had served over forty years in politics and was known for his devoted speeches against the Republican Party. He was vice-president under Harry Truman in 1948, but his true contribution came as a senator. Beginning in 1927, Barkley served four consecutive terms as senator for the state of Kentucky, eventually becoming the senate leader for the Democratic Party. Even after his term as vice-president, he was elected to the senate one final time in 1954.

Barkley probably wouldn't complain about the circumstances surrounding his death. He was a renowned orator, and was given the chance to give one final speech, and, of course, he had the opportunity to deliver the perfect line.

A Few Short Prayers

"God, grant me the serenity to accept the things I cannot change; courage to change the things I can; and wisdom to know the difference."

Reinhold Niebuhr   (1930's)

This familiar prayer, created in the early 1930's by renowned theologian Reinhold Niebuhr, has become the official prayer of Alcoholics Anonymous. Commonly known as the "Serenity Prayer," Niebuhr wrote it while attending church on Sunday in a small Massachusetts town.

Since that day, the prayer has been adopted and recited by over 2,000,000 Alcohol Anonymous members. The support group for recovering alcoholics originated in 1935, and the Serenity Prayer quickly became a centerpiece for the famed Twelve-Step recovery program.

When he was creating the prayer, Niebuhr was a member of the faculty at the Union Theological Seminary in New York, residing in Massachusetts at a summer home. He ended up staying with the college for thirty years, gaining a reputation for his writing and research on the relationship between religion and society.

Neibuhr would be placed in a position to fulfill the wishes of his prayer, and show that he had the *"courage to change the things"* he could. During the 1930's he had preached isolationism and pacifism, but had to rethink his views when it became time to defend the nation against Adolph Hitler in World War II.

"Let us not be content to wait and see what will happen, but give us the determination to make the right things happen."

Peter Marshall (1948)

At the opening of the senate on March 10, 1948, Chaplain Peter Marshall gave this short prayer that would be remembered for years. The prayer was a characteristic one for the preacher, who had become known for his inspirational sermons.

As a native Scotsman, Marshall arrived in America at the age of twenty-five with barely enough money to get him through a couple of weeks. He found a job as a laborer in New Jersey, and eventually traveled south to Alabama. As a member of the Presbyterian Church, Marshall possessed such a fondness and insight for the religion that members of his congregation were persuaded to assist him financially through seminary school. Ten years after arriving in the country, he moved to the nation's capital in Washington, DC, to begin preaching. In the early 1940's, Marshall's hard-working background helped him direct his sermons to the common people of the city as well as to some of the top politicians. His sermons at the Capitol became extremely popular, consistently drawing large crowds.

In 1947, Marshall was appointed Senate Chaplain. While the politicians enjoyed his heartening prayers, he was only able to serve for less than two years. At the young age of forty-six, Marshall died from a heart attack.

Mother Theresa — Worldwide humanitarian

"We cannot solve all the problems of the world, but let us never bring in the worst problem of all..."

Mother Teresa   (1994)

At the age of 84, international humanitarian Mother Teresa was still capable of giving some clear-cut advice. When she led a Morning Prayer in Washington, DC, Teresa spoke in support of natural family planning — *"I also know there are great problems in the world — that many spouses do not love each other enough to practice natural family planning. We cannot solve all the problems in the world, but let us never bring in the worst problem of all, and that is to destroy love. And this is what happens when we tell people to practice contraception and abortion..."*

Mother Teresa gave the speech on February 3, 1994, three and a half years before her death. Her lifetime was spent in dedication to altruistic causes. When she was just 18, Teresa joined a group of Irish nuns in Calcutta, India, and became a teacher. But, after nearly twenty years in the convent, she had a desire to leave and work more directly with the poor. For the next several decades, Mother Teresa spearheaded numerous charity operations to help the sick and destitute. Her work spread throughout the world: she persuaded Fidel Castro to allow a mission into communist Cuba, opened a home in Bangladesh for women who been raped, and started a center for AIDS patients in San Francisco.

Her charities caught the attention of people on an international level, and she successfully used that publicity to further her humanitarian causes. In 1979, Mother Teresa was awarded the Nobel Prize for Peace.

"Today is the first day of the rest of your life!"
Charles Dederich   (1958)

This familiar phrase was coined by Charles Dederich, the founder and leader of the controversial group, Synanon. After battling his own alcoholism, Dederich founded the self-help community in 1958 to assist drug and alcohol abusers. Eventually, the group began to take on a cult-like atmosphere, with its members being required to follow strict rules in an effort to establish a utopian society. Dederich, a charismatic spokesman, greeted his followers by declaring, *"Today is the first day of the rest of your life!"*

Synanon, based in California, was originally associated with the familiar support group, Alcoholics Anonymous. During the first few years, Dederich successfully developed it into a community of drug users that helped each other straighten out their lives. However, Synanon eventually split from Alcoholics Anonymous. In the early 1970's, the group went from being just a therapeutic community to becoming more of an alternative lifestyle. In late 1974, Synanon declared itself an official religion, with nearly 2,000 members.

Because of the controversy surrounding Synanon, it lost its tax-exempt status in 1991, and was consequently disbanded.

"Obstacles are those frightful things you see when you take your eyes off your goal."
—Henry Ford
American businessman (1863-1947)

Chapter 6

Business & Economics

John D. Rockefeller—Oil tycoon and millionaire industrialist

"I have no use for men who fail."
John Rockefeller   (late 1800's)

John D. Rockefeller, great oil tycoon, was describing his business partners when he declared, *"I have no use for men who fail. The cause of their failure is no business of mine, but I want successful men as my associates."* His strict criteria seemed to work. In 1855, at the age of sixteen, he was making $3.50 per week as a bookkeeper. By 1900, he was worth about $1 billion.

The secret to Rockefeller's success was his early insight into an industry that was about to revolutionize the world. When it was discovered that oil could be distilled into kerosene for burning lamps, the twenty-three year old Rockefeller teamed up with associate Samuel Andrews and started the Standard Oil Company. They had an immediate impact, and Rockefeller was able to control 90% of the United States' oil market by 1878. Eventually, the enormous success of the corporation brought on accusations of it being a monopoly. In 1892, the government forced the business to break apart.

As his profits reached what were unthinkable amounts at the time, Rockefeller was kind enough to share the wealth. In fact, he became one of the greatest philanthropists in history. By the time of his death, he had contributed over $500 million to different causes.

"But what have you done today?"
Andrew Carnegie   (1881)

When future industrialist Charles Schwab began his career at the Carnegie Steel Company in 1881, he quickly rose through the ranks. As a general superintendent in Pennsylvania, he proudly wired a telegram to steel tycoon Andrew Carnegie to tell him, *"All records broken yesterday."* Carnegie responded by wiring back, *"But what have you done today?"*

This exchange shows just how Andrew Carnegie earned his success. He became a stereotype of the American dream. He arrived from Scotland as a teenager, and began working in a cotton mill for $1.20 per week. By the time he was in his mid-thirties, he was making over $50,000 per year. As his steel operations expanded, the money kept rolling in, and Carnegie became more and more successful. As a result, he became one of the greatest philanthropists of his day, donating several hundred million dollars to charity.

The lesson of Carnegie's blunt telegram was not lost on Charles Schwab. He eventually became president of the Carnegie Steel Company in 1897, helping to guide the organization through several profitable mergers.

108—"What Made Them Say That?"

"A man who has a million dollars is as well off as if he were rich."
John Jacob Astor   (early 1800's)

John Jacob Astor, the richest man in the United States in the early 1800's, provided this seemingly obvious law of economics. Although poor as a youth, Astor arrived in New York City from Germany at the age of twenty and quickly began to make his fortune. By the 1830's, he had established an enormous wealth of nearly $100 million

When Astor came to the states in 1783, he wasted no time becoming involved in the profitable fur trade. He began by dealing directly with the Native Americans, establishing posts along the Missouri and Columbia rivers. Within a few years, he had earned a substantial profit, so Astor began to expand. He created the American Fur Company in 1808 and the Pacific Fur Company in 1810. Before too long, he was trading furs throughout the world, especially with China—and he was making a huge amount of money in the process. Eventually, after establishing himself as the richest man in the United States, Astor moved away from the fur industry and took advantage of the increasing real estate value of New York City during the 1830's and 1840's.

"The customer is always right."
Harry Selfridge   (1909)

Wise words for any businessman to live by. This radical idea was announced by London resident Harry Gordon Selfridge after opening the doors of his successful department store in 1909. Selfridge and Co., Ltd. was located on the busy Oxford Street in London, and its existence would change the rules of consumer marketing throughout the world. Selfridge's concept, *"The customer is always right,"* helped create an environment in which shoppers could browse for pleasure rather than necessity.

Harry Selfridge refined his skills and business savvy while working for a trading firm in Chicago. In 1906, he visited London and decided that the liberal mood of the city would be a proper atmosphere to test his new marketing ploy. When Selfridge and Co. opened three years later, it was an immediate success.

Although the concept of "*The customer is always right,*" was cutting edge in the early 1900's, consumer outlets throughout the world have since adopted the maxim. People no longer judge the quality of a transaction based solely on economics. Harry Gordon Selfridge helped introduce a new variable into the game — service.

> ***"It is all one to me if a man comes from Sing Sing Prison or Harvard. We hire a man, not his history."***
>
> **Henry Ford   (early 1900's)**

Entrepreneur Henry Ford had a funny way of describing the hiring practices of his enterprise, Ford Motor Company. He made the unlikely comparison between the notorious Sing Sing Prison (a rugged high-security prison opened in New York in the late 1820's) and Harvard College (a prestigious institute for higher learning in Massachusetts). Regardless which of these two institutions a man was derived from, Ford wanted him at Ford Motor Company only if he could effectively do the work. And those guidelines certainly worked.

In 1913, with the adoption of standardized parts and the assembly line, Henry Ford was able to transform the technique for automobile production. This new approach had one major setback: there was a monthly labor turnover of 40 to 60 percent.

To combat this problem, Ford began to choose his employees more carefully. When he found the type of laborer that he was looking for, he provided them with a daily wage that was double what was being offered by his competitors in the industry. The result was phenomenal. His workers became more effective, operating costs decreased, and the profits of the Ford Motor Company doubled in a two-year period.

A Little Out of Context

"The public be damned!"
  William Vanderbilt (1882)

"I owe the public nothing!"
  J.P. Morgan (1912)

The first of these infamous statements was the reaction of railroad executive William Vanderbilt when a reporter asked him his opinion on the sentiment that the railroads should be run for the public benefit. While the words are often repeated as an example of corporate greed, the *entire* story is seldom told.

William Vanderbilt, although a successful businessman in his own right, became a railroad powerhouse in the early 1860's when he joined forces with his father, industrialist Cornelius Vanderbilt. The two operated several major railroads and did a terrific job serving the public. Whatever their intentions, the fact that they wanted to remain competitive forced them to provide a quality product. When, in 1882, the reporter questioned William about his railroad company's obligation to the public, he responded, **"The public be damned! I am working for my stockholders!"**

William Vanderbilt

His point was simple—he was running a successful railroad to increase the investment he and others had made in his company. Therefore, his first priority was to make money. Fortunately for the rest of the world, the side effect of that was an efficient railroad system that benefited the general public as a whole. While Vanderbilt wasn't bashful in his wording, he probably didn't have the evil intentions that are often implied.

Another business tycoon that had an unfortunate slip of the tongue was legendary American financier, J.P. Morgan. His story is simple—he got a little frustrated. At first, everything seemed to be going his way. After all, his banking firm, J.P. Morgan & Company, had achieved an enormous amount of success in the late 1800's. Morgan was able to use his financial influence to control several major businesses throughout the nation. Among his conquests was U.S. Steel Corporation, the largest steel operation in the world.

But because of his involvement in so many ventures, Morgan's decisions began to have a tremendous impact on the economy in the United States. This had its downside: when the economy suffered, the public quickly accused him of forming money-trusts and competing unfairly. In 1912, during a time of particular economic discontent, Morgan was accused of some shady dealings, and he was investigated before the U.S. House of Representatives. Feeling that he was being attacked only because of his success, he shouted, **"I owe the public nothing!"**

J.P. Morgan

Like Vanderbilt's rallying cry, *"The public be damned,"* Morgan's statement has been used to exemplify the greed of big business. In his defense, J.P. Morgan did give millions of dollars to charity throughout his lifetime, and many credit him with saving the economy after an extremely unstable period in the 1890's. In reality, his rise to fame was as clean-cut as they come. Morgan began by working as an agent in his father's banking firm at the age of twenty-three. Through obvious talent and good instincts, he was able to expand the operation into a powerhouse of domestic and worldwide finance.

"Every man has a right to be wrong in his opinions, but no man has a right to be wrong in his facts!"
Bernard Baruch   (early 1900's)

As a financial advisor to President Woodrow Wilson, Bernard Baruch knew better than to rely on tips or uncertain inside information. And his reliability was much appreciated. By World War I, he had already achieved success as a businessman, and his expertise was called upon to convert industry in the United States from peacetime to wartime production. Baruch's decisions had such a positive influence on the economy that he was later asked to advise presidents Harding, Coolidge, and Hoover.

With a great reputation already established, Baruch was faced with a new challenge in 1933. In the midst of the Great Depression, President Roosevelt approached him to help draft the National Industrial Recovery Act. Baruch helped develop the legislation that detailed ways to revive the national economy.

"I have seen the future, and it works!"
Lincoln Steffens   (1917)

Returning from Russia in 1917, American journalist Lincoln Steffens may have been a little bit misled. Amazed by the communist ideology where the resources of the nation are shared equally among the entire community, Steffens excitedly declared to economist Bernie Baruch, *"I have seen the future and it works!"*

Even before his visit, Lincoln Steffens had gained a reputation as a liberal reporter, and he wasn't a big fan of capitalism. He wrote articles exposing the corruption of big business and the harsh economic conditions in large cities. His writing helped start the journalistic "Muckraking" movement in the early 1900's, in which journalists exposed the abuses in society and pressed for government reform.

However, when Steffens boasted to Baruch, he probably didn't succeed in convincing the economist. Baruch had earned a fortune as a businessman in New York City, and he had relied on the ideals of free trade to do so. As a true believer in capitalism, Baruch played a tremendous part in shaping the economy after World War I and again after the Great Depression.

"The chief business of the American people is business."
Calvin Coolidge   (1925)

It's as simple as that. On January 17, 1925, President Calvin Coolidge delivered this famous line before the American Society of Newspaper Editors. He explained, *"...the chief business of the American people is business. They are profoundly concerned with producing, buying, selling, investing, and prospering in the world."*

Serving as president from 1923 to 1929, Coolidge held the office during one of the most prosperous times in American history. After the end of World War I, the "Roaring Twenties" became a time of industrialization and mass production. Basically, people were making a fortune, and the economy was booming. Coolidge, while being known as a man of few words, carried to the table a philosophy of morality and hard work.

As the country boomed economically and opportunities to become rich were more common, many people became worried about the possible consequences. When Coolidge spoke to the editors, he touched on the delicate balance existing in the newspaper business. A newspaper had to report according to its ideals, yet it still had to provide a product that was profitable. He warned that making money cannot be allowed to win over morality — *"I think there is little cause for fear that our journalism, merely because it is prosperous, is likely to betray us. But it calls for additional effort to avoid even the appearance of the evil of selfishness..."*

Predictions a Little off the Mark

> *"Stocks have reached what looks like a permanently high plateau."*
> **Irving Fisher** **(1929)**

Have you ever said something that you wish you could take back? Irving Fisher, a professor of economics at Yale University, did just that in 1929 when he declared, **"Stocks have reached what looks like a permanently high plateau."** Two weeks later the stock market crashed, beginning the infamous Great Depression.

During the 1920's, the people of the United States prospered with the help of modern industry and an aggressive economy. The decade, known as the "Roaring Twenties," also resulted in the rise of self-indulgence and careless spending. To keep up with this new trend, industries began mass-production of goods hoping that the public would continue to buy at the same astounding rates. New concepts like credit, or "buy now, pay later," brought on rising inflation. Finally, the demand for products couldn't keep up with the production. This concerned many experts, but others (such as Fisher) didn't see any backlash waiting in the future.

Unfortunately, during the first part of the 1930's, economic conditions in the United State became dreadful. In 1933, one quarter of the American workforce was unemployed. Among those hurt by the Depression was Irving Fisher himself. Besides having his reputation severely tarnished, he also lost his fortune.

But Fisher wasn't the only one who missed the mark when it came to the future of American business. Thomas J. Watson, chairman of the IBM Corporation, admitted in 1943, **"I think there is a world market for maybe five computers."** Watson had already helped make IBM (International Business Machines) an industrial powerhouse after joining with the company in 1924. At the time, however, IBM was making its biggest impression by selling items like clocks and typewriters. In the early 1940's, with the research on computers still in the infant stage, Watson just didn't see how something so complicated could be practical.

And there were others that were skeptical about computers. In the 1970's, Ken Olson, president and founder of the Digital Equipment Corporation, made the confident declaration, **"There is no reason anyone would want a computer in their home."**

Obviously, both Watson and Olsen were wrong. In fact, only eight years after Watson's remark, IBM entered into the computer market. It was Watson's son, though, who truly took IBM into the computer age. Thomas Watson, Jr. was chairman of the company through the 1960's and 1970's when it began to dominate the world market for mainframe computers. In 1981, IBM introduced its first personal computer—a tremendous success. Unfortunately for IBM, the age of minicomputers opened up the doors for other companies to compete with the corporate giant. Consequently, the company quickly lost the stronghold that it had maintained in the industry for the previous twenty years.

There were other fads besides the computer that not everyone saw coming. In 1927, H.M. Warner (of Warner Brothers fame) asked the now silly question, **"Who the hell wants to hear actors talk?"** Perhaps just as bad, the inventor of the television, Lee DeForest, once remarked, **"While theoretically and technically television may be feasible, commercially and financially it is an impossibility."**

They say that hindsight is 20-20, so it might not be fair to laugh at those who were aiming a little off the mark. Instead, the rest of us can be thankful that their original predictions didn't always come true.

"One of the greatest disservices you can do to a man is to lend him money that he can't pay back."
Jesse Jones (mid 1930's)

Jesse Jones had a tricky job. President Herbert Hoover appointed him to serve on the Reconstruction Finance Corporation in 1932 to help the nation's suffering economy during the Great Depression. His job was to provide banks and companies with emergency funding during the Depression. But this wasn't easy. Jones understood that the dispersion of money had to be handled delicately. In his own words, *"One of the greatest disservices you can do to a man is to lend him money that he can't pay back!"*

Jesse Jones had built his fortune by creating the South Texas Lumber Company in 1902. With his success, he began to erect buildings in downtown Houston. He became so influential as a developer that, by the 1930's, it is said that Jones owned more buildings than any other man. While most of these buildings were in Houston, he had also developed in New York City, Dallas, Saint Louis, and other areas across the country.

A true businessman, Jones wasn't satisfied with his success even after making a fortune. In 1917, he began to reorganize the American Red Cross, turning it into a valuable charity organization during World War I. He also purchased the *Houston Chronicle* in 1926, and became the newspaper's publisher. It was his obvious skill for business that made President Hoover, and later President Roosevelt, seek Jones' help during the Great Depression.

"...in order to earn better than a 'C', the idea must be feasible."
Professor at Yale University (1965)

In 1965, a Yale University student by the name of Frederick Smith wrote an engaging paper for one of his classes. In it, he expressed the need and opportunity for a group of private freight planes to concentrate solely on delivering packages. Unfortunately, he received the disappointing grade of a 'C', and his professor of management responded, *"The concept is interesting and well-formed, but in order to earn better than a 'C', the idea must be feasible."*

Six years later, Fred Smith raised nearly 90 million dollars from investors willing to back the idea he had set forth in his paper. In 1973, Smith's new company, Federal Express Corporation, made its first mail deliveries by air. Ten years later, the Tennessee based company reported annual revenues of over one billion dollars.

With Federal Express Corporation able to provide reliable overnight delivery using a fleet of private aircraft, Smith more than proved that his idea was feasible. Even today, the company remains a leader in mail delivery, and it has kept up with technology by utilizing new features such as the World Wide Web. Despite all of this, however, Smith was never able to change the disappointing grade on his paper.

"There's no such thing as a free lunch."
Milton Friedman   (mid 1900's)

Economist Milton Friedman always believed in the concept that, if something appears too good to be true, then it probably is. It is he that first coined the maxim: *"There's no such thing as a free lunch."* This piece of wisdom has since been adopted as a basic rule for capitalistic economics.

Serving as an advisor to several federal agencies, Friedman became a respected figure in the world of commerce prior to World War II. In 1946, he joined the economics department at the University of Chicago. He became an outspoken advocate of the free market, and a strong opponent of government intervention in the economy.

His number one rule, *"There's no such thing as a free lunch,"* is based on the obvious nature of an economic transaction. Simply put, each benefit must always have an offsetting cost, even if that cost is not immediately apparent. Friedman warned that it is important to know all potential costs — don't expect a *"free lunch."* In 1976, he received a Nobel Prize for his comprehensive work in the field of economics.

"Do not worry about your problems with mathematics, I assure you mine are far greater."
— Albert Einstein
Scientist and mathematician (1879-1955)

Chapter 7

Science & Technology

Galileo Galilei—On trial for heresy

"And yet it moves..."
Galileo Galilei   (1630's)

    Galileo Galilei, one of the great pioneers of modern science, made this assertion at the conclusion of his infamous trial. Through his own scientific observations, Galileo had become a believer in the concept that the earth revolved around the sun, an idea that was first proposed by Nicholas Copernicus.
    This theory was a direct contradiction to the beliefs of the Roman Catholic Church, which declared that the earth was the center of universe. Galileo was warned about making such bold statements, and he was threatened by the Church not to support the Copernican theory. After making his own appeal to the Pope, Galileo was allowed to continue to discuss his position so long as he maintained that it didn't hold any more truth than the Church's teachings.
    In his *Dialog Concerning the Two Chief World Systems* (1632), Galileo gave the impression that he was backing off of his beliefs. In truth, though, he wasn't too subtle about sharing his original ideas about the earth and the sun. The Church was

enraged by the obvious subtext in the work, and Galileo was placed on trial for heresy. He was found guilty.

After some serious threats, Galileo was ordered by the Church to renounce his theory that the earth revolved around the sun—and he did. Yet, as his punishment was being determined, he muttered the phrase, *"And yet it moves..."* This simple statement was a powerful stance against authority. It declared that, no matter what anyone may say or do, it cannot change scientific fact. The earth will still move.

"There is no royal road to geometry!"
Euclid   (300 BC)

Even over 2,000 years ago, learning math was frustrating. When Ptolemy I, King of Egypt, was studying under the great Greek mathematician Euclid, he pleaded with his teacher that there must be an easier way to master geometry. As it was, he had to slowly learn each tedious theorem. Euclid had an immediate reply to the request: *"There is no royal road to geometry!"*

The King was studying Euclid's main work, *Elements*, a comprehensive thirteen-volume study of geometry. Written around 300 BC, the work remained a respected textbook for centuries to come. In fact, versions of the book are still used in geometry courses today. In *Elements*, Euclid discussed all aspects of the field, including plane geometry, solid geometry, and properties of numbers. His contributions make him one of the most influential mathematicians of all time, earning him the title of "father of geometry."

As for Ptolemy I, he had no choice but to concentrate on the tedious theorems. Forunately, his education was effective, enabling him to begin the Ptolemaic Dynasty that ruled Egypt for hundreds of years.

The Hippocratic Oath

"I swear by Apollo the Physician..."

The doctors of today probably don't direct their professional pledge to the God Apollo. Still, this is the translation of the original Hippocratic Oath, recited by numerous physicians before entering into the practice of medicine. The oath promises ethical dealings in medicine, and it has stood the test of time — upcoming doctors have taken it for 2000 years. Even today, an overwhelming majority of medical schools require their students to take some version of the oath upon graduation.

The Hippocratic Oath is named for the Greek physician Hippocrates, who claims the title as the "father of medicine." About 400 BC, he began to practice medicine using deductive reasoning and study, making major strides in understanding health and hygiene. He wasn't the author of the original oath, but it is said to represent his beliefs.

Not surprisingly, few schools use an exact translation of the original oath. It actually forbade participation in surgery, euthanasia, and abortions. Nonetheless, the modern oaths share the same central theme as the original: use the skills of medicine to ethically serve the best interests of the patient.

The Original Oath (Translated by Ludwig Edelstein)

I swear by Apollo the Physician and Asclepius and Hygieia and Panaceia and all the gods and goddesses, making them my witnesses, that I will fulfil according to my ability and judgment this oath and this covenant:

To hold him who has taught me this art as equal to my parents and to live my life in partnership with him, and if he is in need of money to give him a share of mine, and to regard his offspring as equal to my brothers in male lineage and to teach them this art - if they desire to learn it - without fee and covenant; to give a share of precepts and oral instruction and all the other learning to my sons and to the sons of him who has instructed me and to pupils who have signed the covenant and have taken an oath according to the medical law, but no one else.

123—Science & Technology

I will apply dietetic measures for the benefit of the sick according to my ability and judgment; I will keep them from harm and injustice.

I will neither give a deadly drug to anybody who asked for it, nor will I make a suggestion to this effect. Similarly I will not give to a woman an abortive remedy. In purity and holiness I will guard my life and my art.

I will not use the knife, not even on sufferers from stone, but will withdraw in favor of such men as are engaged in this work.

Whatever houses I may visit, I will come for the benefit of the sick, remaining free of all intentional injustice, of all mischief and in particular of sexual relations with both female and male persons, be they free or slaves.

What I may see or hear in the course of the treatment or even outside of the treatment in regard to the life of men, which on no account one must spread abroad, I will keep to myself, holding such things shameful to be spoken about.

If I fulfill this oath and do not violate it, may it be granted to me to enjoy life and art, being honored with fame among all men for all time to come; if I transgress it and swear falsely, may the opposite of all this be my lot.

Modern Version (as approved by the American Medical Association)

I do solemnly swear, by whatever I hold most sacred.

That I will be loyal to the Profession of Medicine and just and generous to its members.

That I will lead my life and practice my art in uprightness and honor.

That into whatsoever house I shall enter, it shall be for the good of the sick to the utmost of my power, holding myself far aloof from wrong, from corruption, from the tempting of others to vice.

That I will exercise my art solely for the cure of my patients, and will give no drug, perform no operation, for a criminal purpose, even if solicited, far less suggest it.

That whatsoever I shall see or hear of the lives of men or women which is not fitting to be spoken, I will keep inviolably secret.

These things do I swear. I bow my head in sign of acquiescence.
And now, if I will be true to this, my oath, may prosperity and good repute be ever mine; the opposite, if I shall prove myself forsworn.

"Eureka!"
Archimedes   (250 BC)

Stepping into his bath and noticing the water overflow from the tub, Greek physicist Archimedes couldn't hold back his excitement. His outcry, *"Eureka!"* translates to "*I found it!"* The water that was displaced by his body helped him figure out the answer to a problem that had previously had him perplexed.

As the legend goes, Hiero II, the leader of ancient Syracuse, had approached Archimedes around 250 BC with a strange dilemma. Hierro II wanted to determine whether a crown that he had been given was made of pure gold or with cheaper alloys. At first befuddled, Archimedes finally found the answer after the bathtub episode. He came up with the theory of hydrostatics, which says that a floating object placed in water has a weight equal to the amount of water it displaces. Since pure gold has a different density, or weight per volume, than other alloys, Archimedes reasoned that he could determine if the crown was indeed pure gold by dropping it in water and seeing the amount that overflowed. This sudden revelation is what brought about his exclamation, *"Eureka!"*

In addition to his work in hydrostatics, Archimedes also had a great influence in the field of geometry and physics. Among his theoretical research, he is credited with developing the principle of the lever, which in turn led him to the creation of the catapult.

"Ask her to wait a moment—I am almost done."
Carl Friedrich Gauss   (mid 1800's)

Carl Friedrich Gauss didn't like to be disturbed. When servants rushed into the room to inform him that his wife was dying, they were given this response from the German mathematician. Gauss was working intensely on a project and wanted just a little more time to finish.

While his priorities may have been a little harsh, Gauss

certainly achieved success with that dedication to his work. He became interested in advanced mathematics while in his late teens—in fact, by his early twenties, he had already contributed lasting theories to arithmetic, algebra, and geometry. During the first part of the 19th century, he wrote several classic works summarizing his mathematical theories. Gauss even expanded his studies into the field of astronomy, developing a new method for calculating the orbits of planets.

Despite being an expert in many fields, Gauss is perhaps best known for his work in physics. He concentrated mainly on the properties of magnetism and electricity, providing extremely important research in the field. It's obvious that Gauss was addicted to his work, as evident by his reaction to his wife's final moments. Upon his death in 1855, there was very little in the way of mathematics, astronomy, and physics that he had not spent time studying and experimenting with.

"Mr. Prime Minister, what good is a baby?"
Michael Faraday   (1830's)

British physicist Michael Faraday had an odd way of explaining to a skeptical visitor the potential of his new discovery. According to scientific urban legend, the Prime Minister of England was visiting Faraday's laboratories in the 1830's, just as he was beginning to experiment with electricity. The Prime Minister was impressed by the sparks that were being produced, but couldn't help ask the question, *"What good is it?"* To this, Faraday answered, *"Mr. Prime Minister, what good is a baby?"*

Although electricity wouldn't have a significant impact on society during Faraday's lifetime, he understood that, like a newborn baby, it would become useful as it developed. Spurred on by this belief, he became one of the most influential experimental scientists in the field.

It was the next generation of scientists, such as the legendary Thomas Edison, that would help make electricity a common tool in society. In 1882, Edison helped develop the world's first sizable electric power station, located in New York City.

126—"What Made Them Say That?"

Louis Pasteur—An advocate of science with a practical use

"Chance favors only the prepared mind."
Louis Pasteur   (1854)

Renowned French scientist Louis Pasteur wanted his students to be prepared, so he passed onto them this advice in 1854. Working at France's University of Lille, Pasteur was concentrating on the study of theory with practical applications. With this being his constant focus, he held his classes near factories, encouraging daytime workers to attend at night. That way, his students would be able to use the technical information that he was teaching them even when they weren't in class. Pasteur preached the importance of continuous experimentation, knowing that the next big breakthrough would come as a result of numerous trials, and a little luck. In his own words, *"Where observation is concerned, chance favors only the prepared mind."*

A relentless researcher, Pasteur was obviously prepared. His experiments in microbiology resulted in the process of pasteurization, where the dangerous germs in milk are destroyed by heating them to a high temperature and pressure. The discovery not only held scientific significance, but it became a solution to one of the huge problems plaguing France at the time.

Throughout his career, Pasteur continued to dedicate his research to battling real problems. Therefore, much of his experimentation was in developing vaccines for diseases like rabies, tuberculosis, and smallpox.

"Whenever you fall down, pick something up!"
Oswald Avery   (early 1900's)

While working on a variety of experiments at the Rockefeller Institute in New York, bacteriologist Oswald Avery managed to keep a positive perspective. Avery was entering into uncharted territory during the 1930's and 1940's as he explored the field of genetics. Because much of his research was new, his predictions were sometimes a little off the mark. Still, he didn't get frustrated—instead, Avery used his setbacks as stepping-stones. He shared his simple rule with his associates at the institute: *"Whenever you fall down, pick something up!"*

Eventually, after thirty years of tedious study at the institute, Avery did finally *"pick something up."* In 1944, he discovered that genetic information was not transferred through a protein as top scientists had originally believed. Instead, he proved that deoxyribonucleic acid, or DNA, was the material that housed the genetic codes. His observations proved that DNA was the building block of all life, and immediately started an onslaught of research leaning in that direction.

Even with Avery's amazing find, genetic researchers still struggled for the next decade to completely uncover the mystery of DNA. In 1953, two young scientists, James Watson and Francis Crick, finally made a tremendous breakthrough when they determined the structure of the genetic material—a double helix.

"How exceedingly stupid not to have thought of that!"
Thomas Huxley   (1859)

Thomas Huxley took the news hard. After reading a copy of Charles Darwin's *The Origin of Species* in 1859, the British biologist couldn't help himself from making this remark. While working as the surgeon aboard a British ship, Huxley studied sea life, and he became extremely interested in the origin and creation of living things. Upon reading Darwin's new book, which introduced the theory of natural selection and evolution, Huxley felt that he had found his answers. What bothered him most, however, was that these answers were so simple— *"How exceedingly stupid not to have thought of that!"*

Apparently, Huxley wasn't alone in his opinion of Darwin's work. *The Origin Species* was an immediate success, causing an enormous reaction from both its supporters and critics. Because of its huge impact, it became known as the *"book that shook the world."* In fact, the controversy of evolution still exists today, well over a century after the theory's introduction.

Having himself written several scientific papers in the field of biology, Thomas Huxley wasted no time in offering his public support of Darwin's work. Charles Darwin himself remained relatively reserved, but Huxley engaged in any debate that he could find. His dedication helped the theory of evolution gain acceptance from the public, despite its obvious conflicts with the traditional belief of creation in the Bible.

"Everything that can be invented has been invented."
Charles Duell   (1899)

Think again! This statement is said to have been made by the director of the United States Patent Office, Charles H. Duell, to President William McKinley in 1899. It is even reported that Duell asked McKinley to abolish the Patent Office entirely, as it would soon be of no use. Of course, whether the conversation ever took place remains a mystery. In actuality, there were several thousand more patents given in 1899 than there were in 1898.

While Duell may not have been convinced that all invention had ceased, he certainly couldn't have predicted the vast changes that would soon take place in the United States. Only a few years later, in 1903, the Wright Brothers successfully flew the world's first airplane. That same year, Henry Ford started Ford Motor Company and introduced the assembly line. This revolutionized mass production almost instantly.

In fact, the pace of technology and invention not only hasn't slowed down, it has created a snowball effect—inventions only lead to more inventions. Today, in the midst of the computer age, it's nearly impossible to predict what advancements will exist in the upcoming decades.

"Mary had a little lamb..."
Thomas Edison   (1877)

Besides being recognized by millions as the start of a popular nursery rhyme, these words were also the first ever to be recorded and then successfully played back again. On December 4, 1877, notable inventor Thomas Edison recited the verse as a test for his newly designed phonograph.

The nursery rhyme, "Mary Had a Little Lamb," was written in 1830 by American author Sarah Josepha Hale. She created hundreds of poems, but this four-line verse quickly became the most popular in the entire English language. It was forty-seven years later when Thomas Edison turned the crank of his experimental phonograph and recited, *"Mary had a little lamb, its fleece was white as snow, and everywhere that Mary went, the lamb was sure to go."* He and his staff had been working on the phonograph for the entire year, with varying degrees of success. On this attempt, Edison's rendition of "Mary Had a Little Lamb" was clearly played back, and it became the first successfully recorded human voice.

Edison obtained a patent for the phonograph in 1878. The public's response to the new invention was remarkable. People crowded around to witness demonstrations, some refusing to believe that the playback was not some sort of hoax.

A Positive Perspective

"I haven't failed. I've just found 10,000 ways that won't work."
Thomas Edison   (early 1900's)

American inventor Thomas Edison didn't hit the bull's eye every time. But, this remark is a testament to the attitude and determination that enabled him to prosper. In the early 1900's, Edison was trying to create a new kind of storage battery, a task that would result in thousands of failed experiments. When responding to a critic who was quick to point these failed attempts, Edison replied, **"I haven't failed. I've just found 10,000 ways that won't work."** He continued his research and ultimately was successful in creating the new battery.

Thomas Edison

Known for renowned inventions like the phonograph in 1877 and the electric light bulb in 1879, Thomas Edison achieved over 1,000 patents in his lifetime. Remarkably, he did this with very little organized schooling. Instead, he was working as a newspaper salesman on the Grand Trunk Railway by the age of twelve. By the time he was fifteen, he was publishing his own weekly paper. Even at this young age, Edison was experimenting with printing presses and mechanical equipment, using a freight car as a laboratory.

Because of his early start, Edison's first major invention, a telegraphic repeating instrument, came before he was thirty. Appropriately enough, he was working as a telegraph operator at the time.

List of Major inventions by Thomas Edison

(Remember! Edison obtained over 1,000 patents in his lifetime. This is just a small selection..)

Alkaline Storage Battery
Cement Works System
Electric Distributing Center
Electric Generator
Electric Locomotive
Electric Meter
Electric Pen
Fuse Block
Incandescent Lamp
Kinetoscope (Motion Picture Camera)
Loudspeaking Microphone
Ore Mineral Separator
Mimeograph
Phonograph
Printer for Stock Ticker
Tasimeter
Telegraph Repeater
Typewriter
Vote Recorder
Underground Electric Conductor

"We haven't got the money, so we've got to think!"
Ernest Rutherford   (early 1900's)

Sometimes you have to resort to plan B. Nobel prize-winning scientist Ernest Rutherford made this confession as he tried to rally his colleagues to continue their tedious research. During the early 1900's, the physicist concentrated his attention on upcoming fields like radiation and atomic energy, both of which were still too unexplored to be profitable. Fortunately, he wasn't concerned about finances. And, over time, his ability to *"think"* revolutionized nuclear physics.

After the discovery of radiation in 1896 by French physicist Antoine Becquerel, Rutherford wasted no time in beginning to study it on his own. He found that radiation was divided into three main classes — he labeled them alpha, beta, and gamma. Building from that, he was able to link radiation to atomic energy. That ultimately opened the doors to its potential.

In 1908, Rutherford won the Nobel Prize for his research, and he was knighted in 1914. Perhaps even more flattering, the chemical element Rutherfordium was named in his honor.

"I can't afford to waste my time making money!"
Louis Agassiz   (mid 1800's)

It's important to prioritize. Swiss-American Louis Rodolphe Agassiz made this telling statement when an emissary approached him in the mid-1800's hoping to persuade the naturalist to address a society. Agassiz refused, feeling that preparing a lecture of this sort would cut into his time for research. The emissary assured Agassiz that he would receive a significant payment for the effort. Frustrated, the determined scientist replied, *"I can't afford to waste my time making money!"*

Perhaps as a result of his dedication, Agassiz became one of the most knowledgeable biologists of the 19th century. He originally studied and taught in Europe, but moved to the United States in 1846. In America, he taught natural history at Harvard

University, remaining there for twenty-five years. Today, his theories still remain a hot topic of discussion—Agassiz was, after all, a major opponent of Charles Darwin and the theory of evolution. As a religious man, Agassiz believed that animals adjust to their environment through a series of unique and independent changes brought about by a Supreme Being.

Despite the controversy of evolution, Agassiz remained a tremendous influence in the field with his extensive explorations.

"I don't believe in it. But, I understand that it brings you luck whether you believe in it or not."
Niels Bohr (early 1900's)

You have to believe in something! Danish physicist Niels Henrik David Bohr, one of the leading contributors to nuclear physics, was asked by a visitor if he believed that the horseshoe he had hanging on his wall would really bring him good luck. Being a respected scientist, Bohr replied, *"Of course I don't believe in it."* He then quickly added, *"But, I understand that it brings you luck whether you believe in it or not."*

Bohr may have been a little superstitious, but he was still a remarkable physicist. During the 1910's, he developed the theory of the atomic structure, which would earn him a Nobel Prize in physics in 1922. Bohr's understanding of the properties of the atom enabled him to become one of the first people to grasp the power of nuclear energy.

In 1945, Bohr traveled to Los Alamos, New Mexico, to develop the world's first nuclear bomb. He had previously been working alongside several top Jewish scientists in Europe. The bomb's detonation was successful, and it ultimately ended the fighting against Japan in World War II.

After the war, Bohr devoted his time to working on peaceful uses for atomic energy, organizing the Atoms for Peace Conference in 1955.

Albert Einstein—Legendary theoretical scientist

"God does not play dice."
Albert Einstein   (1927)

     Nobel Prize winner Albert Einstein was doubtful when he heard about a new hypothesis concerning the Quantum Theory. The complicated theory, which dealt with the nature of matter, had just been given a controversial twist when the hypothesis known as the Uncertainty Principle was introduced in 1927. Proposed by physicist Werner Heisenberg, the Uncertainty Principle stated that the exact position and momentum of subatomic particles can never be truly defined. In other words, they behave randomly, with no distinct pattern.

     Einstein, already a renowned scientist, refused to believe this idea of randomness. He maintained that, though scientists may not be able to understand those particles at the moment, it certainly didn't mean that they were beyond understanding—eventually, through enough experimentation and studying, all of the answers would be obtained. In response to the Uncertainty Principle, Einstein simply replied, *"God does not play dice."*

His reaction was that of a true scientist. Through Einstein's work, along with the other great researches in history, many questions that seemed at one time to be unanswerable now have very rational explanations. Of course, there are plenty of mysteries, like black holes, still existing in the scientific world. Whether they, too, will be solved one-day remains to be seen. Einstein, in any case, felt that God would never leave anything completely up to chance. After all: *"God does not play dice."*

"Could you patent the sun?"
Jonas Salk   (1954)

You're not supposed to answer a question with a question. Jonas Salk did, though, when he was asked by television commentator Edward R. Murrow about who owned the rights to his new polio vaccine. Salk replied, *"Well, the people, I would say. There is no patent. Could you patent the sun?"*

Salk's answer was somewhat surprising. The new vaccine could have certainly made him extremely wealthy. The poliomyelitis virus, commonly known as polio, is a terrible infection that attacks the central nervous system and often results in paralysis. In the early 1950's, nearly 60,000 people fell victim to the illness each year—and most of these people had not yet reached teenage years. However, as the result of Salk and other physicians, there have been very few cases of polio since the introduction of the vaccine in 1954.

When Salk answered, *"There is no patent,"* he was beginning an argument that is carried on even today. The issue is the ownership of intellectual property rights when it affects the public well-being. Salk's belief was that his vaccine was a naturally occurring substance. So, like the sun, it couldn't be patented by one individual. Of course, a counter-argument is that it was he who made the valuable discovery, and should therefore benefit from it. With the field of biotechnology making rapid advancements into the next century, the question still remains open-ended.

Top Secret!

"The Italian navigator has just landed in the New World..."
Enrico Fermi   (1942)

This encoded message changed the world. Sent over the telephone by Enrico Fermi to Washington, DC, on December 2, 1942, it announced that the first self-sustaining nuclear reaction had been successful. The scientific advancement would ultimately lead to the atomic bomb and an end to World War II.

The race for a grasp on nuclear power began in August 1942, with the creation of the top secret Manhattan Project. The enormous undertaking, which occupied several top scientists for years, was created after Albert Einstein wrote several letters to President Roosevelt telling him of the potential of nuclear fission. Einstein urged the President to devote more resources into studying it. At the time, the nation was heavily involved in a world war, so Roosevelt didn't hesitate to agree.

While much of the research for the Manhattan Project was conducted in Los Alamos, New Mexico, it was at the University of Chicago that Enrico Fermi and his team had their first major success. They were experimenting in a squash court that had been turned into a laboratory at the university's Stagg Field stadium. There, Fermi successfully demonstrated a chain reaction. His telephone message to Washington, DC, **"The Italian navigator has just landed in the New World..."** confirmed the success to the government. It was necessary for the message to be encoded because top scientists in Germany and other axis countries were working towards the same goal—and, no doubt, they were keeping a close eye on the Americans.

This success in Chicago was just the first step. Now, the newfound technology had to be used to create a weapon of mass destruction. This gave American physicist Robert Oppenheimer some mixed feelings. As he watched the first successful explosion of a nuclear bomb after years of serious experimentation, he didn't know exactly how to respond. Oppenheimer had been the organizer of the Manhattan Project in Los Alamos, New Mexico. In the summer of 1945, at the height of World War II, the team of scientists finally succeeded in their goal.

Oppenheimer had already made significant contributions to the project with his earlier work, and he understood the potential of what had been created. Upon the explosion, he exclaimed, **"I am become death, the shatterer of worlds!"** He was reciting a line from a collection of verses known as the *Bhagavad-Gita*, the most significant literary work in Hindu philosophy.

While the creation of an atomic bomb ultimately brought an end to World War II, it also introduced the constant threat of nuclear war. This completely changed the view of war throughout the world. Before, when two powerful nations were fighting against eachother, it would only result in significant (but eventually recoverable) damage. But now, with the addition of nuclear weapons, came the concept of MAD (Mutual Assured Destruction). Nations could not only damage eachother, they could completely destroy one another. This sentiment is what led to the Cold War, where the United States and the Soviet Union both raced to make sure that they did not let the other have an edge with nuclear weapons.

Seeing this change in the world, Robert Oppenheimer dedicated his later life to studying the relationship between science and society, becoming an advisor to the government on atomic energy.

"I just invent, then wait until man comes around to needing what I've invented."
Buckminster Fuller (1948)

Sounds like a plan. In 1948, American inventor Buckminster Fuller created the somewhat off-the-wall geodesic dome (a large spherical structure built with interlocking parts and containing no internal supports). While his new product was certainly interesting, it wasn't exactly clear how it could be useful.

What's more, this wasn't the first time that Fuller had been creative in his inventions. In 1932, he founded Dymaxion Corporation—named by combining the words *dynamic, maximum,* and *ion.* With his company, he turned many of his obscure ideas into reality, concentrating on products that were both energy and material efficient. An example of his creations was the Dymaxion car, an extremely fuel-efficient, three-wheeled automobile.

Fuller hit it big, though, with the geodesic dome. Because his structure could be put together quickly, it was convenient as a shelter to hold fairs and exhibits. And, since it required no internal support, it enabled large crowds of people to fit together in a small space. Fuller had designed it to be built at an enormous size and still maintain structural integrity. This feature made his unusual domes useful in housing equipment and machinery. Just as Fuller had predicted, it didn't take long for man to come around to needing what he had invented.

"We have discovered the secret of life!"
Francis Crick (1953)

In the spring of 1953, biophysicist Francis Crick ran into Eagle Pub in Cambridge, England. When he saw his colleague, American chemist James Watson, at the bar, he shouted, *"We have discovered the secret of life!"* The two had just uncovered a secret that scientists had been working on for decades—the molecular structure of deoxyribonucleic acid, or DNA.

Surprisingly, Crick's bold statement wasn't an exaggeration—the two men really had discovered the secret of life. It had been suggested over ten years earlier that DNA carried the bulk of genetic information from one generation to the next. Unfortunately, nobody could tell how it did this, primarily because nobody knew about DNA's structure. This information was so crucial to the scientific world that a race began among researchers to find it. Among the contestants were Francis Crick and James Watson, who performed their research at the Cavendish Laboratory at the University of Cambridge.

The two young scientists, both under the age of forty, discovered that the makeup of DNA is a double-helix, similar to a spiral staircase, with specific bases paired up in a various patterns. This finding earned them a Nobel Prize in 1962.

"I couldn't reduce it to a freshman level. That means we really don't understand it."
Richard Feynman   (1960's)

American physicist Richard Feynman didn't have the tight grasp he had hoped for when it came to the complicated concept of Fermi-Dirac statistics. Feynman was working as a professor at the California Institute of Technology when an interested faculty member asked him to explain his theories on space-time probabilities. Eager to assist, Feynman assured his colleague that he would prepare a lecture on the subject that even a freshman could understand. However, after a frustrating few days, he returned and remarked, *"I couldn't do it. I couldn't reduce it to freshman level. That means we really don't understand it."*

While Feynman may not have felt confident about his understanding of quantum electrodynamics, the rest of the scientific world had a different opinion. For years, his mastery of the subject was virtually unparalleled, and he received a Nobel Prize for physics in 1965. In fact, during World War II, Feynman was still in his twenties when he was called upon to work at the Los Alamos National Laboratory in New Mexico to help develop and test the first nuclear bomb. After success there, he spent several years teaching at Cornell University and Caltech, until his expertise was needed again. This time his task was to investigate what caused the sudden explosion of the space shuttle Challenger in 1986.

"We shall not cease from exploration
And the end of all our exploring
Will be to arrive where we started
And know the place for the first time."
—T.S. Eliot
Writer and Poet (1888-1965)

Chapter 8

Exploration

"'Tis a sharp remedy, but a sure one for all ills."
Sir Walter Raleigh   (1618)

Feeling the blade that would soon cut off his head, Sir Walter Raleigh didn't see any need to lose a positive perspective. Despite being a powerful figure in England, he had just been sentenced to death by King James. At the cutting block, Raleigh's executioner granted his strange request to run his hand along the edge of the ax. Raleigh, pleased with the quality of the blade, smiled and commented, *"'Tis a sharp remedy, but a sure one for all ills."* He was then asked which way he would like to lay his head on the block. Considering what was about to happen, he calmly answered, *"It is no matter which way the head lies."*

Raleigh's rise to fame occurred under England's legendary Queen Elizabeth, who took an instant liking to him. He already had a notable reputation as an explorer, having headed expeditions to start America's first colonies. Under the Queen, Raleigh became one of the most influential men in England, and she gave him the honor of having him knighted.

However, when Queen Elizabeth learned that Raleigh had secretly married one of her close friends in 1592, he quickly fell out of favor. Her successor, James I, liked him even less—he was paranoid that Raleigh was plotting against him. The King hit Raleigh with a list of accusations, and he was sentenced to the Tower of London for thirteen years. Despite being released for a time and leaving England, Raleigh returned only to be given the death sentence by James I in 1618.

"Dr. Livingston, I presume?"
Henry Stanley   (1871)

This could be the most famous greeting in the history of the world. It was given by Sir Henry Morton Stanley to Dr. David Livingston when they met in 1871. Dr. Livingston was a Scottish missionary and explorer who spent thirty years traveling across the continent of Africa. On his final expedition, Livingston couldn't get any word out on his activities, and the entire world became concerned about his welfare and his whereabouts.

In 1869, Sir Henry Morton Stanley, a British explorer and journalist, was sent by the *New York Herald* to find the missing Livingston. After eight months of searching, Stanley found the explorer in rather poor health near the present-day Congo. It was here that he greeted him with the legendary line, *"Dr. Livingston, I presume?"* Stanley helped nurse him back to health, and Livingston was soon ready to start exploring again. In fact, Stanley accompanied him on a journey around Lake Tanganyika.

Dr. Livingston's career as an explorer, which ended with his death in 1873, remains unrivaled even today. His journeys provided a tremendous amount of information on the geography and people of Africa. Livingston single-handedly helped heighten interest worldwide of the often-ignored continent.

"Because it's there!"
George Mallory (1924)

When asked the question of why he would ever attempt to climb Mount Everest, mountaineer George Mallory gave a simple and famous answer: *"Because it's there!"* Mallory had already led a major British expedition up the north side of the world's highest peak in 1921, and he was preparing for another attempt in 1924.

Unfortunately, Mallory would never make it down from his second attempt. Although expecting a tough climb, he was met with extremely harsh conditions, including strong winds, avalanches, and cold temperatures. Mallory and his climbing partner, Andrew Irvine, disappeared. Their bodies were not found until over seventy years later, at an elevation of about 27,000 feet above sea level. It is still unknown whether they actually made it to the summit.

Remarkably, nobody successfully climbed to the peak of Mount Everest until 1953, nearly thirty years after Mallory's attempt, when a British expedition led by John Hunt made it to the top. By the year 2000, nearly 700 people had conquered the rigorous mountain, and almost 150 had lost their lives in an attempt. Yet, all of them shared George Mallory's reason for undertaking such a dangerous task: *"Because it's there!"*

Daniel Boone—Rugged frontiersman of the late 18th century

"I can't say I was ever lost, but I was bewildered once for three days."
Daniel Boone   (1820)

    American pioneer Daniel Boone wanted to set the record straight. In 1820, as famed painter Chester Harding was creating the only life portrait of Boone, he asked the explorer if he had ever been lost. Boone, who was in his eighties at the time, thought back on his life and remarked, *"I can't say I was ever lost, but I was bewildered once for three days."*

    Growing up in the primitive areas of Pennsylvania and North Carolina, Daniel Boone learned to hunt and navigate through the woods while he was still a teenager. With these skills, he began to explore areas around the Kentucky River during the 1760's and 1770's. As an expert in the area (after all, he never did get lost), Boone was hired in 1775 to create a road to Kentucky that could be used by the colonists for trading purposes.

    The building of this road led to an immediate settlement of the area, known as Boonseborough. The settlement managed to survive despite numerous attacks by Native Americans. In fact,

Boone himself was once captured, though he escaped to come back and defend the village.

Despite playing a major role in the settling of Kentucky, Daniel Boone was never able to claim any of the land. In the 1780's, the titles for his property were deemed invalid, so he moved to West Virginia and later Missouri.

"I guess I flew the wrong way!"
Douglas Corrigan   (1938)

As he landed in Dublin, Ireland, after flying across the Atlantic Ocean, pilot Douglas Corrigan was forced to give this explanation to a group of angry officials. Corrigan had recently requested permission from the Federal Aviation Authority to make a transatlantic flight from New York to Ireland. His request was denied—the experts agreed that his single-engine plane, which he had rebuilt himself, was in no condition to make such a journey. Accepting the ruling, Corrigan said he would fly his plane from New York back to his home in California.

On July 17, 1938, he took off from Brooklyn en route to Long Beach, California. However, shortly after takeoff, Corrigan made a complete turn, and started heading over the ocean. Over twenty-eight hours later, he landed in Dublin. When officials approached him, he claimed that he had headed in the wrong direction due to faulty equipment. Corrigan explained, *"My compass froze. I guess I flew the wrong way."* The authorities were not convinced, but they only revoked his license for five days—less than the amount of time it took for him to return by boat.

When Corrigan arrived back in America, he was greeted with a hero's welcome. He had joined the ranks of legends such as Charles Lindberg by making a solo, non-stop flight across the Atlantic. And, for his stand against the authority, he forever earned the nickname "Wrong-Way" Corrigan.

The Final Frontier...

> *"History will remember the inhabitants of our time as the people who went from Kitty Hawk to the moon in 66 years."*
> **Buzz Aldrin** **(1998)**

In 1998, Buzz Aldrin had the honor of rededicating the Wright Brothers National Memorial at Kitty Hawk, North Carolina. He spoke to a crowd at Kill Devil Hill on the outer banks and remarked on the historic events that began a short distance from where he was standing. On December 17, 1903, Orville and Wilbur Wright made history when they created the first heavier than air machine to fly through the air. The machine flew without any reduction in speed, and it landed at a place not lower than the one from which it took off. In short, the Wright brothers had flown the world's first airplane.

Neil Armstrong walking on the moon

Aldrin was an appropriate selection for the dedication, having been one of the pioneers to expand on what the Wright brothers had accomplished that day. On July 20, 1969, he accompanied Neil Armstrong and Michael Collins on the space mission Apollo 11. The men successfully landed on the moon, becoming the first in history to do so. While Collins stayed on the spacecraft and orbited the moon, Armstrong and Aldrin boarded the lunar lander, known as the "Eagle".

After a bumpy flight, which resulted in Armstrong having to override the computerized trajectory in order to avoid hitting boulders, Aldrin and Armstrong landed on the moon's surface. When they had touched down, Armstrong called back to Mission Control in Texas, saying the famous lines, **"Houston, Tranquility Base here. The Eagle has landed."**

Of course, an equally legendary statement was soon to be made. As Neil Armstrong became the first man to set foot on the moon he uttered the words, **"That's one small step for a man, one giant leap for mankind."** The entire country watched as history was made on live television.

The lunar landing of 1969 was a true testament of just how far man's ability to conquer gravity had come in less than an average lifetime. In fact, space travel had become a true reality less than a decade earlier. It was Russian Cosmonaut Yury Gagarin who, on April 12, 1961, took the vessel Vostok 1 past the point of no return. He was exposed to about six times the force of gravity when he shouted, **"Poyekhali"**, which translates to **"Let's go!"** Moments later he became the first man ever launched into space.

After orbiting the earth one time in 108 minutes, Gagarin successfully returned to earth near Saratov, Russia. Immediately, he became a worldwide hero—except, perhaps, in the United States. The scientists of the American space program had hoped to beat the Soviets, but they weren't able to send their first astronaut until twenty-three days later.

But, on that day in 1961, it was Yury Gagarin who began the seemingly impossible idea of space exploration. Before he joined the cosmonaut program a year earlier, he had just over 200 hours of flying experience. In fact, Gagarin didn't know that he had been selected as the pilot of Vostok 1 until four days before the mission. After the historic launch, the cosmonaut continued his training before being killed in a routine flight at age thirty-four. Because of his accomplishment, Gagarin's ashes were buried in the Kremlin Wall.

"Houston, we've had a problem!"
Crew of the Apollo 13   (1970)

On April 13, 1970, NASA'a Mission Control in Houston received this timeless and disturbing message from the crew of the Apollo 13 space vessel. Apollo 13 was to be the third spacecraft to take astronauts to the moon, but the mission went south after an explosion in one of the oxygen tanks.

The crew, consisting of astronauts Jim Lovell, Jack Swigert, and Fred Haise, found themselves very low on oxygen and several days away from home. The situation was dismal, to say the least, but the men were trained not to panic. Engineers at NASA were immediately called in to solve the problem, and several high risk and unorthodox ideas were brought to the table. In an attempt to preserve oxygen, the temperature inside the vessel was lowered to just above freezing.

The entire world watched anxiously as Apollo 13 tried to make it back home before the oxygen on the vessel ran out. And, after a rough ride, the spacecraft landed on April 17 with all three astronauts surviving.

"...If I see two towers, I have to walk."
Philippe Petit   (1974)

At around 7:00 AM on August 7, 1974, the everyday street dwellers of New York City looked up to see a man walking on a thin tightrope across the Twin Towers of the World Trade Center—1,350 feet above the sidewalk. When he was later arrested for his stunt on a charge of disturbing the peace, French aerialist Phillippe Petit gave this simple explanation: *"If I see three oranges, I have to juggle; if I see two towers, I have to walk."*

Petit, who secured his line across the 130-foot gap using a crossbow, was 25-years old when he put on the outrageous show. He had walked on a tightrope across buildings before, and once even across the top of a suspension bridge. Still, the newly constructed Twin Towers caper was without a doubt the culmination of his career. For the thousands of spectators below, the small rope that Petit walked on was just about invisible, and he seemed suspended in mid-air as he danced between the two structures.

The Twin Towers were often criticized during construction for their enormous size and somewhat monotonous exterior, but Petit helped bring to them a little bit of excitement. Eventually, the towers became a symbol of New York City, and, when they were destroyed by a terrorist attack on September 11, 2001, they became a symbol for the entire world.

"We hold these truths to be self-evident, that all men are created equal; that they are endowed by their Creator with certain unalienable rights; that among these are life, liberty, and the pursuit of happiness."
—United States Declaration of Independence (1776)

Chapter 9

Equal Rights

"We must indeed all hang together, or, most assuredly, we will all hang separately."
Benjamin Franklin   (1776)

These words might have saved the United States of America. When the Continental Congress met in 1776, it wasn't exactly smooth sailing for the members. John Hancock, as the president of the congress, had the nearly impossible job of keeping the frustrated delegates on the same page as they created the most important document in the nation's history—the Declaration of Independence. In the midst of differing opinions, Hancock warned, *"There must be no pulling different ways. We must all hang together."* To this, legendary statesman Benjamin Franklin responded, *"We must indeed all hang together, or, most assuredly, we will all hang separately."*

While Franklin's words weren't fancy or poetic, they did remind the men at the convention that they were in an absolute win or lose situation. Like many of the delegates, Franklin had been loyal to England throughout his earlier life. When King George III came to power, though, life for the colonists became tough. They found themselves victims of mistreatments such as being taxed without any representation in parliament. When it became too much to bear, Franklin had to make a difficult choice. In a quest for independence, he and the other delegates openly became enemies of the British state, risking the crime of treason if the colonies failed to gain independence.

No doubt, there was a great deal of concern from each representative in the days leading up to the signing of the Declaration of Independence. Fortunately, the men took Franklin's advice, and were able to *"hang together"* to form the new nation.

"There was one of two things I had a right to—liberty or death..."
Harriet Tubman   (1886)

As she looked back on her daring escape from slavery in 1849, abolitionist Harriet Tubman recalled being faced with these simple options. She explained to Sarah H. Bradford, the woman who would write her biography in 1886, *"There was one of two things I had a right to—liberty or death; if I could not have one, I would have the other! For no man should take me alive!"* To her, death was less terrible than being taken away by a slave-trader from her husband and family to spend the rest of her days as a field hand.

Fortunately, Tubman managed to successfully escape to the northern free states. However, escape wasn't enough for her. She later made nineteen trips back to the south to free other slaves, including her own parents. Leading the slaves to freedom through the immortal "Underground Railroad," Harriet Tubman began to be referred to as the Moses of her people.

When the Civil War began in 1861, Tubman continued to fight slavery by aiding the Union army in any way she could. She served as an aide, nurse, and even a spy during the war.

"Eternal vigilance is the price of liberty!"
Wendell Phillips (1852)

Speaking at an Antislavery Society in Massachusetts, political reformer Wendell Phillips tried to rally support to end the practice of slavery. His speech was in 1852, over a decade before the Civil War was fought. Phillips' cry, *"Eternal vigilance is the price of liberty!"* is consistent with his actions. He was tenacious in his abolitionist beliefs, becoming one of the most radical leaders of the time.

The purpose of Phillips' address was to verbally attack the mob that had killed the abolitionist editor Elijah Parish Lovejoy. His speech was so effective, that it helped stimulate the antislavery movement in the years leading up to the Civil War. Even after the war, when slavery had ended in the United States, Wendell Phillips wasn't satisfied. He continued to rally support for blacks, becoming one of the leading spokesmen in an effort to give them equal treatment and fair justice.

Aside from the issue of slavery, Phillips was outspoken about other controversial issues in the mid-1800's. Among his causes were women's equality and worker's rights.

154—"What Made Them Say That?"

Sojourner Truth—Activist for equal rights.

"Ain't I a woman?"
Sojourner Truth   (1851)

Abolitionist Sojourner Truth asked this question repeatedly on May 28, 1851, as she spoke at one of the earliest woman's rights conventions in Akron, Ohio. She stated, *"That man over there says that women need to be helped into carriages, and lifted over ditches, and to have the best place everywhere. Nobody ever helps me into carriages, or over mud-puddles, or gives me any best place!"* Truth then followed with, *"And ain't I a woman?"*

Sojourner Truth, originally named Isabella, was making the argument that upper class, white women aren't the only ones who should be recognized in the rising suffrage movement. Born as a slave, Truth ran away at age 30, and made her way to New York City with the help of northern abolitionists. Shortly after her escape, New York passed the emancipation of all slaves, so she no longer had to hide.

Despite being free, Sojourner Truth felt it was her responsibility to fight against the slavery that still existed in other parts of the country. She used her skills as a terrific speaker and traveled around New England, preaching against slavery and in support of women's rights. After the Civil War, when slaves were freed across the nation, Sojourner Truth helped provide the new refugees with aid until they could support themselves.

"You cannot fight against the future!"
William Gladstone   (1866)

As he relentlessly campaigned for a Reform Bill in 1866 that would extend voting rights to the poorer classes of England, future Prime Minister William Gladstone delivered a stern warning to parliament. At the time, he was leading the Liberal Party and attempting to make radical changes in the British government. It was Gladstone's belief that, no matter what decision was made concerning a specific bill, the working class of Britain would eventually achieve their rights. He exclaimed, *"You cannot fight against the future!"* He then drove home the point by announcing, *"Time is on our side!"*

The Reform Bill of 1866 did not pass. But, Gladstone was right—time was on his side. One year later, Benjamin Disraeli, another future Prime Minister, would pass a similar bill, opening the door for reform concerning the rights of the working class.

Even though he didn't get what he wanted the first time around, Gladstone still succeeded in making significant adjustments to the British government. In 1868, he was elected to the first of four terms as Prime Minister. While holding the position, he made sweeping changes concerning the justice system, military, and social standards. He represented the ideals of the common people, and with their support was able to remain one of Britain's leading political figures for over thirty years.

"Justice is truth in action!"
Benjamin Disraeli (1851)

When he spoke before the House of Commons on February 11, 1851, future British Prime Minister Benjamin Disraeli had already built a reputation as a champion of the working class. Serving his fourteenth year in the Parliament, it's no surprise that the timeless comment, *"Justice is truth in action,"* was aimed directly to the common people of Britain. Disraeli hoped to help their cause by extending to them the right to vote.

From 1874 to 1880, Disraeli served as Prime Minister, and he had the opportunity to deliver the *"justice"* that he had promised over twenty years earlier. His term was marked by radical legislation that improved the housing and working conditions for the poorer class. The nation also prospered overseas as he expanded the British Empire around the Mediterranean Sea.

Disraeli's involvement in the British government would span more than forty years, making him one of the most respected politicians in the nation's history. He had a profound influence on the Conservative Party, though his terms were often marked by radical government reform.

"The only question left to be settled now is: Are women persons? And I hardly believe any of our opponents will have the hardihood to say they are not."
Susan B. Anthony (1872)

As one of the leaders of the women's suffrage movement in the mid-1800's, Susan B. Anthony had a simple argument for why woman should be allowed to vote—they were *"persons."* She had fought for the right to vote for over twenty years, and finally cast a ballot in the 1872 presidential election. This, of course, was against the law—women wouldn't be allowed the right to vote until the constitution was ratified on August 18, 1920. Anthony was fined $100, which she refused to pay.

After this protest, Anthony pointed out the hypocrisy of the law. She stated, *"Webster, Worcester, and Bouvier all define a citizen to be a person in the United States, entitled to vote and hold office."* She then asks, *"Are women persons?"* With that answer being obvious, the question as to whether or not women should vote should have been equally as obvious.

When it was clear that women were indeed persons, Anthony's next line of reasoning fell into place: *"Every discrimination against women in the constitutions and laws of several states is today null and void, precisely as is every one against Negroes."* Unfortunately, she died in 1906 — fourteen years before the cause that she spent over fifty years fighting for was finally won.

"Don't mourn for me—Organize!"
Joe Hill   (1915)

Time is of the essence. This was a last request made by labor leader and Swedish immigrant, Joe Hill. In the early 1900's, thousands of immigrants arrived in the United States only to find jobs that had poor working conditions and little reward. Hill rose up as one of the best-known combatants in the fight for employee rights. As a member of the Industrial Workers of the World (IWW), Hill organized strikes, wrote essays, and composed protest songs dedicated to the cause. But this all came crashing down when, in 1914, he found himself involved in one of the most controversial murder cases of the century.

Joe Hill was already somewhat of a marked man in California because of his involvement in recent strikes. He was also beginning to earn a mixed reputation in his new location, Salt Lake City. It wasn't all that surprising that, when a former policeman was shot and killed by a masked gunman, Joe Hill was convicted of the crime. Other labor leaders, such as "Big Bill" Haywood, founder of the IWW, argued that it was set-up. In the end, Hill was sentenced to an execution by firing squad.

Joe Hill understood that the fight would continue even after his death in 1915. That explains his last bit of advice for Haywood, *"Don't mourn for me — Organize!"* For this, he became one of the most famous "martyrs" in the fight for labor rights.

Let Freedom Ring!

"I have a dream that one day this nation will rise up and live out the true meaning of its creed..."
Martin Luther King, Jr.   **(1963)**

On August 28, 1963, Reverend Martin Luther King, Jr. delivered one of the greatest speeches in history. His *"I Have a Dream"* speech was presented on the steps of the Lincoln Memorial in Washington, DC, to a crowd of over 200,000 civil rights supporters.

Born in the southern state of Georgia, King dedicated his life to fighting segregation and discrimination. He began his career as an activist while he was a student at Morehouse College, and later followed in his father's footsteps by becoming a minister. He preached against the wrongful treatment of blacks that had been existing for years, and helped to organize the movement that would begin to change that.

Martin Luther King, Jr.

In 1963, King and other civil rights leaders combined their efforts and organized the March on Washington. This was an enormous breakthrough for the cause, and people from all over the country joined in to show their support. As the marchers congregated at the Lincoln Memorial, King stood up to deliver his speech. He explained to the protesters exactly what he was trying to accomplish: **"I have a dream that one day this nation will rise up and live out the true meaning of its creed: 'We hold these truths to be self evident, that all men are created equal.'"** His words told the story, but it was King's powerful delivery that created such a stir throughout the country.

An excerpt from Martin Luther King, Jr.'s famed "I Have a Dream" speech:

I have a dream that one day this nation will rise up and live out the true meaning of its creed: "We hold these truths to be self-evident: that all men are created equal."

I have a dream that one day on the red hills of Georgia the sons of former slaves and the sons of former slaveowners will be able to sit down together at a table of brotherhood.

I have a dream that one day even the state of Mississippi, a desert state, sweltering with the heat of injustice and oppression, will be transformed into an oasis of freedom and justice.

I have a dream that my four children will one day live in a nation where they will not be judged by the color of their skin but by the content of their character. I have a dream today.

I have a dream that one day the state of Alabama, whose governor's lips are presently dripping with the words of interposition and nullification, will be transformed into a situation where little black boys and black girls will be able to join hands with little white boys and white girls and walk together as sisters and brothers. I have a dream today.

I have a dream that one day every valley shall be exalted, every hill and mountain shall be made low, the rough places will be made plain, and the crooked places will be made straight, and the glory of the Lord shall be revealed, and all flesh shall see it together. This is our hope. This is the faith with which I return to the South.

With this faith we will be able to hew out of the mountain of despair a stone of hope. With this faith we will be able to transform the jangling discords of our nation into a beautiful symphony of brotherhood. With this faith we will be able to work together, to pray together, to struggle together, to go to jail together, to stand up for freedom together, knowing that we will be free one day.

"Si se puede!" ("Yes we can!")
Cesar Chavez   (1960's)

In an effort to rally a group of tired and hungry farm workers in the 1960's, labor leader Cesar Chavez didn't see any need to be overly eloquent. The simple statement, *"Si se puede,"* which translates to *"Yes we can,"* was exactly what the workers needed to hear. It became a slogan among the farmhands, giving them confidence to speak out against the harsh working conditions and demand better treatment.

In 1966, Chavez organized the United Farm Workers of America (UFO). Before its establishment, migrant farm workers in California were constantly placed in a terrible working environment. They were paid low wages, forced to work in intolerable conditions, and had no influence on hiring and firing procedures. Chavez gathered the workers and convinced them that together they could change the current situation. Motivated by the cry of *"Yes we can,"* Chavez and his supporters organized a national boycott of grapes, a major crop in California. This boycott gained him and his cause attention across the country, and it helped the bargaining position of the average farm worker.

Chavez also organized marches and rallies to show the plight of the struggling migrant worker to the rest of the nation.

"I have a brain and a uterus..."
Patricia Schroeder   (late 1900's)

Fair enough. This is the answer of United States Congresswoman Patricia Schroeder upon being asked how she was able to both serve as an elected official and be a mother. She simply explained, *"I have a brain and a uterus—and I use both."* Schroeder was fairly adept to being a woman and succeeding in a man's world. Even as a teenager she ignored gender norms by earning her pilot's license. With it, she established a flying service to finance her schooling in the early 1960's.

In 1973, Schroeder was elected as a delegate from Colorado to the United States House of Representatives. She served in the House for twenty-four years, longer than any other woman in history. Shortly after her election, she broke new ground by becoming the first woman to sit on the Armed Services Committee.

Being both a member of congress and a mother, Schroeder naturally became a leading spokesperson for some of the problems facing women. In 1977, she helped found the Congressional Caucus for Women's Issues, which worked to pass legislation dealing with women's health. She also became chair of the Committee on Children, Youth, and Families in 1991.

"You have the right to remain silent..."
Police Officers   (late 1900's)

If nobody has ever said this to you, it's probably a good thing. The statement is used by police officers as they begin to recite the list of rights for an arrested individual. The official name for this list is the "Miranda Warnings," named after the famous *Miranda V. Arizona* court case.

The Miranda case involved a 23 year-old man named Ernesto Miranda who, in 1963, was charged with the crimes of kidnapping and rape. After two hours of police questioning, Miranda confessed to the crime—this confession resulted in a conviction and sentence of over twenty years. There was one problem, though. During his questioning, Miranda never requested an attorney. His lawyers, when they appealed the verdict, reasoned that he was not aware of his rights and his confession shouldn't have been admissible.

Although there was no sign of police misconduct during the questioning, it was argued that the questioning process was extremely intimidating in itself. After a 5 to 4 decision, the court overruled the Miranda conviction. This decision set a new precedent—if a police officer ever fails to inform an arrested person of their rights, any statements made by the accused during the arrest can't be used in court. In order to prevent this, officers will read the individual their Miranda warnings immediately upon arrest.

"Let the word go forth from this time and place, to friend and foe alike, that the torch has been passed to a new generation of Americans born in this century, tempered by war, disciplined by a hard and bitter peace."
—John F. Kennedy
American president (1917 – 1963)
Inaugural address, 1961

Chapter 10

American History

Talking About a Revolution

> "*I believe there are more instances of the abridgment of freedom of the people by gradual silent encroachments of those in power than by violent and sudden usurpations.*"
> **James Madison   (1788)**

The high ideals of the United States are nothing new. In fact, they've been there from the beginning. Dating back to the American Revolution, the war that gave the United States its independence, it can be seen that a new concept of human rights was being formed. The men who fought the war were also the ones who helped create the Declaration of Independence and the Constitution, two documents that outlined concepts like freedom of speech, freedom of thought, and the right to pursue happiness.

Take, for example, George Washington. When he was the commander of the Continental Army, Washington gathered his officers at his headquarters in New York shortly after the end of the war. The year was 1783, and the United States had won the war and gained its independence, but the Constitution had not yet been written. There was no solid government, and the new nation was at a crossroads. The future was uncertain.

More than anyone, George Washington knew that individual liberty had to be the foremost focus in shaping the new nation. **"If men are to be precluded from offering their sentiments on a matter that can invite the consideration of mankind,"** he told his officers, **"reason is of no use to us."** In other words: if people aren't free to speak their minds, the end result is chaos. Washington continued, **"Freedom of speech may be taken away and, dumb and silent we may be led, like sheep to the slaughter!"**

Because of his heroics during the American Revolution, George Washington could have easily assumed the role of a king. However, he had just fought against the monarchy of Britain, and it didn't seem like a good idea for the United States to follow in that path. As a result, he limited himself to only two terms as the nation's first president.

James Madison, one of the most prominent speakers on individual freedom and liberty, is another man who helped lay the groundwork for American thinking. At the Virginia Convention in 1788, he worked to create the state's Constitution. In his words, the document was designed to prevent the **"abridgment of freedom of the people by gradual silent encroachments…"**

James Madison

Madison's public career, which would span over forty years, began with his election to the Continental Congress at the age of twenty-nine. He was the youngest member in the Congress, but he was able to gain a reputation as a competent and moral politician. Madison argued for a strong government but, like everyone else in the nation at the time, was extremely wary of allowing that government to infringe on individual liberty in any way.

Madison's finest hour was perhaps in 1787, when he worked as one of the key members in forming Constitution of the United States. He arrived to Philadelphia early for the Constitutional Convention, and became a leading spokesman during the endeavor. His role in shaping document, as well as his distinguished political career, resulted in Madison's election as the fourth president of the United States in 1809.

And, don't forget Benjamin Franklin. When the 81-year old walked out of Independence Hall after the secret meetings of the Constitutional Convention, he was met by a mob of anxious citizens and asked what the delegates had created. That's not an easy question to answer on the spot. Benjamin Franklin managed to do so: **"A republic—if you can keep it!"**

This statement reflects Franklin's understanding of what it meant to establish a government for the people and by the people. He knew that it could only exist if the citizens were up to the task.

Benjamin Franklin — Co-signer of the Declaration of Independence

"...I have the happiness to know it is a rising and not a setting sun."
Benjamin Franklin (1787)

    Benjamin Franklin had a poetic way of declaring victory. When the delegates of the Constitutional Convention gathered in a small room at Independence Hall, they knew they were embarking into uncharted territories. They were shaping the laws of a nation created by the people and for the people—a nation that in no way resembled the monarchies that had ruled Europe for centuries.

    As the delegates toiled over the Constitution, George Washington took his position at the front of the room. Presiding over the convention, he sat on a chair that contained a carving of the sun, half-hidden below the horizon. The legendary Benjamin Franklin, at the age of 81 and in failing health, took immediate notice of that carving. He kept studying it as the arguments over the wording of the Constitution grew tense and heated. Each moment had the potential to make or break the new nation, but Benjamin Franklin couldn't stop thinking about that sun on the back of the chair.

Finally, after much debate, the Constitution was created and a new government was born. It was then that Benjamin Franklin stood before the delegates and told of his dilemma — *"I have often looked at that picture behind the president without being able to tell whether it was a rising or setting sun. Now at length I have the happiness to know that it is indeed a rising, not a setting sun."* His message was simple—the United States of America had a bright future.

"There, I guess King George will be able to read that!"
John Hancock   (1776)

Among his many accomplishments, John Hancock should be credited with inscribing the most famous signature in history. As the presiding officer of the Continental Congress in 1776, the American patriot had the privilege of being the first man to sign the Declaration of Independence. Writing his name in large letters in the center of the page, Hancock declared, *"There, I guess King George will be able to read that!"* It was a bold statement—after all, the Declaration of Independence claimed that the American colonies were independent of Britain, and each man who signed it placed himself at great risk of treason.

Introduced to the public on July 4, 1776, the honored document was basically a list of complaints against King George III. But, more importantly, it fed the fire of the American Revolution, which had begun a year earlier. Ironically, King George's entry into his diary on July 4 read, *"Nothing of importance happened today."*

While each delegate shared in the grievances against King George, John Hancock's dislike for the King was personal. In 1768, he had rebelled against paying import duties (one of the leading causes of the Revolution) by smuggling goods, and British officials seized his ship. Hancock held strong against his accusers, and the incident gained him fame in his home state of Massachusetts, where he would later serve as governor.

The Presidential Oath

"I do solemnly swear that I will faithfully execute the Office of President of the United States, and will, to the best of my ability, preserve, protect, and defend the Constitution of the United States."

If you ever find yourself saying these lines, your career is probably going pretty well. Outlined in Article II of the Constitution, this oath has been recited at every presidential inauguration. The first man to take it was George Washington, who added the words, **"So help me God,"** at the end. The presidents that came after him followed this example.

The pledge is customarily taken with the right hand on the Bible, and the left hand slightly raised. The Constitution also permits the word *"affirm"* to replace the word *"swear".* A few presidents, such as Franklin Pierce (1853) and Herbert Hoover (1929), have chosen to use this version.

Franklin D. Roosevelt holds the distinction of reciting this oath more than any other man. He was inaugurated as president four different times (1933, 1937, 1941, 1945).

Different presidents have recited this oath in different locations, but the most unusual may have been the setting for Lyndon B. Johnson. He was sworn in on the presidential airplane, *Air Force One*, on November 22, 1963. This urgency was a result of President Kennedy's assassination.

These days, the president isn't the only one who has to take an oath when he gets into office. In the United States, all officials who enter into a position of civil service have a pledge of their own. This includes all members of the House of

Representatives, everyone in the Senate, enlisted personnel in the military, and United States' attorneys.

Similar to the President's oath, theirs begins with the standard, yet important, line, **"I do solemnly swear that I will support and defend the constitution of the United States against all enemies, foreign and domestic."** It concludes with the individual promising, **"I will well and faithfully discharge the duties of the office upon which I am about to enter."** This particular phrasing has existed since the late 1800's. When the First Congress assembled in 1789, a simpler oath was used. It consisted only of, **"I do solemnly swear that I will support the constitution of the United States."** It was in 1861, when loyalties began to shift as people chose sides for the upcoming Civil War, that the oath was expanded to avow a greater faithfulness to the Union.

A list of those who have recited the Presidential Oath of the United States *(and their years in office)*:

George Washington (1789-97)
John Adams (1797-1801)
Thomas Jefferson (1801-09)
James Madison (1809-17)
James Monroe (1817-25)
John Quincy Adams (1825-29)
Andrew Jackson (1829-37)
Martin Van Buren (1837-41)
William Henry Harrison (1841)
John Tyler (1841-45)
James Polk (1845-49)
Zachary Taylor (1849-50)
Millard Fillmore (1850-53)
Franklin Pierce (1853-57)
James Buchanan (1857-61)
Abraham Lincoln (1861-65)
Andrew Johnson (1865-69)
Ulysses S. Grant (1869-77)
Rutherford B. Hayes (1877-81)
James A. Garfield (1881)
Chester A. Arthur (1881-85)
Grover Cleveland (1885-89)
Benjamin Harrison (1889-93)
Grover Cleveland (1893-97)
William McKinley (1897-1901)
Theodore Roosevelt (1901-09)
William H. Taft (1909-13)
Woodrow Wilson (1913-21)
Warren Harding (1921-23)
Calvin Coolidge (1923-29)
Herbert Hoover (1929-33)
Franklin D. Roosevelt (1933-45)
Harry S Truman (1945-53)
Dwight D. Eisenhower (1953-61)
John F. Kennedy (1961-63)
Lyndon B. Johnson (1963-69)
Richard M. Nixon (1969-74)
Gerald R. Ford (1974-77)
Jimmy Carter (1977-81)
Ronald W. Reagan (1981-89)
George Bush (1989-93)
William J. Clinton (1993-2001)
George W. Bush (2001-present)

"There is always room at the top!"
Daniel Webster   (early 1800's)

When famed lawyer, Daniel Webster, was advised not enter into the legal profession because it was already overcrowded, *"There is always room at the top,"* was his rock-solid rebuttal. Knowing that a statement this bold should never be made unless it is backed up with results, Webster found *"room at the top"* by becoming one of the most influential and acclaimed lawyers of his time.

In the years from 1817 to 1823, Daniel Webster argued several significant cases before the U.S. Supreme Court and the legendary Chief Justice John Marshall. He became known for his constant defense of a strong federal government. Most notable was the case of *McCulloch v. Maryland* in 1819, which limited a state's right to tax federal institutions.

Webster's skills as an eloquent speaker served him not only as a lawyer, but in his efforts to become a politician. From 1827 to 1852, he served as a congressman, a senator, and also as the secretary of state. He seemed to find *"room at the top"* wherever he decided to focus his energy.

"...the one that never proves ungrateful or treacherous, is his dog."
George Vest   (mid-1800's)

There are a few court trials throughout the ages that were so significant that they have literally shaped history—George Vest was never involved in any of them. He did, however, deliver what is perhaps the greatest closing argument ever.

Vest, who later became a Missouri senator, found himself representing an odd client in the mid-1800's. There had been a dreadful shooting in which the victim was a foxhound named "Drum". The man who shot the dog claimed he was being attacked. George Vest didn't believe him. A known dog-lover, he took the case in an effort to bring justice to the dead canine.

When Vest stood up to make his closing statements, he began by explaining how unreliable even the most trusted individuals can be – *"The best friend a man has in the world may*

turn against him and become his enemy." He insisted, *"The one absolutely unselfish friend that a man can have in this selfish world, the one that never deserts him, the one that never proves ungrateful or treacherous, is his dog."*

While his speech was very short, it obviously won over the jury (undoubtedly a group of dog lovers). The initial fine was supposed to have been less than $200 — Vest's client was awarded $500.

"Thomas Jefferson still survives..."
John Adams   (1826)

As he uttered his last words, John Adams was completely unaware that what he was speaking was a lie. The second president of the United States and one of the original signers of the Declaration of Independence, Adams took comfort in the notion that his old friend and political adversary would survive him. On July 4, 1826, his last words were, *"Thomas Jefferson still survives,"* revealing that Adams was completely unaware that Jefferson had died just a few hours earlier.

Both Adams and Jefferson had lived lives dedicated to the United States of America, and both had played a large part in helping the nation gain its independence. But their relationship had been a rocky one.

Adams had defeated Jefferson in the presidential election of 1796. He became president, and Jefferson served in the less coveted position of vice-president. With the nation still trying to find its place in the rest of the world, the two men, both from different political parties, butted heads on almost every issue — especially foreign policy.

In the next election, it was Jefferson who defeated Adams. Adams was bitter. He felt that the country had turned against him, and he was so hurt that he refused to attend Jefferson's inauguration.

Several years later, the two men reconciled and began an extensive correspondence for the last twenty years of their lives. It remains an amazing coincidence that both of these presidents died on July 4, the 50th anniversary of the Declaration of Independence.

A Bitter Rivalry

"I didn't shoot Henry Clay and I didn't hang John Calhoun!"
Andrew Jackson   (1837)

When asked if he regretted leaving anything undone during his time in office, Andrew Jackson had a quick response. Jackson, who served as the seventh president of the United States (1829 to 1837), pointed out two simple things: **"I didn't shoot Henry Clay and I didn't hang John Calhoun!"** Not surprisingly, he had some issues with the two men.

Andrew Jackson

During Jackson's first term as president, his vice-president was South Carolina native John Calhoun. The two were constantly at odds with each other. The pinnacle of their disagreements came over the doctrine of nullification—a piece of legislature which gave individual states the right to nullify any federal law it saw as oppressive.

Calhoun's home state of South Carolina found itself in the center of the nullification issue when the federal government declared taxes on imported goods, seriously hurting the state's port cities. South Carolina wanted to nullify the law, arguing that the local state government was more apt to choose what was best for its citizens than the federal government. Obviously, John Calhoun took the side of his home state, proclaiming that the people in South Carolina should be given the opportunity to make their own choices. Andrew Jackson, on the other hand, felt that a single state should never be allowed to ignore the majority. If that happened, then the Union would ultimately fall apart.

In April 1829, right in the middle of this heated debate, a presidential dinner was held. This dinner created an awkward situation where all men present had to be on their best behavior regardless of personal opinions. At the end of the night, President Jackson offered a toast that he finished by nodding to Calhoun and saying, **"Our Federal Union! It must be preserved!"** Calhoun raised his glass back and responded, **"The Union, next to our liberty, most dear."**

The subtle exchange was filled with tension. Andrew Jackson had hoped to sneak in a cheap-shot by mentioning the importance of maintaining the union, but John Calhoun shot back. In the end, a compromise was made regarding South Carolina, and both sides of the nullification argument declared a victory.

A close supporter of John Calhoun was Congressman Henry Clay, which leaves no surprise that Henry Clay and Andrew Jackson weren't the best of friends. In fact, Clay had run for president against Jackson on several occasions—but, he never did win the office. When Andrew Jackson became president, Clay became the leader of the new Whig Party, which basically was created only to oppose Jackson's administration.

In all, Henry Clay made three unsuccessful attempts to become President of the United States. His beliefs on certain sensitive issues (like slavery) didn't go over well with the public. But Clay stood by his principles, holding his ground by declaring, **"I had rather be right than be President."**

Despite failing to obtain the country's highest office, Henry Clay's political career wasn't a disaster. In 1803, at the age of twenty-six, he was elected to the Kentucky state legislature. Just three years later, he became a senator. For most of the years from 1811 to 1825, he served in the House of Representatives, eventually rising to become Speaker of the House.

While the public must not have liked Henry Clay enough to make him the president, he did have his share of supporters. He became popular when he rallied support for the War of 1812, and he helped create the Treaty of Ghent that ended the war. Afterwards, Henry Clay devoted his attention on domestic affairs, helping to establish a solid road system and a national bank.

"You can go to hell—I'm going to Texas!"
Davy Crockett   (1835)

Davy Crockett never had the reputation of a graceful loser. As a pioneer, adventurer, and defender of the Alamo, he's become almost more of a legend in American folklore than a real historic figure. Yet, much of the myth that has been built around him is a result of his real behavior. He was speaking to his victorious opponents after losing a congressional election in Tennessee when he told them, *"You can go to hell—I'm going Texas!"* And, true to his word, he left Tennessee for Texas.

It was a gutsy move. Davy Crockett was born and raised in Tennessee. He also served in the state legislature and two terms as the state's representative in Congress. Unfortunately, Crockett's political views put him in conflict with one of the most powerful politicians of the day—Andrew Jackson. His defeat in the 1835 congressional election was to one of Jackson's cronies.

In Texas, Davy Crockett led a small group of Tennessee volunteers in the fight against Mexican rule. In 1836, these men, Davy Crockett included, lost their lives at the infamous Alamo.

"Go west, young man!"
Horace Greeley   (1850's)

Apparently, it takes just a simple phrase to motivate thousands of Americans to drop everything and head west in search of some awaiting fortune. It all started in 1848, when gold was discovered in the hills of northern California. This began one of the most massive migrations in human history. People from the east coast of the United States immediately began to pack up what little they had and take off across the country. The west was still largely unsettled, and it seemed like the land of opportunity. Horace Greeley thought so. Greeley was an American journalist who, in 1841, founded the *New York Tribune*. His *Tribune* was one of the first affordable daily newspapers in the area.

Offering advice to a clergyman who had to give up the ministry after he lost his voice, Greeley remarked, *"Go west, young man!"* Originally, an Indiana newspaper editor named John Soule had used the phrase, but it wasn't until Greeley said it that it caught on. The public responded to the new catchphrase by gathering in large and small groups to head west. In 1859, with the help of new railroads, Greeley's newspaper continued to stir up public interest by reporting on life in California.

Greeley used his newspaper for other reasons as well. In 1860, he played a significant role in getting Abraham Lincoln nominated for the presidency. Later, he tried earning the office of president for himself, but was defeated by Ulysses S. Grant.

"The Chinese built the Great Wall, didn't they?"
Charles Crocker   (1860's)

When the vision of building a transcontinental railroad across the United States became popular in the 1860's, it was quickly tempered by the harsh realization of how difficult it would be. The amount of labor necessary to carry out such a rugged task was almost unthinkable. The work was dangerous and exhausting, and there just didn't seem to be any steady source of manpower to see it through. That's when Charles Crocker, a businessman overseeing the railroad's construction, suggested hiring the Chinese people for laborers. This proposition met immediate criticism—his superintendents felt that the Chinese were too small to handle the rigorous work. To this, Crocker simply replied, "The Chinese built the Great Wall, didn't they?"

He was right—the Chinese people did build the legendary Great Wall, beginning in 3rd century BC, to protect China's northern border. And, they would prove themselves again in the task of railroad building. In the 1850's, a piece of a line beginning in Sacramento, California was completed using Chinese labor. But that was a small task compared to extending the tracks across the rugged Sierra Nevada Mountains.

Nonetheless, Crocker called on the Chinese. By the late 1860's, the workforce for the transcontinental railroad consisted of several thousand Chinese laborers, and the speed and efficiency of construction was remarkable. The railroad would transform a trip across the country—what had taken several months by wagon, now took about a week by train.

Famous Firsts

"Mr. Watson, come here! I want you!"
Alexander Graham Bell   (1876)

When he prepared to test his newly invented telegraph machine on May 24, 1844, Samuel Morse decided to try something a little more interesting than "Testing 1-2-3". The chosen words were from the Bible's book of Numbers, verse 23:23. The phrase— **"What hath God wrought!"** Morse sent this message from the Capitol Building in Washington, DC to a man named Alfred Vail, located in Baltimore. Vail had provided early financial support to aid Morse in the experiments.

Unlikely as it may seem, Samuel Morse was a professor of painting and sculpting at New York University when he became interested in the electric telegraph. Using both technical and financial assistance from others, he conducted several experiments that led to his patenting of the telegraph in 1840. He also developed a code, appropriately referred to as Morse Code, intended to be used with his new invention.

In 1843, Congress agreed to provide Morse with the money to build an experimental line between Washington, DC and Baltimore. It was on that line that Morse transmitted the world's first telegraph message.

Over thirty years later, in 1876, Alexander Graham Bell had his chance at a famous first. Just three days earlier, he had received patent #174,465 from the United States Patent Office—his patent, of course, was for the telephone.

On March 10, he and his assistant, Thomas A. Watson, were about to test a new transmitter when Bell accidentally spilled battery acid on himself. Located in a different room than Watson, he called for him by yelling, **"Mr. Watson, come here! I want**

you!" Thomas Watson heard the cry, but not from down the hall—he heard it through the transmitter that the two men were preparing to test.

When Watson told Bell what had happened, the battery acid seemed fairly insignificant. After all, he had just made the world's first telephone call.

The invention of the telephone had an immediate impact. In 1878, President Rutherford B. Hayes had the relatively new device installed in the White House. The telephone was already two years old but, since no other places in Washington had one, it didn't seem to be particularly necessary for the White House to have one either.

When the telephone was put in, Alexander Graham Bell himself went thirteen miles away from the White House to test it. President Hayes made the first phone call, and Bell began talking to him on the other end of the line. That was when Hayes had his moment to shine

Alexander Graham Bell testing the first telephone

and speak the first words ever by a President of the United States over the phone—his choice: **"Please, speak more slowly."**

Hayes may have intended to say something more eloquent on his first occasion, but that's what goes down in the history books. Nonetheless, the telephone call was a success, and Bell probably honored the President's request and spoke more slowly.

"From where the sun now stands, I will fight no more forever."
Chief Joseph   (1877)

It was the year 1877 when Chief Joseph and the Nez Pérce tribe were ordered by General Oliver Howard to move from their land in Oregon to a reservation in Idaho. They were given 30 days. Chief Joseph refused to cooperate. Instead he planned to take his people to Canada where they could be given freedom, just as the famous Chief Sitting Bull had already done. As he led the tribe in that direction, the chase began. The United States calvary made it their mission to stop Chief Joseph. Several skirmishes took place along the way, but the Nez Pérce refused to give in. Carrying the sick and wounded with them, the tribe marched persistently over the harsh Rocky Mountains for 1,800 miles.

But, the 700 people that made the journey weren't all trained warriors. Many of them were women and children, and it became too much for Chief Joseph to watch his people suffer. *"It is cold and we have no blankets. The little children are freezing to death,"* he declared when, after 105 days, he finally surrendered to General Howard. *"I am tired; my heart is sick and sad. From where the sun now stands, I shall fight no more forever."* Chief Joseph didn't realize that his people were only fifty miles from the Canadian border.

"I am chief here and the people look up to me. There, I would be a poor half-breed Indian."
Parker Quanah   (late 1800's)

Comanche Chief Parker Quanah knew his place in the world. His mother, Cynthia Ann Parker, was a white woman who had been captured by his tribe in the 1840's. In 1845, she gave birth to Quanah, a half-white and half Native American child. In 1860, she was released back to the white world.

Quanah would grow up to become a great war chief for the Comanche Indians, leading his people to battle the white settlers in Texas. However, with his tribe vastly outnumbered and overpowered, he was forced to surrender. After the fighting had ended, Quanah quickly adapted to the white culture. He became fluent in both English and Spanish, and learned the agricultural techniques of the settlers. At his peak, Quanah was considered the richest Native American in North America.

Despite his tremendous success, Quanah remained loyal to his tribe. He was constantly engaged in business with the white settlers, but refused to leave his Comanche heritage. After being asked why he was so intent on staying separate from the white world where his mother had come from, he explained, *"As far as you can see I am chief here and the people look up to me. There, I would be a poor half-breed Indian."* With that outlook, he made it a point to distance himself from the white world except in business. His loyalty to his heritage was so great that, by 1890, Quanah had become Chief over all of the Comanche tribes.

"Tell the people it is no use to depend on me anymore now."
Crazy Horse   (1877)

Aware of what his future held, Sioux warrior Crazy Horse delivered this solemn declaration to his tribesman. The Chief was courageously leading his followers against white expansion in the western United States. However, the U.S. army was relentlessly pursuing him, and his days were numbered. At the end of the long chase, Crazy Horse had a message sent back to his tribe: *"Tell the people it is no use to depend on me anymore..."* He was later killed by a United States soldier.

During the 1870's, as white settlers chased Native Americans from their homes, the Sioux Indians had depended on Crazy Horse for his leadership. He had joined forces with Sitting Bull, successfully fending off the U.S. Army on several occasions. On June 25, 1877, he led his warriors against General Custer in the infamous Battle of Little Bighorn. Taking place in the Black Hills of Montana, Custer's calvary was completely destroyed.

It was at this point that the Army began to pursue Crazy Horse. He was able to survive on the run for almost a year, but the chase ended on May 6, 1877 in Nebraska. With no option left, Crazy Horse surrendered and was taken prisoner.

"Not one cent for scenery!"
Joseph Cannon   (early 1900's)

Not everyone is blown away by a pretty picture. Joseph Cannon, the powerful Speaker of the House in the early 1900's, gave this bold opinion after listening to a proposition for a bill that preserved timberland for the sake of aesthetics. Growth was rampant at the turn of the century, so several pieces of legislation (most namely the Weeks Law) were designed to allow the federal government to buy private land to create undisturbed national forests. Joseph Cannon's reply to the idea of using public money for this purpose, *"Not one cent for scenery,"* told volumes about his character.

A conservative Republican from Illinois, Cannon became the leader of the House of Representatives in 1903. He presided over the House with a heavy hand, making himself one of the most powerful Speakers in American history. His traditional outlooks sometimes conflicted with the progressive legislation that was common at the beginning of the century. Not surprisingly, this resulted in more than a little tension among the Democrats and less conservative Republicans. But, for the first decade of the 1900's, Cannon kept a tight grip on the majority of the bills that passed through the House.

Perhaps it is fortunate that some bills concerning forest conservation were able to squeeze through. As a result, dozens of national forests were formed, many still existing today.

"What this country needs is a really good five-cent cigar!"
Thomas Marshall   (1920)

Does this seem like too unreasonable of a request? It is the celebrated remark of Thomas Marshall, the 28th Vice-president of the United States. While serving under President Woodrow Wilson, Marshall was listening to a Senate debate where the opponents rambled on about exactly what the country needed. Perhaps a little bored, Marshall leaned over to the Senate's assistant secretary, Henry Rose, and muttered, *"What this country needs is a really good five-cent cigar."*

Having practiced law in Indiana for over thirty years, Marshall became well liked for his charm and wit. In 1909, he was elected as the Democratic governor of Indiana, and earned a reputation for his work on labor rights and social reform. In 1912, a number of Democrats supported the idea of having Marshall represent the party in the upcoming election, but Woodrow Wilson was chosen instead. Marshall did receive the vice-presidential nomination.

During his term as Vice-president, Marshall became a solid supporter of Wilson in his dealings with social legislation. Still, he was perhaps more nationally known for his sense of humor than his political tendencies.

"When our boys come home from France, we will have the hags flung out!"
William Spooner   (1910's)

Copy that? This remark was made by Reverend William Spooner during World War I in an effort to reassure his students at New College of Oxford. Unfortunately, it isn't exactly what he meant to say. The statement is known as a "spoonerism," named for the Reverend himself. A spoonerism is a linguistic mix-up in which a phrase such as "coffee table" becomes "toffee cable". So, when Reverend Spooner stated, *"When our boys come home from France, we will have the hags flung out,"* he was meaning to say, *"we will have the flags hung out."*

As the dean and warden of New College from 1903 to 1924, Reverend Spooner became known for his constant flip-flops. When a student missed yet another one of his lectures, Spooner reproached him by saying, *"You have tasted two worms"* (he was trying for "wasted two terms"). Then the professor then told the student that he ought to leave Oxford on the next *"town drain"*.

A professor of divinity and history, Reverend Spooner certainly was an intelligent man. If anything, his thoughts moved faster than his tongue. Whatever the explanation, his most remembered contribution to the world won't be his great teachings, but instead his creation of the "spoonerism."

Presidential Assassinations (and Some Close Calls)

"I will make this speech or die!"
Theodore Roosevelt (1912)

As he clutched his hand over a bullet wound in his stomach, President William McKinley delivered one final, and interesting, order. McKinley was greeting visitors after he had given a speech at the 1901 Pan-American exposition in Buffalo, New York, when anarchist Leon Czolgosz shot him twice. Immediately, the spectators attacked Czolgosz and began to beat him ferociously. The only thing that kept them from killing the President's attacker was the wounded McKinley's remark to his guards, **"Don't let them hurt him!"**

McKinley wouldn't survive the attack. Despite being rushed away for an emergency operation, he died on September 14, 1901, eight days after the shooting. His young vice-president, Theodore Roosevelt, was left to carry out the term. As for Leon Czolgosz, he didn't have much time to be grateful to the President for sparing his life—he was executed one month later.

It's not surprising that McKinley's audience was so quick to pounce on his assassin. During McKinley's term as president, the United States transformed from a relatively isolated nation into a world power. McKinley became extremely popular and his successor, Roosevelt, was able keep up the country's optimism.

Theodore Roosevelt went on to serve two terms as president. But, when he was campaigning a final time for the presidential election of 1912, he was shot in the chest just before giving a speech in Milwaukee, Wisconsin. Luckily, Roosevelt had prepared a long speech. The bullet went through the several page copy he was carrying in his pocket, as well as the metal case for his eyeglasses. Although wounded, Roosevelt was not seriously hurt. After the commotion had cleared, he declared, **"I will make this speech or die!"** His security men obviously disapproved, but Roosevelt refused to be intimidated by any attempt on his life. As promised, he continued with his speech.

The assassination was attempted made by an extremely peculiar man named John Schrank. Schrank claimed that eleven years earlier the ghost of President William McKinley had visited him in a dream. In his dream, McKinley had warned him not to let a murderer become president. Apparently, Schrank thought that Roosevelt was the man whom McKinley was referring to. From this, he decided that it was his duty to assassinate President Roosevelt. After the failed attempt, Schrank was found to be insane and later committed.

Theodore Roosevelt

What's more, Theodore Roosevelt wasn't the only President to have a close call with a madman. Almost seventy years later, and only two months into his presidency, Ronald Reagan was the victim of a failed assassination. He was leaving the Washington Hilton Hotel on March 30, 1981, when a lone gunman fired several shots. Though one of the bullets hit his ribcage, Reagan was not seriously injured. As he entered the hospital to have the bullet removed, he realized his fate was at the hands of his doctors. Despite the injuries, Reagan had the presence of mind to plead with the surgeons, **"Please tell me you're Republicans!"**

Whatever the political beliefs of the doctors, the bullet was removed successfully and the President was soon back at work. He had been the eighth American president to become the target of an assassin's bullet, and the fourth to survive. Surrounded by a large group of people, Reagan was undoubtedly a difficult man to hit. In fact, three other men were also wounded in the burst of shots. White House press secretary James Brady was struck by a bullet above the eye, and was seriously wounded. He later became an outspoken advocate for gun control.

The lone gunman, 25 year-old John Hinckley, was immediately subdued. He was later found not guilty on a plea of insanity—instead, he was committed to a mental hospital.

Helen Keller—Successful in overcoming her handicaps

"My teacher learned about me and broke through the dark, silent, imprisonment...."
Helen Keller   (1925)

That's a big thank-you. On June 30, 1925, Helen Keller made these remarks at a convention in Cedar Point, Ohio. Keller was not the first speaker of the night, however—Anne Sullivan was. Sullivan had been Helen Keller's teacher since Helen was six years old, and it was she who had broken through the *"dark, silent, imprisonment."*

At just 19 months old, Helen Keller caught a fever that would leave her blind and deaf for the rest of her life. Knowing she was completely isolated from the rest of the world, her father took her to see the inventor Alexander Graham Bell. Bell had developed a system of writing for the blind, and he recommended taking Helen to the Perkins Institution for the Blind located in Boston. There, in 1887, they met up with Anne Sullivan.

Because Helen could neither see nor hear anything, Sullivan had to get creative. She would give objects to Helen, and then manually spell the names of the objects with Helen's hands. It was a tedious task, but Helen Keller was up for it. Slowly, she started to break out of her shell, and from there she learned at an astounding rate. Helen soon learned to read Braille, and began speaking at age eleven. As an adult, Keller became an international humanitarian, helping to improve the quality of life for the disabled.

Sullivan would continue to stay by Helen Keller's side, forming a relationship that lasted almost fifty years.

> ***"Never in our full life could we hope to do such work for tolerance, for justice, for man's understanding of man..."***
> **Bartolomeo Vanzetti   (1927)**

It's probably not easy to speak so eloquently just moments after hearing that you've been sentenced to death. But, Italian immigrant Bartolomeo Vanzetti managed to do so as he gave the concluding statement in one of the most famous and controversial trials in history. Vanzetti and Nicola Sacco, who worked respectively as a fish peddler and a shoemaker, had been accused of murdering a paymaster and his guard on April 15, 1920 in South Braintree, Massachusetts. The trial lasted for seven years, ending with a sentence of death for both men.

Unfortunately, the facts of the trial were shaky at best. Many felt that the incriminating evidence was inadequate, and the testimony given clearly contradicted itself. Both men had admitted to being anarchists, and it appeared that they were being treated unfairly because they were immigrants with unpopular beliefs. The trial quickly caught the attention of the public, and it placed a spotlight on the unjust treatment of settlers from abroad.

Despite the fact that the final decision of the court was against him, Vanzetti felt that he had served his purpose. His unfortunate situation had allowed him to become something of a martyr. When his fate was finalized, Vanzetti gathered enough courage to stand before the court and declare, *"Never in our full life could we hope to do such work for tolerance, for justice, for man's understanding of man as now we do by accident."* He then attacked the court's decision — *"The taking of our lives—lives of a good shoemaker and a poor fish-peddler—all! That last moment belongs to us—that agony is our triumph!"*

"Gentlemen do not read each other's mail!"
Henry Stimson   (1929)

It's seldom that major political decisions are based on common courtesy. Nonetheless, this is the reasoning provided by Secretary of State Henry Stimson in 1929 as he disbanded the nation's sole codebreaking and counterintelligence operation. Serving under Herbert Hoover, Stimson's decision to shut down the "Black Chamber" was certainly controversial. The organization had, after all, proved successful in deciphering coded messages from adversary nations in the past. But, Stimson decided that it was no longer necessary.

While the disbanding of the Black Chamber may have stunted counterintelligence operations temporarily, it didn't stop them. Instead, the art of codebreaking was shifted to a more conventional division of the State Department, and new techniques continued to develop and improve. A great emphasis on message decoding and other spy-operations developed in 1941, when the United States became involved in World War II. With advances that had been made before the war, the government was able to use its counterintelligence operations to help secure an allied victory.

"The income tax law is a lot of bunk."
Al Capone   (1931)

You have to admit, it's hard to argue with that sentiment. Notorious gangster Al Capone used this logic when he was convicted for income tax evasion in 1931. During the years of prohibition, Capone headed up an enormous organized crime operation in Chicago. Scarface, as he was sometimes known, was involved in a wide variety of bootlegging and gambling. His illegal acts left hundreds dead in various gang wars.

Despite Capone's obvious connection to organized crime, the authorities could not make any charge stick. Finally, after appearing immune to federal discipline, he was brought down on the charge of tax evasion. The prosecutors were able to give numerous examples of huge purchases and lavish spending that would indicate that Capone was making an enormous amount of money. He wasn't, however, paying taxes on the amount of income that was necessary to maintain his lifestyle. The evidence was overwhelming, and he was convicted. But Capone didn't feel the charges brought against him made any sense. In his words, *"The income tax law is a lot of bunk. The government can't collect legal taxes from illegal money."*

After his conviction, Al Capone was given a large fine and sentenced to serve eleven years in prison. Because he was such a high profile criminal, he was sent to the infamous prison, Alcatraz, located in the Bay of San Francisco.

"There is no greater inequality than the equal treatment of unequals."
Felix Frankfurter   (1950)

Seem a little harsh? Associate justice of the United States Supreme Court, Felix Frankfurter, didn't think so when he made the claim during the controversial trial *Dennis vs. United States*. At the conclusion of the case, Frankfurter upheld a previous decision to convict eleven defendants.

The accused party in *Dennis vs. United States* was a group of communists who had plotted to overthrow the government by force. This was in 1950, when the Cold War was heating up and the entire nation was on edge about the threat of communist infiltration. Nonetheless, as the case was argued, many believed that the conspirators were just exercising their freedom of speech—they were being targeted simply because they were communists. After all, no physical crime had been committed.

Justice Frankfurter felt differently. Believing that the government has a right to protect itself, he recognized that the accused were guilty of "sedition" (a crime similar to treason but with no violent acts). He argued that a conspiracy to overthrow the government could only lead to a violent ending. Frankfurter defended himself against those who claimed he was too harsh on the communists by explaining, *"To take appropriate measures in order to avert injustice, even towards a member of a despised group, is to enforce justice."*

Franklin Roosevelt—Calming the nation during the Great Depression

> *"...the only thing we have to fear is fear itself—nameless, unreasoning, unjustified terror which paralyzes needed efforts to convert retreat into advance."*
>
> **Franklin Roosevelt (1933)**

When Franklin D. Roosevelt stood up to make his first inaugural address on March 3rd, 1933, it definitely wasn't the best of times. He was well aware that his presidency was beginning during the darkest period of the United States since the Civil War. Almost a quarter of Americans, over 13 million, had lost their jobs, and the economy was at an all-time low. The period appropriately became known as the Great Depression.

Running on the promise of a "New Deal," Roosevelt had defeated then-President Herbert Hoover by an overwhelming margin. He made no secret of the country's bleak situation in his inaugural speech, "*Only a foolish optimist can deny the dark realities of the moment.*" But, he knew it was his job to lift the morale of the nation— *"We are stricken by no plague of locusts!"*.

The greatest danger during the Depression was not hunger, not housing, and it was not disease. The one thing that threatened the American people most at that time was panic. Roosevelt understood this more than anyone. After just a few introductory words in his inaugural, he recited the line that would become one of the most famous in American history *"...the only thing we have to fear is fear itself"*.

Roosevelt managed to keep everyone calm in a time of great distress. Because of his leadership, he was able to fulfill another prediction in his inaugural: *"This great Nation will endure as it has endured, will revive and will prosper."*

"Roosevelt or ruin!"
Charles Coughlin   (1933)

That doesn't leave much room for indecision! Father Charles E. Coughlin gave this choice to the American people during his popular radio broadcasts of the early 1930's. Starting out as a small-town pastor, Coughlin began to give weekly sermons over the radio in 1926. His shows were so well received that he branched away from religion and ventured into politics and economics. By 1935, over one-third of Americans were listening to his programs. That's a larger listening audience than Rush Limbaugh, Howard Stern, and Paul Harvey — *combined.*

Coughlin used his popularity and influence to help Franklin Roosevelt win the election in 1933. In the heart of a Great Depression, Coughlin criticized the Hoover administration for its economic decisions and he assured the American public that Roosevelt's radical reforms were the only solution to the Depression. Over the radio he declared, *"It is Roosevelt or ruin!"* and the sentiment caught on across the country.

Ironically, Father Coughlin, who was perhaps Roosevelt's greatest supporter in the beginning, would later become his worst critic. He believed that Roosevelt's reforms weren't carried out as promised — instead, Roosevelt was putting the country in a worse state. By 1936, Father Coughlin, who had introduced the slogan *"Roosevelt or ruin!"* would come on the radio and announce, *"Roosevelt AND ruin!"*

When he became too controversial, Coughlin was eventually asked by the Catholic Church to leave the radio business and simply return to his work as a parish priest.

"There is no Democratic or Republican way of cleaning the streets!"
Fiorello La Guardia   (1933)

Well said. This is the declaration of Fiorello La Guardia, one the most influential mayors in the history of New York City. Elected to the first of his three terms in 1933, La Guardia quickly became popular with the community, and he also had an immediate influence. His claim, *"There is no Democratic or Republican way of cleaning the streets,"* was true on several levels. In addition to helping in the beautification of New York City, La Guardia also helped reduce political corruption, upgrade slum areas, and improve health conditions in the city.

Standing at only 5'-2", La Guardia was known affectionately as the "Little Flower" by his constituents. He was elected as a Republican, but in reality he had many liberal philosophies. His connection with both political parties helped La Guardia deal with opposition from all directions when he set out to pass reforms.

Raised by a Jewish mother and an Italian father, La Guardia was the obvious candidate to govern the huge immigrant population of New York City in the 1930's. In fact, he had served as an interpreter at the immigrant checkpoint of Ellis Island before taking office. His good ties with the community were also strengthened with a radio program that he broadcast over the city each week.

"The Attilas come and go. The Hitlers flash and sputter out. But freedom endures."
Harold Ickes   (1941)

In May of 1941, the people of the United States watched in fear as Germany went on a rampage, conquering several nearby nations in Europe. The Germans had begun to bomb England, and there were no signs that they would stop until they took over the world. It was then, with all of America holding its breath, that Secretary of the Interior Harold Ickes stood before a large crowd at New York's Central Park and delivered his famous "I am an American" speech.

"What has happened to our vaunted idealism?" he asked, "Why have some of us been behaving like scared chickens?" There had been a lot of talk about the United States staying out of World War II altogether, letting the European nations deal with it themselves. Ickes made it clear that the United States couldn't just look the other way.

If Britain and other nations were attacked, he explained, then the American people were also in danger. "*We cannot retain our liberty if three-fourths of the world is enslaved.*" Ickes, confident in the task ahead, said what the public needed to hear — and he was correct. *"Liberty never dies. The Genghis Khans come and go. The Attilas come and go. The Hitlers flash and sputter out. But freedom endures."*

"The buck stops here!"
Harry Truman   (1952)

That's the attitude you have to have if you're going to be the President of the United States. This expression was actually popularized by a small sign President Harry Truman kept on his desk. The saying is derived from the maxim, *"passing the buck,"* which means relaying a certain responsibility to someone else. The phrase *"passing the buck"* is believed to have originated during poker games of old west. At the time, a knife with a buckhorn handle was placed on the table and pointed to the player whose turn it was to deal. If that person didn't want the responsibility of dealing, it was said that he *"passed the buck"* — the knife was then turned to the next player.

Harry Truman recognized that, as President of the United States, the idea of *"passing the buck"* was simply not an option. On December 19, 1952 he gave a speech at the National War College and described his outlook. *"It's easy for the Monday morning quarterback to say what the coach should have done, after the game is over,"* Truman explained, *"But when the decision is up before you — and on my desk I have a motto which says 'The Buck Stops Here' — the decision has to be made."*

Truman certainly had his share of big decisions. He served as President for two terms, helping the country to recover after World War II.

God Bless America!

"I pledge allegiance to the Flag of the United States of America, and to the Republic for which it stands; one Nation under God, indivisible, with liberty and justice for all."

Sound familiar? For generations, these words have been repeated by millions of citizens across the nation. The Pledge of Allegiance to the U.S. flag was first recited in public schools throughout the country on October 12, 1892, in honor of the 400th anniversary of Christopher Columbus's discovery of America.

The words are originally believed to have been written by Francis Bellamy. He worked as an assistant to the owner of the children's magazine, *The Youth's Companion*, where the pledge first appeared. Bellamy, a socialist minister from Boston, was appointed as chairman of the committee that organized the events for the Columbus Day celebration in 1892.

The original version of the Pledge of Allegiance was the more condensed, **"I pledge allegiance to my Flag and to the Republic for which it stands: one nation, indivisible, with liberty and justice for all."** The expanded wording, which is known today, was finalized in 1954.

There are a few more words that are universally recognized by the American public. The line, **"Oh say can you see by the dawn's early light,"** is, of course, the first line to the national anthem of the United States — the "Star Spangled Banner". Ironically, a lawyer named Francis Scott Key wrote the song while he was on board a British Frigate.

During the War of 1812, Key had come onto the British ship under a truce in order to arrange the release of American prisoners. The day was September 13, 1814 and, that night, the British decided to bomb Fort McHenry in Baltimore. Unable to leave, Francis Scott Key had to sit in the middle of the Chesapeake Bay all through the night and watch as an American fort suffered a tremendous assault.

The next morning, Key looked onto the shore and witnessed that the flag of the United States — the Star-Spangled Banner — was still waving over the fort. The Americans had not surrendered. It was that sight that inspired him to write the national anthem.

Key's lyrics hit land soon after. They were originally distributed in a handbill that was passed around Baltimore. At that time, it was entitled "Defence of Fort M'Henry". Later, the words were put to the music of a British drinking song called "To Anacreon in Heaven".

The new patriotic song quickly caught on, but that didn't make it the "national anthem". It was the combined efforts of an executive order by President Wilson in 1916 and an act of Congress in 1931 that officially made "The Star-Spangled Banner" the national anthem of the United States.

The first verse of Francis Scott Key's four verse poem. This is what is recognized today as the words to the "Star-Spangled Banner:"

Oh, say can you see, by the dawn's early light,
What so proudly we hailed at the twilight's last gleaming?
Whose broad stripes and bright stars, through the perilous fight,
O'er the ramparts we watched, were so gallantly streaming?
And the rockets' red glare, the bombs bursting in air,
Gave proof through the night that our flag was still there.
O say, does that star-spangled banner yet wave
O'er the land of the free and the home of the brave?

"I am a free man, an American, a United States senator, and a Democrat—in that order."
Lyndon Johnson   **(1958)**

Senator Lyndon B. Johnson had his priorities in order. He offered this "Political Philosophy" during a statement to the press in 1958. Having already served as a senator for nearly a decade, Johnson also admitted to being, *"a liberal, a conservative, a Texan, a taxpayer, a rancher, a businessman, a consumer, a parent, a voter, and not as young as I used to be nor as old as I expect to be—and I am all these things in no fixed order."*

Johnson became a senator in 1949 after serving in the House for almost a dozen years. His experience in government enabled him to move so quickly through the ranks that in five years he was the majority leader. At the time, the Democratic senate was serving under a Republican president, Dwight Eisenhower. But, Johnson was able to keep the tension to a minimum by working closely with fellow Democrat and Speaker of the House, Sam Rayburn. The outcome was successful legislation for both parties during the late 1950's.

In 1960, presidential candidate John F. Kennedy announced that he wanted to run with Lyndon Johnson on the ticket as Vice-president. Kennedy was victorious, but he was later assassinated in 1963. Johnson was sworn in as president just a few hours afterward. In 1964, he won the presidential election on his own right with a huge margin of victory over Barry Goldwater.

"Have you left no sense of decency?"
Joseph Welch   **(1954)**

This question led to the inevitable downfall of Senator Joseph R. McCarthy. It was asked on June 9, 1954, in the midst of the *Army vs. McCarthy* Congressional Hearings. McCarthy's theories of Communist infiltration were getting out of control when Boston lawyer Joseph N. Welch finally confronted him.

The inquiry, which took place from April 22 to June 17, was the result of McCarthy accusing the Army of having communists mixed up in its ranks. McCarthy also claimed that the Army was taking actions to cover this up.

Welch, who represented the Army, brought the hearings to a climax after McCarthy broke a personal agreement with him. McCarthy insinuated that a young lawyer at Welch's law firm had communist tendencies. Upon hearing this accusation, Welch stood up and screamed, *"Have you no sense of decency, sir, at long last. Have you left no sense of decency?"*

The spectators, surprised by the verbal attack, broke out into applause. More significantly, however, the entire country had seen the event on national television, and McCarthy's reputation would never recover.

"You have the God-given right to kick the government around!"
Edmund Muskie   (1968)

That's an unusual assertion to be made by a politician, but Edmund Muskie didn't let that stop him. As the running mate of Hubert Humphrey in the 1968 election, the senator from Maine was campaigning in Indiana when he reminded his audience of their *"God-given right to kick the government around!"* He then told them, *"Don't hesitate to do so."*

Unfortunately for Muskie, the people of America decided to kick him around a little. He and Hubert Humphrey lost the election to Richard M. Nixon in an extremely close popular vote. Muskie didn't get discouraged, though—he remained a large influence in the Democratic Party. Even before his Vice-presidential campaign, his political career had been impressive. He had been elected to the Maine House of Representatives when he was only thirty-two, eventually becoming the governor of the state.

After his failed campaign with Humphrey, Muskie tried on his own to earn the Democratic presidential nomination in 1972, but he again came up short. As something of a consolation prize, he was chosen to serve as Secretary of State under President Carter.

John F. Keenedy—Inspiring President of the early 1960's

"And so, my fellow Americans: ask not what your country can do for you—ask what you can do for your country!"

John F. Kennedy   (1961)

John F. Kennedy, upon becoming the youngest person to be elected president at age 44, wanted to make the right impression. And he did just that when, on January 20, 1961, he recited these timeless words in his inaugural speech. Coming from a prominent family, Kennedy got an early start to his political career by being elected into the House of Representatives before he was thirty. But he had proven himself under pressure before. During World War II, he was decorated for saving three soldiers after a Japanese Destroyer sank his vessel.

Elected as president in 1960, Kennedy delivered his inaugural address at the Capital in Washington, DC, declaring, *"My fellow Americans: ask not what your country can do for you—ask what you can do for your country! My fellow citizens of the world: ask not what America will do for you, but what together we can do for the freedom of man!"*

Both the American people and the ideals of freedom would be tested during Kennedy's presidency. In 1961, he ordered the Bay of Pigs invasion, which became a failed attempt to overthrow Cuban dictator Fidel Castro. Only a year later, the Cuban Missile Crisis had the country holding its breath when Soviet missiles aimed at the United States were found in Cuba. Other issues, like Civil Rights, were also stirring up the nation at this time. Through all of this, Kennedy managed to still hold onto his popularity with American people.

"I think 'Hail to the Chief' has a nice ring to it."
John F. Kennedy   (early 1960's)

This should have been obvious! *"Hail to the Chief"* is the official theme song for the office of President of the United States, and it is played at public appearances made by the president. And, not surprisingly, Kennedy named this tune when he was asked about his favorite song.

"Hail to the Chief" was not written as a presidential theme song. Originally, in 1812, James Sanderson wrote it for a dramatic rendition of the poem, "The Lady of the Lake". It took on its political connection in 1815, when a version of it was played at a ceremony celebrating George Washington's birthday on February 22.

In the 1840's, during the terms of President Tyler and President Polk, *"Hail to the Chief"* began to be used to announce the entrance of the president. The tradition carried over to other presidents, and the song was eventually declared as the official music for the office. So, while Kennedy may have been the only one to admit it outright, it's probably safe to say that, when it comes to favorite songs, *"Hail to the Chief"* at least makes each president's top three.

"You, the great silent majority of my fellow Americans—I ask for your support."
Richard Nixon (1969)

This was President Richard Nixon's plea to the American people as he addressed them on November 3, 1969. Nixon was discussing his plans for a slow withdrawal of American troops from Vietnam.

His term *"silent majority"* may have been a correct way to describe many of those who supported him. At the time, large numbers of young Americans were publicly protesting the Vietnam War. They would hold rallies, organize protests, carry signs, and chant slogans. Most of them were so opposed to the war that they felt it would be better to take the loss and bring home the American soldiers immediately. Because of their aggressive tactics, the rest of the nation had no choice but to hear them.

President Nixon realized, however, that just because this group spoke the loudest and earned the most attention, they did not necessarily represent the feelings of the entire public. In fact, the president felt that there were more people, a *"silent majority,"* who felt that a sudden withdrawal was not the proper way to end the war. Instead, America could achieve peace with honor by pulling out slowly and not leaving the South Vietnamese allies completely abandoned. As a result, he ordered the withdrawal of 25,000 troops in the summer of 1969, which was to be followed by cutting nearly 65,000 troops by the end of the year.

"Fellow Americans, our long national nightmare is over."
Gerald Ford (1974)

After one of the most controversial episodes in American history, Gerald Ford tried to be an optimist. The people of the nation were beginning to lose faith in the presidency after the infamous Watergate scandal resulted in the resignation of President Richard Nixon in 1974. As Vice-president, Ford inherited the rest of Nixon's term. He understood that his first order of business was to earn back the trust of the American public. Therefore, it was important to assure the people that *"our long national nightmare is over."*

The *"nightmare"* of Watergate began on June 17, 1972, when five men were caught in the Democratic Party's campaign headquarters at the Watergate office complex in Washington, DC. However, the attempted wiretapping and burglary were only the start of the controversy. After the events, it was suspected that a massive cover-up by powerful government officials hindered the investigation. The accusations reached as high as President Nixon himself.

Facing almost certain impeachment, Nixon became the first president to resign on August 9, 1974. After inheriting the presidency, Ford immediately pardoned Nixon for any crimes that he might have been guilty.

"Obviously a major malfunction."
Stephen Nesbitt   (1986)

In utter disbelief, NASA Public Affairs Officer Stephen Nesbitt uttered these words just moments after the space shuttle Challenger exploded. Nesbitt had been reporting to the general public watching the take-off on television. When the explosion occurred, he was still reciting his usual script, *"...velocity 2,900 feet per second, altitude nine nautical miles, downrange seven nautical miles..."* Though Nesbitt continued to speak completely unaware of anything unusual, the viewers around the nation had already seen the Challenger explode.

When Nesbitt did finally look to see the disaster, there was a forty-second pause in his telecast. He finally broke the silence by calmly announcing, *"Flight controllers are looking very carefully at the situation."* He then added the now famous assertion, *"Obviously a major malfunction."*

The explosion of the Challenger had a tremendous impact on the nation. First, many had witnessed it on live television, and were totally unprepared for anything other than a routine take-off. Second, among the seven members of the flight crew killed in the disaster, one was a civilian. Christa McAuliffe was a high school teacher from New Hampshire who had been chosen to join the astronauts in the mission.

Ronald Reagan—Putting pressure on Gorbachev

"Mr. Gorbachev, Tear down this wall!"
Ronald Reagan (1987)

Throughout the Cold War, the Berlin Wall stood as a symbol of tension between the democratic United States and the communist Soviet Union. Unfortunately, with 299 guard towers, the wall was much more than a symbol for the people of East and West Berlin, whom it kept permanently separated.

On June 12, 1987, Ronald Reagan spoke at the Brandenburg Gate in West Berlin to a crowd of 20,000, his back to the Berlin Wall. This speech marked the beginning of the end for the Cold War, and the eventual destruction of the Berlin Wall.

General Secretary Mikhail Gorbachev of the Soviet Union had been preaching the concept of "glasnost," or "openness." But, in reality, he had done very little to show that he intended to allow Eastern Europe free access to the rest of the world. On this day, speaking to Berliners who had had enough of empty promises, Ronald Reagan personally challenged Gorbachev and the Soviets. *"General Secretary Gorbachev, if you seek peace, if you seek prosperity for the Soviet Union and Eastern Europe, if you seek liberalization: Come here to this gate! Mr. Gorbachev, open this gate! Mr. Gorbachev, tear down this wall!"*

Reagan affirmed his belief that the wall would come down, stating, *"This wall will fall. For it cannot withstand faith. It cannot withstand truth. The wall cannot withstand freedom."*

It motivated the German audience. Even loud speakers were placed in a way to allow the people trapped in East Germany to hear the president speak. Only two years later, in late 1989, the people of Berlin took it upon themselves to reunite their city and litrally tore down the Berlin Wall.

"Terrorist attacks can shake the foundations of our biggest buildings, but they cannot touch the foundation of America."
George W. Bush   (2001)

The term "September 11th" took on a whole new meaning in the year 2001. On that day, the United States suffered from the most brutal terrorist attack ever to take place on American soil. The nation watched as many of its esteemed landmarks came under attack. After the chaos, President George W. Bush reminded the people of the United States, *"Terrorist attacks can shake the foundations of our biggest buildings, but they cannot touch the foundations of America. These acts shatter steel, but they cannot dent the steel of American resolve."*

The tragedy began early in the morning on September 11th, when four commercial airline jets were hijacked by nineteen terrorists. Two of these jets flew into the twin towers of the World Trade Center. The 110-story towers, rising to over 1,300 feet, had already become a symbol of American ingenuity and a distinguished part of the New York City skyline. Ultimately, the damage from the jetliners resulted in the collapse of the buildings, killing nearly 3,000 innocent citizens and rescue workers.

The third hijacked plane flew into the pentagon in Washington, DC, killing over 100 workers. The final airplane crashed down into a field in Pennsylvania. The passengers on this jet had become aware of the attack and refused to cooperate with the hijackers. The events of September 11th did not strike terror into the nation as the terrorists had hoped. Instead, it united the people in the United States and restored a new feeling of patriotism throughout the country.

"These are the times that try men's souls. The summer soldier and the sunshine patriot will, in this crisis, shrink from the service of their country; but he that stands it now, deserves the love and thanks of man and woman."
—Thomas Paine
American patriot (1737-1809)
Opening lines of his pamphlet, *The Crisis* (1776)

Chapter 11

American Wars

"Taxation without representation is tyranny!"
James Otis   (1761)

This legendary line is responsible for the American Revolution. The directness and accuracy of the statement helped the colonists realize their unfortunate situation, and it became a rallying cry in the days leading up to the war. The concept, *"Taxation without representation is tyranny!"* was originally uttered by statesman James Otis in 1761, fifteen years before the start of the fighting. He was, of course, speaking to the frustrated and overtaxed citizens of the American colonies. Otis was referring to the onslaught of orders and writs issued by the British government without the colonists' consent or representation in Parliament. His speech made him a leader in the early stages of America's struggle for independence.

After becoming established for his stance against the heavy-handed rule of Britain, Otis joined the Massachusetts legislature. He continued to speak out against unfair taxation, and furthered his reputation by helping to define America's opposition to the Stamp Act in 1765.

"If this be treason, let's make the most of it!"
Patrick Henry   (1765)

The Stamp Act was wrong, and the colonists weren't about to stand for it. In 1765, Great Britain placed a tax on all legal documents and other paper products in the American colonies. The tax was passed without any debate in Parliament from the American public—it was taxation without representation.

With frustrations mounting, a twenty-nine year old from Virginia rose up to lead the American people in protest against the Stamp Act. Patrick Henry, who would play a vital role in preparing the country for the revolution a decade later, had only been a member of the Virginia House of Burgesses for a couple of weeks when the legislation was passed. He delivered a motivating speech before the House against the Stamp Act, concluding with the remarks, *"Caesar had his Brutus, Charles the*

First his Cromwell, and George the Third may profit from their example!"

Lots of people were outraged by the Stamp Act, but they felt that Patrick Henry had gone too far when he directly insulted the King of England. The American Revolution was still over ten years away, and loyalty to the King was expected in the colonies. Voices cried out, *"Treason! Treason!"* To this, Patrick Henry shouted back, *"If this be treason, let's make the most of it!"*

And they did. People in the colonies began to ignore the tax stamp—even courts wouldn't require it on legal documents. If nothing else, the Stamp Act ultimately united the colonists against a common enemy—Great Britain.

"Don't one of you fire until you see the whites of their eyes!"
William Prescott   (1775)

This immortalized order found its place in the history books during the American Revolution's Battle of Bunker Hill fought near Boston, Massachusetts on June 17, 1775. The American troops were led by Colonel William Prescott and General Israel Putnam. Both men had gained their experience fighting along side the British in the French and Indian War.

As the British launched their initial attack, Prescott and Putnam had an unsettling realization—they were low on ammunition. In an effort to conserve what they did have, an order was passed through the lines. Men who fought at the battle recalled the exact words being: *"You men are all marks men. Don't one of you fire until you see the whites of their eyes!"*

The American troops allowed the British to advance to dangerously close range, and then opened fired. Surprised and confused, the British were forced to retreat on their first assault. Eventually the Americans did run out of ammunition. At this point, they had no choice but to withdraw.

Despite the final outcome of the battle, the British (who suffered over twice as many casualties as the Americans) realized that it was going to be a tough war. To this day, it is not entirely known whether it was Colonel Prescott or General Putnam who gave the famous order. Prescott, though, is usually credited.

How Samuel Adams Started the American Revolution

"This meeting can do nothing more to save the country!"
Samuel Adams   **(1773)**

These words, spoken by American Patriot Samuel Adams on December 16, 1773, began the infamous Boston Tea Party. This, in turn, led the way for the Revolutionary War. Earlier that night, 5,000 colonists had gathered at the Old South Meeting House in Boston to debate the action that should be taken to combat a tax that the British had imposed on imported tea. The tax was just one of a long list of grievances that the people of the colonies had suffered. They were tired of falling victim to taxation without representation.

Boston Tea Party

But all of the debating and arguing seemed to be accomplishing nothing. Seeing this, Adams announced, **"This meeting can do nothing more to save the country!"** This was a signal to the thousands of patriots outside of the meeting hall, telling them to resort to harsher measures.

Dressed as Native Americans, the crowd ran to the waterfront where three British ships were waiting to off-load shipments of tea. The protesters boarded the ships and tossed 342 chests of tea into the water, destroying over 30,000 pounds of the commodity. The message to the British was clear—the colonists would no longer stand quietly and watch their rights be ignored. And, more importantly, the Boston Tea Party set the stage for the American Revolution, which began less than two years later.

But that was just the beginning. When it was time for the war to begin, Samuel Adams made sure he had front row seats. On April 19, 1775, Paul Revere made his famous midnight ride to alert the people of Massachusetts that the British were coming. Revere brought the news to Adams, who was staying in Lexington with fellow member of the Continental Congress, John Hancock. Because the two were such prominent figures, they were obvious targets for the British soldiers. Taking cover nearby, Adams and Hancock were just feet away from the location that would go down in history as the starting point of the American Revolutionary War.

Samuel Adams

They watched as the Minutemen, civilians from Massachusetts who were ready to fight the British at a minute's notice, prepared for the incoming troops. Enjoying the anxiety, Adams replied to Hancock, **"What a glorious morning is this."** As the first shot was fired in Lexington, known as the "shot heard around the world," the Revolutionary War was underway. The fighting was only a skirmish, and the British troops kept marching until they reached Concord, where a larger battle ensued.

Samuel Adams came out of the engagement unscathed, giving him the opportunity to sign the Declaration of Independence one-month later.

"Don't give up the ship!"
James Lawrence   (1813)

This command has become nothing short of the unofficial motto for the United States Navy. It was given by Captain James Lawrence after being mortally wounded on June 1, 1813.

Gaining his experience fighting against the Barbary pirates, Lawrence became commander of the U.S. frigate *Chesapeake* during the War of 1812. He had an inexperienced crew, but that didn't stop him from accepting a challenge to battle his ship against the highly experienced crew of the *HMS Shannon*.

Not surprisingly, the *Chesapeake* was overwhelmed, and Lawrence suffered a serious injury. As he was carried to the deck below, he shouted the order, *"Tell the men to fire faster! Don't give up the ship!"* Motivated by their commander, every ranking officer continued to fight until they were either killed or wounded. Lawrence died four days later.

In honor of Lawrence, the words *"Don't Give Up the Ship"* were stitched into a flag and given to Navy commander Oliver Hazard Perry. With this flag on display, Perry went on to capture an entire British fleet at the Battle of Lake Erie on September 10, 1813. It was after this victory that Perry relayed the legendary line, *"We have met the enemy and they are ours..."*

"Patriotism, in the exclusive meaning, is surely NOT made for America!"
Frances Wright   (1828)

Hold on—hear the woman out. As one of the first women to gain national fame for her public lectures, social reformer Frances Wright had this to say at an Independence Day address on July 4, 1828. Born in Scotland, Wright knew that the people in Europe viewed "patriotism" as a *"love of the public good."* In her speech, she pointed out that this definition just wasn't fitting for the United States: *"Patriotism, in the exclusive meaning, is surely NOT made for America!"* Wright explained the views of the American people, *"It is for them more especially to know why they love their country; and to feel they love it, not because it is their country, but because it is the palladium of human liberty!"*

Frances Wright had fallen in love with America while touring the country from 1818 to 1820. She detailed her experiences in her book, *Views of Society and Manners in America.* A few years later, she moved to the States for good.

While here, Wright joined with British socialist Robert Owen to develop a communal village built on utopian ideals. Located on 20,000 acres in Indiana and Illinois, they created a society known as New Harmony. The experiment with the utopian society wasn't a complete success, but Wright did gain a reputation by lecturing her utopian ideals across the country. Among the topics she supported were equal rights for women, freedom of slaves, and universal education.

"To the victor belong the spoils of the enemy."
William Marcy   (1832)

That's one of the basic rules of war. But, in 1832, Senator William L. Marcy originally coined the famous phrase in a completely different context.

Senator Marcy was a friend of President Andrew Jackson—and Jackson was often criticized for making sure that his friends always rose successfully through the political ranks. When Marcy spoke before the senate in support of future president Martin Van Buren (another Andrew Jackson supporter), he acknowledged that he saw *"nothing wrong in the maxim that to the victors belong the spoils of the enemy."* From this point, the idea of placing people in office without using a merit system became known as the "spoils system."

In truth, the idea of *"to the victor belong the spoils"* is true in politics and in war. Andrew Jackson believed that a president should surround himself with people that he trusted and who looked out for his interests. It was also an opportunity to get those who opposed him out of powerful positions. Laws regulating the "spoils system" began to come into effect soon after Jackson's term. Of course, even today political positions are often obtained by more than just merit.

Same Words—Different Meaning

"Our country right or wrong!"

After the War of 1812, naval officer Stephen Decatur was sent to the coast of North Africa for a special mission. His goal: to end the reign of terror caused by pirates working the coasts of the nations Algiers, Tunis, and Tripoli. With a little negotiating, not to mention a young and powerful United States navy ready to back him up, Decatur returned from his mission as a success. In 1815, back in America, a banquet was held in his honor. It was there that Decatur gave one of history's most memorable toasts: **"Our country! In her intercourse with foreign nations may she always be in the right; but our country right or wrong!"**

Decatur believed what he was saying—he always put his country first. From 1801 to 1805, while still in his early twenties, he rose through the naval ranks during a war against Tripoli. Later, Decatur became a ship commander in the War of 1812, engaging in several battles against the British fleet. His patriotism and experience are the reasons that he was chosen to combat the pirates in North Africa—and, that's mission that he is most remembered for today.

Over fifty years after the campaign in North Africa, the sentiment behind the comment, **"Our country right or wrong,"** still existed. On January 17, 1872, Missouri senator Carl Schurz spoke to his colleagues and paraphrased the famous words. This time, though, he put a new twist on Decatur's original lines, noting, **"My country right or wrong—when right, to keep her right; when wrong, to put her right!"**

They might have used a similar phrase, but Decatur and Schurz were expressing different ideas when they declared the **"country right or wrong."** Decatur was an unwavering patriot who felt that the United States was always right, regardless of the action. Schurz held a different perspective. Originally a German citizen, he was also a member of the Union army during the Civil War. These experiences led Schurz to believe that it was the duty of the nation's leaders to steer the nation in the correct course—*"when right, to keep her right; when wrong, to put her right."*

After his term in senate, Schurz became a respected political writer, contributing several articles to the popular news journal, *Harper's Weekly*, during the 1890's.

Here's a head to head comparison of the lives of Stephen Decatur and Carl Schurz—the men who believed *"our country, right or wrong:"*

Stephen Decatur

Born: 1779, Sinepuxent, Md.

Age 19: Becomes a midshipman in the US Navy.

Age 22: Joins the Tripoli Squadron as a first lieutenant, gains fame for a raid into the Tripoli Harbor.

Age 29: Serves as a judge for the court-martial of James Barron, a fellow navy lieutenant accused of making serious battle blunders.

Age 33: Commands three vessels in the War of 1812.

Age 36: Because of a stellar military record, is sent to Algiers to end the raids of pirates off the coast. Success in this endeavor leads to his famous toast.

Age 41: Is challenged to a duel by his long-time enemy James Barron. Mortally wounded, he dies shortly after.

Carl Schurz

Born: 1829, Cologne, Germany

Age 19: Attends the University of Bonn and participates in Revolutionary uprisings against the oppressive German government.

Age 23: Flees to the United States after the movement fails.

Age 27: Settles in Wisconsin, and becomes a strong supporter of Abraham Lincoln.

Age 34: Serves under General Sherman in the Civil War.

Age 37: After the war, gains fame as a correspondent and editor for several major newspapers.

Age 40: Becomes senator for the state of Missouri.

Age 77: Dies in 1906. Spends last forty years of his life active in American politics with the help of his influential newspaper career.

"The man and the hour have met!"
William Yancey   (1861)

William Yancey knew that such an event didn't happen too often—but, in February 1861, the political leader from Alabama was certain that it had. After strongly supporting the succession of the southern states prior to the Civil War, Yancey made the remark while introducing the newly inaugurated president of the Confederacy, Jefferson Davis.

From 1861 to 1865, Jefferson Davis *"met the hour"* by serving as the first and only president of the Confederate States of America. Prior to the Civil War, he had represented the United States in the military, as a senator, and as the secretary of war. An advocate for slavery and states' rights, Davis originally was opposed to the idea of the southern states seceding. When his home state of Mississippi broke from the Union, though, he didn't have much choice but to resign his seat in the senate.

Soon after, Davis was elected as president of the Confederacy for a six-year term. It was a tough job—the southern states were short of finances, and foreign nations refused to recognize them as a separate country. Still, Davis was able to prepare for the Civil War by establishing a respectable army and recruiting competent leaders like Robert E. Lee. The result was the bloodiest war in American history, which ended with the Confederate Army's surrender in 1865. Davis was captured soon after and found guilty of treason. The federal government released him in 1868.

"So you are the little woman who wrote the book that started this great war!"
Abraham Lincoln   (1862)

This is how Harriet Beecher Stowe, author of the historical book *Uncle Tom's Cabin*, was greeted when she met President Abraham Lincoln in 1862.

Her novel, published from 1851 to 1852 in the newspaper *The National Era*, tells the story of "Uncle Tom," a slave who is sold several times until he is eventually beaten to death by his final owner. Stowe was motivated to write the book by her own experience with fugitive slaves; it was also her response to legislation passed a few years before that made it illegal to give help to escaped slaves. The story had an enormous and immediate influence on the country's view of slavery.

Besides becoming a national phenomenon, *Uncle Tom's Cabin* was published in over thirty languages and read throughout the world. By the time Abraham Lincoln became president in 1860, the novel had propelled the issue of slavery into a heated one that had to be dealt with. The result was the Civil War. Lincoln met Harriet Beecher Stowe in the middle of the war, a decade after the book was first published. At first glance, Stowe seemed to be common enough. She had grown up as the daughter of a minister, later married a minister, and lived a relatively quiet life—but Lincoln recognized her significance. Thus, there was no understatement in the words he used to greet her— *"So you are the little woman who wrote the book that started this great war!"*

"Get down, you damn fool!"
Oliver Wendell Holmes   (1864)

This order was yelled by a 23 year-old soldier to a careless civilian during a fierce battle in the Civil War. The civilian had come to watch the Union army fight the Confederates at Fort Stevens, and was peering over the fortress wall for a better view. He was wearing a top hat, making him an easy target under the heavy fire.

Luckily, when the soldier yelled, *"Get down, you damn fool,"* the civilian complied and wasn't hurt. This was especially fortunate since that civilian was President Abraham Lincoln. On July 12, 1864, Lincoln traveled to Fort Stevens, just outside of Washington, DC, and became the first president ever to be directly under enemy battle fire while in office.

The young soldier didn't realize he was yelling to the president, and he didn't get into any trouble for his harsh words. This was also fortunate, because the soldier's name was Oliver Wendell Holmes—he would later serve as a justice on the U.S. Supreme Court. Holmes served on the Supreme Court for thirty years, earning himself the nickname "The Great Dissenter" for his constant arguments against the majority on a variety of issues.

Differing Opinions

"It is well that war is so terrible—we would grow too fond of it!"
Robert E. Lee   (1862)

"War is hell!"
William Sherman   (1879)

Confederate General Robert E. Lee had an interesting view of war. He made the above observation to his right-hand man, General James Longstreet, on December 13, 1862. The two were preparing for the Battle of Fredericksburg in Virginia—the battle ended with a Confederate victory.

General Lee was, and is still to this day, regarded as one of the finest military strategists in history. His leadership of the Confederate troops in the Civil War was only overcome by the overwhelming manpower and resources of the Union Amy. After several impressive early victories, the Confederate troops finally wore down—Lee was forced to surrender to Ulysses S. Grant at Appomatax Courthouse in April 1865.

Robert E. Lee

President Abraham Lincoln recognized Lee's military expertise even before the start of the Civil War. In 1860, he met with Lee in Washington, DC, and offered him the command of the Union forces. Residing in Virginia, Lee declined the offer. Instead, when Virginia seceded from the Union, he resigned from the U.S. Army to join the Confederates.

When General Lee pointed out that he was in danger of growing **"too fond"** of war, he wasn't speaking for everyone. One person who particularly disagreed was Union General William Sherman. While teaching in Michigan in 1879, almost fifteen years after the end of the Civil War, General Sherman declared, *"I am tired and sick of War. Its glory is all moonshine. It is only those who have never fired a shot nor heard the shreaks and groans of the wounded cry aloud for blood, more vengeance, more desolation."* He then summed it up with the famous line, *"War is hell."*

Ironically, Sherman's military career doesn't seem to reflect his hatred for war and bloodshed. After capturing and burning the city of Atlanta, Georgia, in 1864, Sherman began his famous "march to the sea." Here, he led 60,000 men through Georgia, South Carolina, and North Carolina. Along the way, his men completely demolished everything in their path including farms, houses, and businesses. Sherman's hope was to destroy the morale of the south and bring an earlier end of the war.

As a result of his campaign, he became one of the most hated leaders of the Union army.

Here are a few highlights of Sherman's "March to the Sea":

- After a several month campaign, Sherman captures the city of Atlanta in September 1864.
- All civilians are ordered to evacuate the city.
- In November 1864, soldiers are ordered to burn federal buildings, cotton gins, mills, and warehouses—they are also ordered to respect private homes. (This order is not followed, nor is it enforced)
- Sherman and his 62,000 soldiers begin to march out of Atlanta and towards the Atlantic coast in November 1864.
- Marching nearly 15 miles a day, the soldiers destroy everything in their path (farms, railroads, homes, businesses, livestock...)
- The trail of damage is 360 miles long and 60 miles wide.
- In December, the Army captures Savannah, Georgia, and Sherman presents it to Abe Lincoln as a "Christmas Gift."
- South Carolina, the state that Sherman feels is personally responsible for the war, suffers the most damage.
- Sherman meets some opposition from General Johnston in North Carolina, but Johnston is finally forced to surrender.

"Damn the Torpedos! Full speed ahead!"
David Farragut   (1864)

It was at the Gulf city of Mobile, Alabama, where Admiral David Farragut uttered these legendary words. He was fighting in one of the most critical naval battles of the Civil War.

Serving as one of the last remaining ports on the Gulf Coast still under Confederate control, Mobile stood as an inevitable showdown spot between the north and south. On August 5, 1864, Admiral Franklin Buchanan, commander of the Southern forces, huddled his small fleet in an effort to fend off the Union navy and hopefully keep the South's supply lines open.

The Union troops, headed by Farragut, closed in. The convoy was led by the monitor *TECUMSEH* which, less than 100 yards from the Confederate ships, ran over a mine in the water. The entire Union fleet watched as their lead ship sank instantly, its bottom blown away. Surprised and confused, the Union soldiers panicked as they approached the dangerous waters.

With the battle lines broken and order shattered, Farragut had to make a quick decision: *"Damn the torpedos! Full speed ahead!"* His men followed the order, restored the battle lines and moved forward for the attack despite the danger they had just witnessed. As a result of a moment's inspiration, the Union forces went on to become victorious in the Battle of Mobile.

"There stands Jackson's brigade like a stone wall!"
Bernard Bee   (1861)

Ever wonder where he got the name "Stonewall" Jackson? Here's the story. On July 21, 1861 the first major battle of the Civil War took place in northern Virginia, about thirty miles outside of Washington, DC. During the First Battle of Manassas, or Bull Run, the Confederate troops were vastly outnumbered, and it appeared that the battle would end with a Union victory.

Several of the southern brigades found themselves in trouble early, suffering serious casualties and being driven back rapidly. General Bernard Bee was in such a position—he was having little luck maintaining his battle lines as the Union kept charging in with superior numbers. Bee's inexperienced troops were faltering quickly.

On higher ground, another skirmish was taking place. General Thomas Jackson, also outnumbered, was holding his own against the Union troops. General Bee witnessed this, and inspired his troops by yelling, *"There stands Jackson's brigade like a stone wall! Rally behind the Virginians! Let us determine to die here and we will conquer!"* The troops did rally behind Jackson, and the Confederates were able to force the north into a retreat.

More importantly, they were victors in the Civil War's first battle. General Bee, who had played such an important part in the conflict, met his death on the field that day. But his inspirational orders weren't forgotten. Because of his comment on General Thomas Jackson's bravery, Jackson became known by the more familiar name of "Stonewall" Jackson from that day forth.

"Charge BOTH ways!"
Nathaniel Bedford Forrest   (1862)

Confederate calvary commander Nathaniel Bedford Forrest gave this confusing order when his soldiers questioned him after being the victims of a surprise attack.

It was December 31, 1862, and Forrest and his men were attempting a get away after an encounter with Union forces at Parker's Crossroads in Tennessee. As Forrest was preparing to fight through the Union troops, he was unexpectedly attacked from behind by a new set of Union soldiers. In a panic, with enemy lines ahead of them and behind them, Forrest's calvary asked him what he wanted them to do. Without wasting any time, Forrest bellowed, *"Charge BOTH ways!"* His men carried out the order and attacked the Union forces in all directions.

The aggressive response surprised the Union soldiers. And, despite being outnumbered, the relentless Confederates were able to fight their way out.

While Nathaniel Bedford Forrest's genius on the battlefield was undisputed, there was some controversy about his personal life. After the war, he became the first leader of the Ku Klux Klan—he later tried to disband the organization in 1869 when he felt that it had become too violent.

Abraham Lincoln—Holding a nation together

"Fourscore and seven years ago our fathers brought forth on this continent, a new nation, conceived in Liberty, and dedicated to the proposition that all men are created equal."

Abraham Lincoln   (1863)

    This is the opening line to what may be the most significant and legendary speech in history. On November 19, 1863, Abraham Lincoln stood before a respectable crowd to dedicate the Gettysburg National Cemetery in Gettysburg, Pennsylvania—the fierce Battle of Gettysburg had been fought nearly a year earlier.

    Lincoln gave his speech following Edward Everett, who spoke for two-hours. After Everett's remarks, the crowd applauded loudly. When it was Lincoln's turn to speak, he talked for only a few minutes. When he was finished, there was virtual silence. In part, the crowd was shocked, and perhaps disappointed, that he would say so little. Of course, nobody understood the significance of what had just transpired.

    In his short remarks, Lincoln admitted that it was a nice sentiment for the people to come and dedicate the land. But, he made it clear that they were really in no position to do that—those who fought there had already dedicated it more than enough. In his words, *"The brave men, living and dead, who struggled here, have consecrated it, far above our poor power to add or detract."*

It's been a long-time myth that Lincoln wrote the speech on the back of a napkin as he was traveling to Gettysburg. In fact, it appears that he prepared the speech well in advance, giving great thought to each line. For that reason, Lincoln was able to say more in two-minutes that day than Everett did in two-hours.

"I can't spare this man—He fights!"
Abraham Lincoln   (1865)

Those few words are the best compliment that President Abraham Lincoln could have given his top military commander. During the Civil War, Union General Ulysses S. Grant became one of the most controversial figures in the country. After leading his soldiers through bloody battles like Shiloh, he gained the reputation of being a butcher that gave no thought to the number of casualties he suffered. Even in victory, his critics felt that Grant had luck on his side, and that his victories were a result of superior numbers rather than skill. On top of all this, Grant was accused of being a drunk and a negligent slob.

The allegations became so heated that President Abraham Lincoln was urged to remove General Grant from command. To this, the President had only one reply: *"I can't spare this man—He fights!"* Lincoln had a legitimate argument. While Grant did seem to have an unorthodox approach to military strategy, he had only one objective in mind—victory. At the Battle of Fort Donelson, General Grant fought against one of his best friends before the war, Confederate General Simon Buckner. After seeing that defeat was imminent, Buckner asked Grant to list his terms for surrender. Grant answered, *"no terms except unconditional and immediate surrender."* With his back to the wall, Buckner had no choice but to accept the ungenerous demands.

In hindsight, it seems Abraham Lincoln made the correct choice in keeping General Ulysses S. Grant in command. He was the one who would accept the surrender from General Robert E. Lee at Appomatax Courthouse in 1865.

"You furnish the pictures, I'll furnish the war."
William Randolph Hearst   (1897)

When Frederick Remington was sent to Cuba by the *New York Journal* to take pictures of the Cuban fight for independence, he expected to be in violent and exciting territory. Instead, he arrived to find that there was really nothing worth reporting. He wrote a telegram to William Randolph Hearst, publisher of the *New York Journal*, and asked to return due to the lack of action. Hearst replied with the message, *"Please remain. You furnish the pictures, I'll furnish the war."*

Hearst was true to his word. The *New York Journal* had already helped capture the public's attention about the Spanish occupation of Cuba. Hearst portrayed the Spanish rule as unjust and ruthless. And, his papers advocated the concept of Manifest Destiny, an idea that says it is the divine right and duty of America to go beyond its borders and expand into new land.

In February 1898, with the sinking of the American battleship *USS Maine* in Cuba, Hearst was quick to point a finger at the Spanish. Though the true cause was unknown, the American public supported him in the accusation. The public pressure became so strong that President McKinley had no choice but to put an end to the fighting in Cuba. This was the beginning of the Spanish-American War. With photographers like Remington close to the action, newspapers kept the public updated and highly interested in the action. The United States came out victorious, and William Randolph Hearst got his story.

"I want to stand by my country, but I cannot vote for war."
Jeannette Rankin   (1917)

All eyes were on Jeannette Rankin in 1917. As the first woman elected into the U.S. House of Representatives, she stood before the congress and voted "no" for the nation's entry into World War I. Despite the fact that fifty members also voted against the United States' involvement, this outspoken pacifist and leader of the womens' suffrage movement received the most attention. Her wishes were overruled, however, and the country entered into the war.

The representative from Montana had been a social worker prior to her election into congress. Her vote against the entry into World War I received so much attention primarily because she was a woman—it did not, however, stir up as much controversy as her stance in World War II. In December 1941, after the Japanese surprise attack on Pearl Harbor, she once again voted against the United States' entry into the war. This time, she stood alone. As the only member to vote "no", she claimed, *"As a woman, I can't go to war and I refuse to send anyone else."*

Rankin never budged from her stance on pacifism. In 1968, at the age of eighty-eight, she led a demonstration of thousands of women against the military action in Vietnam.

"The culminating and final war for human liberty has come..."
Woodrow Wilson   (1918)

President Woodrow Wilson was sure that he had the perfect plan for a peaceful world. When he gave his "Fourteen Points" speech before congress on January 8, 1918, he was certain that World War I would be the "war to end all wars".

Wilson's "Fourteen Points" were straightforward; most of them simply required Germany to give back any territory that it had taken. But, his "fourteenth point" was a little different. It established the League of Nations for *"the purpose of affording mutual guarantees of political independence and territorial integrity to great and small states alike."* In other words, it was a group of countries that promised to watch each other's backs.

Wilson finished detailing his plan by remarking, *"The moral climax of this, the culminating and final war for human liberty has come, and they* [the people of the United States] *are ready to put their own strength, their own highest purpose, their own integrity and devotion to the test."*

World War I ended ten months later. But, as we all know, it wasn't the *"culminating and final war for human liberty."* But, the lesson was learned, and Germany (the instigator of both wars) was given a stricter sentence at the end of World War II.

"Yesterday, December 7, 1941—a date which will live in infamy..."
Franklin Roosevelt (1941)

Just before 8:00 in the morning on December 7, 1941, Japanese forces launched a surprise attack on the U.S. naval base at Pearl Harbor, Hawaii. The brutal attack left over 3,000 American men either killed or wounded, and it destroyed nearly 200 planes and over twenty ships.

The following day, President Franklin D. Roosevelt stood before Congress and called for a declaration of war against Japan. He began the speech, *"Yesterday, December 7, 1941—a date which will live in infamy—the United States of America was suddenly and deliberately attacked by naval and air forces of the Empire of Japan."* He reassured the country of an inevitable outcome: *"No matter how long it may take us to overcome this premeditated invasion, the American people, in their righteous might, will win through to absolute victory."*

As promised, the United States forced the Japanese to surrender in 1945. The Japanese had hoped that the attack on Pearl Harbor would completely destroy the U.S. navy beyond repair, but that wasn't the case. Several of their main targets, the aircraft carriers, were out to sea at the time of the attack. Even Admiral Isoroku Yamamoto, the Japanese leader who had devised the attack, later warned, *"We have awaken a sleeping giant..."*

"It is foolish and wrong to mourn the men who died."
George Patton (1945)

During some of the most tumultuous periods in history, there are always those who are determined to set the people straight. American General George S. Patton, who led his Third Army through Europe to defeat Germany in World War II, spoke in Boston on June 7, 1945, reminding his audience, *"It is foolish and wrong to mourn the men who died. Rather we should thank God that such men lived!"* Although often criticized for his flamboyant and outspoken personality, few denied Patton's military competence or his ability to motivate the troops.

As one of the military's greatest speakers, Patton was often called upon to inspire his men just before battle. Perhaps his most famous address was to his troops in May 1944, just before the invasion of Normandy. In an effort to boost their confidence, he declared, *"All real Americans love the sting and clash of battle. America loves a winner. America will not tolerate a loser. Americans despise a coward; Americans play to win."* General Patton, despite being one of the top officials in the military, always designed his speeches to connect with the low-ranking privates — the men actually fighting in the battles. As a result, he was highly respected throughout the military, in spite of the tremendous amount of criticism he received by the American media.

"It is better for aged diplomats to be bored than for young men to die."
Warren Austin   (early 1950's)

When asked whether he ever grew tired of the long debates that took place at the United Nations meetings, Warren Austin replied, *"Yes, I do — but it is better for aged diplomats to be bored than for young men to die."* As the primary representative of the United States to the United Nations (UN) from 1946 to 1952, he had plenty of time to see how tedious the proceedings could be.

Warren Austin first became active in international policy and military affairs through his several terms in the senate. His experience made him the perfect candidate in 1945 to negotiate the Act of Chapultepec, a treaty among several nations to provide mutual defense during World War II. The success of his negotiations persuaded President Harry Truman to appoint Austin as the permanent representative to the United Nations. Founded immediately after the end of World War II, the United Nations was formed as a collaboration of countries throughout the world. Its focus was international peacekeeping.

During his six years as a delegate, Austin became responsible for defining the American position on several worldwide issues. In 1948, he helped shape the nation's policy in the creation of the Jewish state of Israel. And, in 1950, he again had to deal with international turmoil when the Korean War began. Austin resigned his position in 1952.

"The whole world of the future hangs on a proper judgment."
George Marshall   (1947)

After the havoc of World War II, the entire continent of Europe was devastated. Aside from the millions left dead from the war, there were also shortages of food, housing, and money. Even though the fighting had stopped, the future of Europe didn't seem too bright. People like Secretary of State George C. Marshall knew that some serious measures needed to be taken. The American public, however, didn't see the destruction firsthand and failed to realize just how bad the situation was.

On June 5, 1947, Marshall spoke at Harvard University to convince the American public that they needed to help restore a down-spiraling Europe. He pleaded, *"The United States should do whatever it is able to do to assist in the return of normal economic health in the world, without which there can be no political stability and no assured peace."* Marshall, who had served as a leading General during World War II, reminded his audience, *"The whole world of the future hangs on a proper judgment."* He then asked, *"What must be done?"*

Soon after the speech, the United States began the European Recovery Program, which became commonly known as the Marshall Plan. Well over $10 billion went to sixteen different European countries for relief. In 1953, George C. Marshall won a Nobel Peace Prize for his efforts.

"You knock over the first one, and what will happen to the last one is the certainty that it will go over very quickly."
Dwight Eisenhower   (1954)

When President Dwight D. Eisenhower declared this at a White House press conference on April 7, 1954, he was using dominoes as an analogy for the current situation in the nations of Vietnam, Cambodia, and Laos. He believed that, if the United States allowed just one of them to fall to communism, it wouldn't be long before they were all under communist rule. Explaining this snowball effect, Eisenhower told the reporters, *"You have*

broader considerations that might follow what you would call the "falling domino" principle. You have a row of dominoes set up—you knock over the first one, and what will happen to the last one is the certainty that will go over very quickly."

Just before the President made his remarks, the French effort to defeat communism in Vietnam had failed after the fighting at Dienbienphu. Eisenhower had refused to join the French earlier, but he now recognized the fragile state that Indochina was in. In September 1954, he provided economic aide for South Vietnam's defense against the communist North, and he signed a treaty putting the area under United States protection.

While serious military involvement in Vietnam didn't begin until the mid-1960's, Eisenhower sent over 500 advisers to the country to monitor the increasingly unstable situation.

"We are all the President's men."
Henry Kissinger   (1970)

This was Secretary of State Henry Kissinger's way of saying that he stood behind his boss. The man he was supporting was President Richard Nixon. At the time, Nixon was already under a tremendous amount of scrutiny for the United States' military involvement in Vietnam. When the North Vietnamese guerrillas entered Cambodia, it became difficult to decide whether or not the fighting should be expanded. In 1969, Nixon decided to authorize bombing in Cambodia to stop the guerrillas—Kissinger and the rest of the presidential staff had to decide if they could handle the harsh opinions American public. That's when Kissinger declared, *"We are all the President's men."*

A recognized expert in foreign policy, Kissenger accompanied Nixon on trips to China and the Soviet Union in 1972, both of which required his tactful skills of diplomacy. When the fighting in Vietnam came to a conclusion, it was Kissenger who was sent to negotiate terms.

Kissinger's famous line, *"All the President's men,"* became the title of a successful motion picture in 1976. But, the film didn't focus on Vietnam or Cambodia (the events that prompted Kissinger to make the statement). Instead, it centered on the investigation of Nixon's involvement in the Watergate.

Another Kind of War

"We will never again permit any foreign nation to have Uncle Sam over a barrel of oil!"
      Gerald Ford   (1974)

  Vice-president Gerald Ford made a big promise in 1974. At a speech in West Palm Beach, Florida, he expressed his frustration of the fact that inflated international oil prices were causing an energy crisis in the United States. Ford wanted to step up the effort to make the nation self-sufficient when it came to energy. He proposed that alternate forms of energy be explored, especially nuclear, solar, and geothermal.
  Years earlier, Gerald Ford probably didn't expect that he'd be the one making these major decisions. He inherited the position of vice-president only after Spiro Agnew resigned in 1973. One year later, Nixon resigned—this made Ford the only man to hold the offices of vice-president and president and not be elected to either of them. And, to make a complicated situation even more complicated, he inherited the nation's highest office during what was perhaps the most difficult time since World War II. Inflation was rampant, unemployment was high, and the Organization of Petroleum Exporting Countries (OPEC) was refusing to export oil to the United States. The members of OPEC were angered by the fact that the United States supported the Israelis over several oil rich Arab nations.

  Ford did his best to deal with the turmoil of the energy crisis, but left plenty for Jimmy Carter to handle when he became president after Ford. When Carter addressed the nation in April 1977, he wanted to convey to the people just how serious the energy problem had become. Like his predecessor, he relentlessly urged research in alternative methods of energy, hoping to end the United States' almost complete dependence on foreign nations for oil. Explaining the crisis, Carter declared: **"This difficult effort will be the moral equivalent of war, except that**

we will be uniting our efforts to build and not to destroy."

Eventually, Carter was able to make bold moves to help increase United States' energy independence. During his presidency in the late 1970's, he deregulated the oil and natural gas that was produced domestically. This had mixed results. While it stimulated the energy industry, it also increased the price of oil. The price increase only added to the country's already high inflation. But, knowing that any sort of wage controls would only result in further troubles, Carter decided that it was best to wait out the temporary rise in oil prices.

The prices did finally go down and the energy crisis wasn't such a crisis any longer. Unfortunately, the United States' dependence on foreign nations for oil never did go away completely.

In the search for alternative forms of oil, here are a few options that have been brought to the table:

- **Wind power** *(gathered by a series of windmills, some as large as 300 feet high, spread over several acres of land)*
- **Solar power** *(seems to be the safest and most abundant, but hasn't advanced as quickly as hoped)*
- **Nuclear power** *(certainly the most powerful, but also the most dangerous)*
- **Geothermal power** *(difficult to extract and store for everyday use)*
- **Ocean Gas power** *(methane on the ocean floor—this seems to be abundant, but very difficult to extract)*
- **Water Power** *(extracted using hydro dams, which are usually massive and obtrusive construction projects)*
- **Biomass power** *(animal or plant products that can be burned for fuel—most likely possibilities seem to be pig waste or corn, but the verdict is still out)*
- **Hydrogen power** *(the third most abundant element on earth, found in water, can be converted to energy—safety and technology are still major drawbacks)*

"I came here to tell you the truth—the good, the bad, and the ugly."
Oliver North   (1987)

Lieutenant Colonel Oliver North found himself in a sticky situation during the mid-1980's. Serving on the National Security Council, he became a key player in the Iran-Contra affair, a scandal that resulted in his dismissal and damaged the reputation of several members in the Reagan Administration.

The Iran-Contra affair centered on two controversial world events. First, there were several American hostages being held by Iranian terrorists in Lebanon. In the hope that these hostages would be released if weapons were sold to Iran, over 1,000 missiles changed hands. However, an embargo against selling weapons to Iran had previously been declared.

At the same time, a group of rebels in Nicaragua were battling for their freedom against communist leader Fidel Castro. President Reagan supported this group of Contras, but his hands were tied by the fact that congress refused to provide any aid to the Contras. This spurred a covert operation that used the money from the weapons sales in Iran to aid the rebels in Nicaragua.

Lietenant Colonel Oliver North, believing that the deal was legitimate, oversaw much of this transaction. In 1986, North was brought before a congressional hearing to disclose everything that he knew about the scandal. Under the offer of limited immunity, North agreed, declaring, *"I came here to tell you the truth—the good, the bad, and the ugly."*

"Leadership is a potent combination of strategy and character. But if you must be without one, be without the strategy."
Norman H. Schwarzkopf   (1991)

After serving over thirty years in the military, General Norman Schwarzkopf knew a thing or two about leadership. He gave his definition of leadership simply as the *"potent combination of strategy and character."* However, understanding that a leader may be thrust into such a position without proper time to prepare, Schwarzkopf explained, *"...if you must be without one, be without the strategy."*

General Schwarzkopf began his military career with two tours of duty in Vietnam. While there, he was wounded twice and came home with the Distinguished Service Medal. But, Schwarzkopf truly earned a name for himself by leading the coalition forces during the Persian Gulf War.

On August 2, 1990, the oil-rich nation of Iraq invaded its essentially defenseless neighbor, Kuwait. Immediately, the United States and the United Nations demanded that the Iraqi president, Saddam Hussein, pull his forces out of Kuwait. He refused. As a result, a coalition of thirty-two nations combined to launch Operation Desert Storm. Headed by General Schwarzkopf, an offensive was launched on January 18, 1991, with massive air attacks over Iraq. This continued for over one month when, on February 24, over 700,000 ground troops moved in and encircled the Iraqis troops in Kuwait. Completely overwhelmed, the Iraqi troops surrendered and Kuwait was liberated.

"...we don't want that smoking gun to be a mushroom cloud."
Condoleezza Rice   (2002)

As the tension between the United States and Iraq mounted in late 2002, national security adviser Dr. Condoleezza Rice explained the situation: *"The problem here is that there will always be some uncertainty about how quickly he* [Saddam Hussein] *can acquire nuclear weapons. But we don't want the smoking gun to be a mushroom cloud."*

At the end of the Persian Gulf War in the early 1990's, inspectors from the United Nations were sent to Iraq to uncover any hidden weapons. The inspectors were making progress, but Iraq wasn't fully cooperating. In 1998, the inspectors had to pull out completely when Saddam Hussein refused to comply. In 2002, however, tensions between the United States and Iraq became particularly high, and inspectors were once again sent in. Just as before, there seemed to be a lack of cooperation.

In March 2003, the United States and other nations invaded Iraq and removed the nation's leaders from power.

"History is a version of past events that people have decided to agree upon."
— Napoleon Bonapart
French leader (1769-1821)

Chapter 12

World History

Tough Love

"Come back with your shield or on it!"

The Spartans meant business. In 7th century BC, the Greek city-state developed into one of the most dominant military powers in history. The attitude of the Spartan people was clearly expressed by the fact that, when mothers sent their sons off to war, they left them with the words, **"Come back with your shield or on it!"** To say the least, they were never accused of spoiling their children.

The militaristic lifestyle of the Spartans started with a man named Lycurgus, a lawmaker who enforced strict class separation and warlike values. His rules influenced every member of Spartan society. Any boy who was deformed or disabled was killed at birth. At the age of 7, all remaining boys were taken away from home to train as soldiers. Each Spartan man entered the ranks of a foot soldier at the age of 20, and he lived on the barracks until he was 30. It wasn't until the age of 60 that the military obligations usually ceased.

Even the Spartan women were held to a high standard. They were encouraged to be fit and were given rigorous training to insure that they gave birth to healthy sons. Later, they were expected to provide unwavering support to their military-minded husbands and sons. If a member of their family was killed in war, they were obligated to show no emotion except for pride.

Because of their militaristic mindset, the Spartan people did enjoy some great success. They vastly expanded their territory and, with the defeat of Athens in 404 BC, Sparta became the dominant Greek state. Unfortunately, the fighting with the Athenians didn't end there. Athens was able to gather itself for yet another war, eventually wearing down the Spartans and achieving a victory of their own.

Here's a quick rundown of the ancient Greek city-state, Sparta, and why it has earned such a solid place in history today:

- Located in a valley and with the protection of mountains on all sides, Sparta is created by invading Greeks in the eighth century BC.

- The government is headed by *two* Kings from *two* different families, with the crown being passed down by heredity.

- Most of the state's political power is in the hands of five "ephors," members of a board that are elected annually. There is also a council of elders and a general assembly of citizens.

- All business of the state is conducted in secret meetings.

- In 725 BC, the Spartans overtake their neighboring state, Messenia. The Messenians revolt *(they outnumber the Spartans ten to one)*, almost destroying Sparta. From this battle, the Spartans learn their lesson, and become a completely military-minded culture.

- With a new attitude, the Spartans once again conquer the Messenians, forcing them to become agricultural slaves known as "helots."

- By 600 BC, Sparta is on the verge of becoming the strongest Greek city, despite its small in population.

- For the next 300 years, Sparta and the cities that it has conquered fight constantly against their greatest rival—Athens.

- After a mix of victories and defeats, the more numerous Athenians finally wear down the Spartans by 300 BC. Sparta is no longer able to hold onto its dominance of Greece.

- Under the rule of the Romans, Sparta once again thrives, but not to the same degree as the Sparta of old.

- By 400 AD, ancient Sparta has completely fallen.

"I'd rather have people ask why I have no monument than why I have one!"
Cato the Elder   (200 BC)

Cato the Elder had his dignity. He was just worried that the rest of Rome didn't.

Around 200 BC, Cato was elected to the position of Censor (a Roman magistrate who sorted the citizens into the proper classes). In this position, he preached the ideals of strict morality and hard work. But, the people of Rome were inheriting a successful empire and this strenuous set of ethics was being replaced by a life of luxury. Cato predicted that this would be the great city's downfall—and he would ultimately be correct. Trying to convince the citizens to understand his old-fashioned thinking, he explained, *"After I'm dead, I'd rather have people ask why I have no monument than why I have one."*

Cato's hatred for the "easy life" led to Rome's Third Punic War. He had built up a great animosity towards the city-state of Carthage, where the people were extremely wealthy. According to Cato, their lives were too comfortable—other than that, the city didn't pose any real threat to Rome. Cato didn't let this stop him, however, as he started to end each speech with the words, *"Carthage must be destroyed!"*

After hearing the line enough, the people of Rome began to agree. In 149 BC, they fought the last of three wars against Carthage. As Cato had hoped, Rome captured the small city and burned it to the ground.

"Nature has formed you, desire has trained you, fortune has preserved you for this insanity!"
Marcus Cicero   (63 BC)

When he spoke these words before the Roman Senate in 63 BC, Roman statesman Marcus Tullius Cicero had just become aware of a conspiracy to have him assassinated. He was directing his speech to a man named Lucius Catiline, Cicero's leading competitor in the election for the consulship a year earlier. Cicero was the victor, and Catiline didn't take it very well. To vent his frustration, he organized a plot to overthrow the government.

When Cicero learned of Catiline's conspiracy, he foiled the plans by drastically increasing government security. Speaking to the senate days later, he assured Catiline that he was prepared for any surprises that might be in store. *"When, O Catiline, do you mean to cease abusing our patience?"* Cicero asked, *"How long is that madness of yours still to mock us?"* There was little doubt that Catiline was crazy with the thought of vengeance. In Cicero's words, *"Nature has formed you, desire has trained you, fortune has preserved you for this insanity!"*

Cicero was successful in putting an end to Catiline's plans, but he couldn't avoid the turmoil of the Roman government. Constantly at odds with the dictator Julius Caeser, he was murdered in 43 BC.

"The dungeon became to me a palace!"
Vivia Perpetua   (202)

In 202 AD, Roman Emperor Septimus Severus figured out a way to put an end to the onslaught of Christian conversions—he threw the new converts into the dungeon. Not surprisingly, many new Christians were forced to hide their beliefs in an effort to remain safe. Still, not all of them chose this path. Vivia Perpetua, a twenty-two year old mother from an upper class family in North Africa, refused to hide the fact that she had recently converted. As a result, she was thrown in prison.

Separated from her son and placed in a dungeon, Perpetua was told that she had no choice but to disown her Christian beliefs. She refused. In fact, the terrible conditions of the dungeon didn't seem to bother her at all. Eventually, the guards even gave her permission to be with her son. Trying her best to care for her baby and herself, she asserted, *"The dungeon became to me a palace!"* Perpetua felt that so long as God and her child accompanied her, there was nothing more that she needed.

When it became obvious that Perpetua had no intentions of giving up on Christianity, the Romans saw no choice but to put her to death. In March of the following year, she was brought into an arena and killed by wild animals.

"He raised me to be a queen. Now he will raise me to be a martyr."
Anne Boleyn (1536)

Anne Boleyn was the second wife of Henry VIII and the mother of Elizabeth I, the future Queen of England. Unfortunately for her, she failed to produce any male offspring. Because of this, and because of his own philandering, Henry VIII grew tired of her. He had Anne Boleyn imprisoned in the Tower of London in 1536, and he made certain that she was convicted of trumped-up charges of adultery and conspiring against the King. With those crimes, her execution was scheduled soon after.

Boleyn didn't have hard feelings for the King, however. Shortly before her beheading in May 1536, she remarked, *"The King has been very good to me. He promoted me from a simple maid to a marchioness. Then he raised me to be a queen. Now he will raise me to be a martyr."* Only one day after her execution, Henry VIII was remarried, this time to Jane Seymour. In all, he would marry six times.

Boleyn's claim of martyrdom held a degree of truth. While Henry VIII was a powerful King, he also had many enemies among the people. He stirred up the most trouble by rejecting the authority of the Pope and the Roman Catholic Church. His execution of Boleyn and others helped pave the way for a revolution by the Christian church.

"I am the Protestant whore!"
Nell Gwyn (late 1600's)

Nell Gwyn didn't want there to be any confusion. When an anti-Catholic mob began attacking her coach with the mistaken belief that she was Louise de Keroualle, the Catholic mistress of Charles II, the English actress calmed them with this remark. She, too, was a mistress of the King in the late 1600's, but she wanted to make clear one important fact—she was a Protestant. Therefore, she pleaded with the crowd, *"Pray, good people, be civil. I am the Protestant whore!"*

Selling oranges at Drury Lane Theater in London as a child, Nell Gwyn drew attention with her wit and charm—not to mention a total lack of fear of being placed in the spotlight. In 1665, at the age of fifteen, she made her first major debut in the play *The Indian Emperor*. Her affair with the King began just a few years later, when she was still a teenager. By then, she was already a favorite among the London public who deemed her "pretty, witty Nell".

While the public may have idolized her, Nell Gwyn wasn't necessarily the King's favorite mistress. Charles II, taking reign immediately after the English Revolution, had thirteen different mistresses and multiple children in his lifetime.

"Paris is well worth a Mass."
Henry IV   (1589)

Henry IV had to make a decision when he was given the chance to become the King of France in 1589. Raised as a Protestant, he wasn't an acceptable King to the Catholic population in France, so couldn't take the throne unless some changes were made. His decision was to convert from a Protestant to a Catholic, and it led to his famed comment, *"Paris is well worth a Mass."* While his conversion instantly satisfied most of the people in Paris, some still doubted his sincerity. Henry IV had, after all, been the leader of the French Protestant group known as the Huguenots since 1576. Fortunately, as a competent leader, he was eventually able to appease the vast majority.

With a focus on the economy, Henry IV helped spur on agriculture and industry in France. He even made the claim that nobody should be so poor as to be *"unable to have a chicken in his pot."* His reign of over twenty years was marked by a strong government, relative peace, and constant growth.

Still, not everyone was convinced that Henry IV was a legitimate leader. He remained sympathetic to Protestant causes throughout his reign and, in 1610, Henry IV was assassinated by Catholic extremists.

Good Queen Bess

I know I have the body of a weak and feeble woman; but I have the heart of a king, and of a king of England, too."

Elizabeth I   (1588)

The courageous leader of the undersized British Navy—a fifty-five year-old woman—spoke these words to her troops as they prepared for battle against the legendary Spanish Armada. Queen Elizabeth I, known by her subjects as the "Virgin Queen" and "Good Queen Bess," assured her soldiers that they had her support—*"I am amongst you at this time, not as for my recreation or sport, but being resolved, in the midst and heat of the battle, to live or die amongst you all."*

Queen Elizabeth I

Receiving the title of Queen at the age of twenty-five, Elizabeth ruled over England for forty-five years. During that time, the country prospered both economically and culturally—in short, it became a world power. Her road to becoming Queen was not effortless, however. Elizabeth was the daughter of the infamous Henry VIII, who had had her mother, Anne Boleyn, beheaded. Her half sister, Mary, served as queen a short time before Elizabeth took the crown. Mary, a devout Catholic, had Elizabeth locked up in the Tower of London because of her Protestant views.

When Elizabeth finally took the throne she was able to win the respect of her supporters with her powerful speeches and commanding presence. Shortly after she spoke to her navy in 1588, they went on to defeat the Spanish Armada in the most critical naval battle in England's history. This battle enabled England to be regarded as the most powerful country in the world, a position that it would hold for centuries to come.

Because England had thrived so much over her forty-five year rule, it's not shocking that her subjects were sad to see her go. When Queen Elizabeth turned over the crown to James VI of Scotland, she delivered an address to Parliament to basically say thank-you to her loyal subjects—it became known as the "Golden Speech." Elizabeth complimented the people by beginning,  **"God hath raised me high, yet this I count the glory of my crown: that I have reined with your loves."** She continued, **"I do not so much rejoice that God hath made me to be a queen, as to be a queen over so thankful a people."**

As the first woman to successfully rule England, Good Queen Bess helped the nation strive domestically and internationally. By steadying the economy, she helped allow for the English Renaissance to come about, a creative movement led by notables such as William Shakespeare.

"I am the State."
Louis XIV   **(1643)**

Tell us what you really think! This is the declaration of French King Louis XIV, who served as the King of France for over seventy years. A believer in the absolute monarchy, and a king's divine right to serve, Louis XIV announced, *"L'Etat, c'est moi,"* which translates, *"I am the State."*

King Louis XIV took his position seriously. Although he was only six years old when he received the crown in 1643, it wasn't too long before he was a major player in making the big decisions. He was an extremely hard worker, spending nearly ten hours each day on governmental affairs. And Louis XIV was a very public king, constantly going out to see the people or entertaining at his castle in Versailles. Most important, he always held onto his absolute rule over France, the most powerful nation in Europe during his reign.

To maintain France's glory, Louis XIV often had the nation involved in foreign wars—there was constant fighting against several neighboring countries such as Spain, Germany, and England. But, back home the country flourished culturally. Louis XIV was involved in creating several art academies within France. After his reign ended, and with the rise of a new generation and new ideals, no king was ever be able to regain the absolute control he had held over France.

"The art of taxation consists in so plucking the goose as to obtain the largest possible amount of feathers with the smallest amount of hissing!"
Jean-Babtiste Colbert   **(late 1660's)**

French statesman Jean-Babtiste Colbert, who served as the nation's minister of finance under King Louis XIV, is responsible for this definition of taxation. Using the concepts of mercantilism, which emphasizes considerable government regulation and foreign trade, he restructured the economic system of France. In an effort to bring more money to the government, Colbert didn't hesitate to levy taxes.

One of the techniques used in Europe at the time to bring in a steady income without much *"hissing"* was the idea of colonization. A powerful nation, such as France or Britain, would take control of other nations and then, through taxation, use those colonies as a supply of revenue. This practice ultimately gave rise to rebellions such as the American Revolution, where colonists grew tired of being exploited. Nonetheless, fair or unfair, the idea of mercantilism was successful in bringing money to the government. Colbert, because he was able to reshape France's economy, is therefore regarded as one of the most influential men in the nation's history.

"Release this guilty man! I don't want him corrupting all these innocent people."
Frederick the Great   (mid 1700's)

King Frederick II gave this somewhat backward order while walking among the convicts of a Berlin prison during the mid-18th century. The Prussian King, perhaps better known as Frederick the Great, was questioning the prisoners about their crimes. After hearing each one proclaim their innocence, the King noticed that one man was sitting quietly in the corner, oblivious to all of the commotion. Frederick II approached the man and asked him to tell his story. The man told the King that he was in prison for armed robbery. When asked if he was guilty, and the man admitted that he was and that he deserved to serve his time in prison. At this point, Frederick II yelled to the guards, *"Release this guilty man! I don't want him corrupting all these innocent people."*

This account is telling of the Frederick II's sense of justice. He reigned over Prussia for forty-six years, helping the empire find a solid place among the European nations. He was a competent military leader, as well, especially during the Seven Years' War of the 1750's. Frederick II's reign was marked by advancements in agriculture, industry, and government—all of which helped him earn the flattering nickname "Frederick the Great".

"Nothing is politically right which is morally wrong!"
Daniel O'Connell   (early 1800's)

Known as the "Liberator," Irish patriot Daniel O'Connell wasn't afraid to take a stand. In the early 19th century, he became outspoken about the British policy that forbade Irish Roman Catholics from holding any seat in parliament. Leading a movement to repeal the law, O'Connell argued his point in simple terms — *"Nothing is politically right which is morally wrong!"*

Daniel O'Connell began the fight for the rights of Irish Roman Catholics when he was just in his early twenties. He formed the Catholic Association in 1823, which constantly pressed for reform. The organization had a huge victory in 1829 when the Catholic Emancipation Act was passed, allowing Roman Catholics to be involved in parliament. Taking advantage of his new rights, O'Connell entered the British House of Commons that same year, representing the county of Clare.

Obviously affectionate towards the Irish people, O'Connell became somewhat controversial figure in the British parliament. He was even arrested and convicted for conspiracy, though the House of Lords quickly reversed the charges.

"Arrest, remand, do anything you can!"
Charles Wood   (1847)

Irish Chancellor Charles Wood was beginning to get desperate. He gave these instructions to Lord Lieutenant Clarendon in 1847, in the midst of the great potato famine in Ireland. The crop failure, which began in 1845, resulted in a nation filled with starvation and disease. Because of the terrible conditions, almost two-thirds of the people were living in poverty. Obviously, a situation like this doesn't help a government make too much money on taxes.

Frantic to find income for his government, Charles Wood decided that his tax collectors needed more authority. He instructed his Lieutenant, *"Arrest, remand, do anything you can!"* And concluded by telling him to do everything *"to the verge of the law and a little beyond."*

This new policy took the already unstable nation of Ireland and turned it completely upside down. The collectors seized whatever they could from the struggling citizens—this included houses, livestock, and furniture. The result was a country full of homeless, starving, and now angry citizens. Violence was rampant, and British troops had to be brought in for damage control. The Chancellor succeeded in collecting funds, but he didn't win any awards in the arena of public relations.

"Power without responsibility—the prerogative of the harlot throughout the ages!"
Rudyard Kipling   (early 1900's)

    To be a poet, you have to have a unique way of looking at things. So, it's not all that surprising that legendary poet and author Rudyard Kipling is responsible for this unusual comparison. He was speaking to the successful British newspaper publisher Max Aitken, an influential figure in conservative political philosophy. Kipling, too, had become a well-respected individual in British politics through his writing. The conversation took place in the early 1900's, when Kipling told Aitken about the similarities between those greedy for unearned power and a lowly prostitute— *"Power without responsibility— the prerogative of the harlot throughout the ages!"*

    The opinion is consistent with Kipling's political agenda— he was a relentless supporter of English imperialism. Kipling took it one step further, though. He believed that it was not only in the best interest, but it was also the *responsibility*, of England to expand English culture into third-world nations. As a modern nation and a world power, England had the duty to help civilize the rest of the world. This is a task Kipling referred to as the "White Man's Burden."

    As the author of internationally recognized works such as *The Jungle Book*, Kipling often relayed his feelings of patriotism and imperialism in his writings. In 1907, his work earned him the Nobel Prize in Literature.

Mahatma Ghandi — Pioneer of non-violent resistance

"I think it would be a good idea."
Mahatma Gandhi   (1931)

     Indian independence leader Mahatma Gandhi had a simple answer to a simple question. In 1931, he came to London as a representative in the Indian National Conference — the conference was designed to determine the future of the nation under British rule. When a reporter asked him, *"Mr. Gandhi, what do you think of Western Culture?"*, the unimpressed Gandhi replied, *"I think it would be a good idea."* Gandhi won the support of his people because he was not intimidated or overly excited by England's standards of living.

     Unfortunately, the conference in 1931 didn't enable Gandhi to achieve what he really wanted — independence for the nation of India. He had already been crusading for the cause for nearly twenty years by using non-violent tactics, and it now appeared that a different approach needed to be taken. But Ghandi refused to turn to violence. Instead, his followers protested British rule by resigning from government offices, boycotting British goods, and sometimes just by sitting in the streets, refusing to move despite being beaten by authorities. This passive resistance won Gandhi, and the Indian people, support throughout the world.

Over time, Gandhi became a powerful force in helping India break away from British rule. His influence was so great, in fact, that he could protest unfair acts by merely going on a hunger strike. The British knew that his death would immediately spark a revolution in India, so they had no choice but to yield to some of his demands. Finally, in 1947, the nation of India succeeded in gaining its independence.

"What is our task? To make Britain a fit country for heroes to live in!"
David Lloyd George   (1918)

Easier said than done! David Lloyd George, one of the most controversial political figures of the 1900's, gave this challenge to his supporters in Wolverhampton, England on November 24, 1918. Serving as Prime Minister of Britain from 1916 to 1922, George had a career in which he was sometimes embraced and at other times hated by the public.

A terrific debater even at a young age, David Lloyd George won his first election before he was thirty. He became controversial, though, by speaking out against England's position in the Boer War. The emotions on the subject were so high that his speeches sometimes ended in riots.

As he rose through the political ranks, George took on an extremely liberal agenda, campaigning for serious social reforms. His programs succeeded in helping the poor, but they resulted in significantly increased taxes on the rich. Obviously, this wasn't appreciated. But, George was able to redeem himself by displaying leadership Britain's victory over Germany in World War I. He also helped establish the Treaty of Versailles, which listed the terms of surrender after the war.

All of his accomplishments aside, David Lloyd George couldn't help from always being surrounded by scandal his entire time in office. It was this scandal that caused his popularity to fade, ultimately leading to his resignation.

"One day there will be only five Kings left—hearts, spades, diamonds, clubs, and England!"
Farouk I   (late 1940's)

Sensing the tension growing among his citizens, King Farouk I had a prediction in the late 1940's. He had taken the throne of Egypt in 1936, and he ruled the nation with a heavy hand. His constant rejection of any form of a democracy, as well as the defeat of Egypt by Israel earlier that year, created an increasing unrest among his people. In 1952, a military coup led by General Muhammed Naguib resulted in Farouk's exile, and an end to the monarchy in Egypt. Even before he was ousted, Farouk could see the changing trends in his country and throughout the world. He explained, *"The whole world is in revolt. One day there will be only five Kings left: hearts, spades, diamonds, clubs, and England!"*

Farouk's prediction, while not entirely true, had some degree of fact. After World War I, several monarchies in Europe ceased to exist, and those that remained lost a significant amount of power. Today, just as Farouk had foreseen, the Kings of hearts, spades, diamonds, and clubs are still alive and well—and there is still a monarchy in England. But, these are not the only "Kings" that remain. Other prominent nations with enduring monarchs include Sweden, Norway, Denmark, and Belgium.

"Our people never had it so good!"
Harold Macmillan   (1957)

Harold Macmillan didn't think there was any room for complaining. At a Conservative Party rally in 1957, the soon-to-be British Prime Minister delivered this now famous line before a crowd of his supporters. The phrase caught on, and his optimism resulted in his great popularity among the English people. Macmillan was referring to the fact that, before World War II, Britain suffered from high unemployment—by 1957, the unemployment rate had dropped way down. His simple slogan, *"Our people never had it so good!"* helped the public realize that the current conditions weren't as bad as some were speculating.

With the support of the people, Macmillan became Prime Minister when Anthony Eden resigned in 1957. Because of the initial reaction, he used the saying, *"Our people never had it so good,"* throughout his term to rally support for the Conservative Party. During his six years as Prime Minister, Macmillan managed to stay on relatively good terms in the public's eye. This is especially impressive because he had to hold office during the difficult Cold War era.

In 1963, after some health problems and pressure from his party for a younger leader, Macmillan resigned the office.

"I am not a gentleman—I am a representative of the Soviet Union!"
Semyon Tzarapkin (1954)

Thanks for clearing that up. In 1954, Soviet Ambassador Semyon Tzarapkin gave this reply during a United Nations meeting when American diplomat Henry Cabot Lodge inquired as to why *"the gentleman"* was asking to take the floor. Resenting the remark, Tzarapkin responded, *"I am not a gentleman—I am a representative of the Soviet Union!"* Lodge didn't hesitate to agree, and added, *"The two are not necessarily exclusive!"*

This uncivil exchange was consistent with the relationship between the United States and the Soviet Union at the time. The two world powers were in the midst of a tense rivalry that began immediately after World War II and would not end until the late 1980's. This ongoing struggle became known as the Cold War. Not surprisingly, Semyon Tzarapkin wasn't too reserved in his distrust for Americans. He, like most of the Soviet Union leaders during the 1950's, favored the ideology of communism, and the concept of communal wealth. America, of course, relied on capitalism, where every man was responsible for his own fortune.

Henry Cabot Lodge was a true capitalist. He became a leader of the Republican Party by serving several terms in senate and then, in 1953, becoming a United States delegate to the United Nations.

Mikhail Gorbachev—Steering Russia away from tyranny

"The Soviet people want full-blooded and unconditional democracy!"
Mikhail Gorbachev   (1988)

    This isn't what you'd expect to hear from a leader of the Soviet Union. Mikhail Gorbachev made the astonishing statement in July 1988. After suffering through decades of heavy-handed communist rule, Gorbachev saw the need to make radical changes. Rallying support for his cause despite his many communist critics, he declared something that went against all precedent— *"The Soviet people want full-blooded and unconditional democracy!"*

    Growing up in Russia under the dictatorship of Joseph Stalin, Gorbachev had witnessed first hand the terror that was a result of the collective rule of communism. When he took office in 1985, huge changes were made immediately. By restructuring the personnel, he cracked down on corruption within the communist party.

    Wanting to make more progress, Gorbachev grew frustrated with the bureaucratic hurdles that he was faced with. In 1986, he instigated dramatic reforms to the Soviet government. With new policies such as "glasnost" (an effort to open Russia up to the outside world) and "perestroika" (rebuilding), Gorbachev proceeded to shift the Soviet Union's position in the world. Perhaps his most radical move, however, was when he came out in favor of "demokratizatsiia" — which translates to "democratization". Gorbachev knew that the Soviet Union couldn't survive under the fierce dictatorships that had ruled it in the past. In fact, he even encouraged economic independence of the Union's occupied countries in Eastern Europe. And, through several meetings with leaders like President Ronald Reagan, Gorbachev helped improve his nation's relationship with the Western world.

"We will bury you!"
Nikita Khruschev (1956)

Be careful what you say in a fit of rage. Speaking to Western ambassadors at a reception in Moscow on November 18, 1956, Soviet Premier Nikita Khrushchev hit the table with his fist and exclaimed, *"Whether you like it or not, history is on our side. We will bury you!"* The comment added fuel to the already heated Cold War, and exaggerated the obvious rivalry between communism and capitalism.

Khruschev had been a supporter of Joseph Stalin early in his career, but Stalin had alienated his followers with violent acts to the party and Soviet population. As a result, Khruschev dedicated himself to steering the Communist Party on a new course when he took power in 1956. He promised a new standard of living, and improvements to agriculture and industry.

In fact, Khruschev even promised a peaceful coexistence with the capitalist nations of the Western world. In his mind, war was not necessary. Communism was a superior system to capitalism and would inevitably win out. Of course, his prediction was incorrect — history was not on his side. Khruschev found himself under scrutiny from his followers because communism failed to produce the increased standard of living he promised. By contrast, the United States was experiencing a tremendous growth in its economy under the theory of capitalism. Ultimately, well after Khrushchev's rule had ended, communism fell and the Soviet Union was dissolved.

A Worthy Compliment

"I think this is the most extraordinary collection of talent, of human knowledge, that has ever been gathered together at the White House—with the possible exception of when Thomas Jefferson dined alone."

John F. Kennedy   (1962)

This is the incredible compliment given by President John F. Kennedy at a White House dinner honoring Nobel Prize winners in 1962. Despite the unbelievable aptitude of his guests, Kennedy knew that he wasn't surrounded by the best that the White House had ever seen. With world-renowned scientists, writers, and other persons of great influence sitting together in the room, it didn't get much better—but there was **"the possible exception of when Thomas Jefferson dined alone."**

Thomas Jefferson

The Nobel Prize is an award given each year in fields such as physics, chemistry, literature, and peace. Alfred Nobel, the inventor of dynamite, established the prestigious award after his death in 1896 by detailing it in his will. Since that time, the award has been recognized internationally, with previous winners including such notables as Marie Curie, Albert Einstein, and Martin Luther King, Jr.

But, even with all of the hype surrounding the Nobel Prize, President Kennedy probably wasn't exaggerating—the greatest talent that the White House has ever seen may have been Thomas Jefferson. Jefferson, the third president of the United States and author of the Declaration of Independence, was also a philosopher, writer, scientist, architect, and inventor. His influence helped the United States gain its independence and, more importantly, he helped insure that the nation always kept its main focus on individual liberty.

A *very* brief timeline of Thomas Jefferson's accomplishments:

- In his early twenties, Jefferson studies law under George Wythe, Virginia's leading legal scholar and later a member of the Constitutional Convention.
- In 1768 (at age twenty-five), Jefferson designs and begins building Monticello, his future home and a masterpiece of architecture.
- Also in 1768, Jefferson is elected to a seat in the Virginia House of Burgesses (state legislature).
- In the early 1770's, Jefferson becomes outspoken against Britain's policies of taxation without representation, helping to stir emotions for the American Revolution.
- In 1775, Jefferson is appointed to the Second Continental Congress in Philadelphia. Because of his superb writing skills, he is elected to draft the Declaration of Independence.
- In 1776, Jefferson and the other delegates of the Convention sign the Declaration of Independence.
- In the early 1780's, after the American Revolution ends in victory for the colonies, Jefferson works to help develop policies for the settlement and governing of the new nation.
- In 1784, Jefferson becomes a foreign minister in Paris, France. He spends five years in the position.
- In 1789, Jefferson returns to the States and becomes Secretary of State under the first president, George Washington.
- In 1793, Jefferson loses the presidential election to John Adams, thus becoming vice-president.
- In 1800, Jefferson defeats Adams to become the third President of the United States.
- In 1808, after two tumultuous terms, Jefferson refuses to run for a third time, dedicating the next two decades to writing, studying, and various hobbies.

"The State has no business in the bedrooms of the nation!"
Pierre Elliott Trudeau   (1967)

You have to draw the line somewhere. As the Minister of Justice to Canada in 1967, Pierre Elliott Trudeau tried to set the record straight to a group of reporters. Representing the Liberal Party, Trudeau attempted to liberalize laws concerning divorce, abortion, and homosexuality. And, despite constant protests from conservatives and members of the Canadian clergy, numerous changes were made in the criminal code as a result of his efforts.

Because of his influence as the Minister of Justice, Trudeau was chosen as the successor to Lester Pearson when Pearson resigned as the leader of the Liberal Party. On April 20, 1968, Trudeau became the Prime Minister of Canada. During the late 1960's, his liberal policies were popular with the Canadian public—in fact, he secured the first majority government in Canada for nearly a decade. Aside from his reforms on the issues in the "bedroom," Trudeau also took an aggressive stance on establishing equal rights among the French and English-speaking citizens of the nation. He liberalized Canada's foreign policy, as well, lessening the concentration on the military.

"Development is the best contraceptive."
Karan Singh   (1974)

At the 1974 World Population Conference in Bucharest, Romania, delegates from several nations debated about one of the most sensitive global issues of the time—overpopulation. It was argued that firm numbers needed to be set to limit the increasing number of people in the world. India's Minister of Health, Dr. Karan Singh, disagreed. Instead, he believed that if a country developed economically and technologically, then the population issues would take care of themselves. His words, *"Development is the best contraceptive,"* became a catch phrase in the effort to control population in third-world countries by increasing the standard of living.

Singh had the evidence to back up his position. In countries like the United States, with an extremely high standard of living, population growth through the number of newborns isn't astounding. In fact, if each couple had only two children, which is near the actual average, then there would be no growth at all. By contrast, women in third-world countries typically have six to ten children—about the same number of children a woman might have given birth to a century ago in the United States. For various reasons, there is a clear correlation between population growth and standard of living, something Dr. Singh noticed nearly thirty years ago.

"It doesn't matter whether the cat is black or white, as long as it catches mice!"
Deng Xiaoping   (1976)

When he became the ruler of a devastated China in 1976, Deng Xiaoping decided to govern by this simple motto.

Xiaoping had been a follower of Mao Zedong when the Chinese Communist Party gained power in the brutal civil war in 1949. This resulted in the creation of the People's Republic of China. Unfortunately, Zedong made several decisions that led to a nation of starving citizens. Among his disastrous reforms was the "Cultural Revolution" of 1966, an attempt to completely rid China of any Western influence. The result was revolt and violence. This prompted Deng Xiaoping split from Zedong, and he became the new leader after Zedong's death in 1976.

In a great contrast to Mao Zedong, Deng Xiaoping wasn't so quick to criticize the Western World. He was consistent with his motto, *"It doesn't matter whether the cat is black or white, as long as it catches mice!"* Zedong had refused to accept ideas and technology if they had originated in Western culture. Xiaoping did away with this bias, and it resulted in major positive strides in agriculture, industry, military, and technology in China.

Under Xiaoping's rule, peasants were permitted to lease farmland and market their crops. Foreign trade began to exist to a degree, and students were even sent to places such as the United States for a better understanding of new technology. As soon as the people got a taste of this new freedom, they thirsted for more. The outcome was variety of pro-democracy protests such as the 1989 Tian'an Men Square demonstration.

"Stand up for freedom of the imagination..."
Salman Rushdie   (1989)

British author Salman Rushdie's novel, *The Satanic Verses*, caused a tremendous commotion throughout the Islamic community. The novel, published in 1988, combined fantasy and philosophical reflections, and was thought by many to be an attack on the Koran and the Muslim faith. The tension became so heated that Iran's Ayatollah Ruhollah Khomeini actually declared that anyone dealing in the book should be killed, announcing, *"All those involved in its publication who were aware of its content, are sentenced to death. I ask all Moslems to execute them wherever they find them."*

Fearing for his life, Rushdie went into hiding. His novel had already been banned in several Islamic nations, and a large bounty existed for his capture and execution. He apologized, announcing his support of the Islamic faith, but to no avail. Finally, in 1989, Rushdie made a statement to the British press, announcing, *"I call upon the intellectual community in this country and abroad to stand up for freedom of the imagination, an issue much larger than my book or indeed my life!"*

Eventually, though his life was still in great danger, Rushdie began to appear in public and grant interviews. By 1995, he was even appearing on television and participating in readings of his controversial novel.

"Let's just start growing!"
Norman Borlaug   (1984)

Renowned agronomist Norman Borlaug decided that age seventy-one was a little too young to retire. Instead, he focused his expertise on helping the dismal agricultural industry in Africa. On a trip to the continent to see firsthand just how bad it really was, Borlaug saw the multitude of starving people, and came up with his plan— *"Let's just start growing!"* He went to work immediately, aiding the famished nations by teaching the locals his modern techniques.

In his younger years, Borlaug had led the frontier of the Green Revolution, a worldwide effort to improve agriculture in less developed countries. He was an expert in helping uneducated farmers upgrade their techniques, and he trained other technicians to teach those principles throughout the world. In 1970, he was awarded the Nobel Peace Prize.

Surprisingly, despite his worldwide influence, Borlaug had never been a part of any programs in Africa. In 1984 he was approached by Japanese philanthropist Ryoichi Sasakawa, who encouraged him to expand to the continent. But, by that time, Borlaug was already over seventy years old, and was a little hesitant to take on the new challenge. Offering him the financial backing, Sasakawa finally convinced Borlaug to bring his expertise to yet another undeveloped corner of the world.

Borlaug's success in Africa was instant. In over a dozen countries—such as Ethiopia, Ghana, and Sudan—he was able to teach local farmers about planting, fertilizing, and harvesting. As a result, crop yields more than tripled.

"General, you'd better put jam in your pockets because we're all about to be toast!"
Unknown Geologist (1991)

In April 1991, Mount Pinatubo, a volcano that had been dormant for over 600 years, started to show signs of life. By June, it was evident that a serious eruption was possible. This was a major concern for those stationed at Clark Air Base in the Philippines. Clark was one of the largest bases outside the United States, and it was located less than twenty miles from the volcano.

The geologists who were examining Mount Pinatubo were stern in their warnings. One geologist drove it home when he told the commander of the base, *"General, you'd better put jam in your pockets because we're all about to be toast!"* The order to evacuate was given just a few days before the eruption.

When Mount Pinatubo did erupt on June 12, it completely devastated the surrounding area. Several feet of ash fell to the ground, and almost a quarter of a million acres of agricultural land was destroyed. Over 500 people lost their lives. As a true testament to its power, Mount Pinatubo literally "blew its top" and was several hundred feet shorter after the eruption.

"The person who has nothing for which he is willing to fight, nothing which is more important than his own personal safety, is a miserable creature and has no chance of being free unless made and kept so by the exertions of better men than himself."
—John Stuart Mill
British philosopher (1806-1863)

Chapter 13

World Wars

"Veni, Vidi, Vici!" ("I came, I saw, I conquered!")
Julius Caesar   (47 BC)

Julius Caesar released this legendary message to Rome after yet another military victory for the great city.

Born into a family that didn't carry an extreme amount of wealth or prestige in Rome, Caeser, with some clever politics, was eventually able to rise through the ranks of a general, statesman, and eventually dictator. And, as the ruler of Rome, he didn't mind having a nation at war. One of his conquests, in 47 BC, took his army to Asia Minor (near present-day Turkey) in the fight for an ancient kingdom. The battle was quick and definitive, and the powerful Roman army came away as victors. Afterwards, Caesar sent back his brief description to the Roman people of what had transpired, saying only, *"Veni, Vidi, Vici."*

Caesar's demise came three years later on March 15, 44 BC—a day that would become known as the Ides of March. That's when several members of the senate betrayed him, and he was assassinated.

"Dieu li volt—God wills it!"
Pope Urban II   (1095)

This rallying cry began a series of wars known as the Crusades, resulting in thousands of European Christians storming across Asia Minor to recapture the Holy Land from the Muslims.

In November 1095, Pope Urban II stood before a crowd of people huddled in a field in Clermont, France. He spoke to them in an effort to stir their emotions about the Christian people's destiny to occupy the city of Jerusalem (the Holy Land). The city was currently controlled by Muslims. He shouted, *"On whom, then, rests the labor of avenging these wrongs, and of recovering this territory..."*. The Pope assured the crowd that a higher power was on their side, *"God has conferred remarkable glory in arms, great bravery, and strength to humble the heads of those who resist you."*

The inspiring talk concluded when Pope Urban II, speaking in French, declared, *"Dieu li volt,"* which means, *"God wills it!"* The crowd reacted with emotion and began to chant back the phrase. Many of the spectators decided to immediately join in the fight, and the first Crusade soon followed. For the next 200 years, several wars were fought against the Muslims in an effort to claim the city of Jerusalem.

> ***"If it were possible to collect all the innocent blood that you have shed in your unhallowed ministry, in one great reservoir, your Lordship might swim in it!"***
> **Robert Emmet   (1803)**

Irish patriot Robert Emmet held a grudge, and rightfully so. In 1803, as he was being tried for treason, he had these words to the court just before being pronounced guilty. The twenty-five year old Emmet was the leader of a group of about 100 men known as the United Irishmen who stormed Dublin Castle in a rebellion against English rule. Unfortunately, Emmet's group behaved more like an angry mob than an organized army, and the attack was quickly dispersed by the British. After a few days in hiding, Emmet was captured and brought to Dublin for trial.

Emmet's trial was a set-up. With his lawyer under the secret payroll of the prosecution, the guilty verdict was inevitable. After being repeatedly silenced, Emmet finally refused to yield to the interruptions of the judges and began to say what was on his mind. Angered by his contempt, the judges ordered him to stop, but Emmet wouldn't. He knew that a death sentence awaited him, and he told the court, *"Let no man dare, when I am dead, to charge me with dishonor. Let no man attaint my memory by believing that I could have engaged in any cause but that of my country's liberty and independence!"*

As expected, Emmet was found guilty, and ultimately hanged in Dublin shortly after his trial.

Oliver Cromwell — Agitator of the British Revolution

"Cruel necessity!"
Oliver Cromwell (1649)

Oliver Cromwell wasn't totally without feeling. As he looked down at the beheaded English King Charles I, the revolutionary hero acknowledged the tragedy by muttering these words before turning and walking out of the room. Cromwell had been a leader of the army that had overthrown the King during the English Revolution of the seventeenth century.

King Charles I had started the trouble by believing in the "Divine Right" of kings — the idea that it was God's will for him to be ruler. Receiving his crown in 1625, Charles I was the King of England, Scotland, and Ireland for nearly twenty-five years before his insolence created tension among the British parliament and ultimately led to the English Civil War. The uprising against King Charles I hit full swing in the early 1640's, and resulted in his imprisonment.

As the fighting between the ruling powers of England continued, Oliver Cromwell rose as a leader of the Independents. Cromwell had at first wanted to keep the monarchical rule, only limiting the authority of the king — but ultimately he didn't believe that Charles I, sor any king, could be trusted. When Charles I was put on trial in 1649, Cromwell supported the punishment of execution. Shortly after, he was appointed as the Lord Protector of England, the first commoner ever to rule the nation.

> **"To have printed liberties, and not to have liberties in truth and realities, is but to mock the kingdom!"**
> **John Pym**   **(1640s)**

Parliamentary leader John Pym and King Charles I just didn't get along. Pym had had enough of the idea of "Divine Right" and, in the days leading up to the English Revolution, he wasn't afraid to let his opinions be known. Pym had served in the Parliament since 1614. By the 1640's, there was a tremendous amount of tension between he and King Charles I — and Pym wasn't alone. He delivered a rallying speech that helped him win the support of the public. In it, he cited a list of grievances against the King, including, *"To have printed liberties, and not to have liberties in truth and realities, is but to mock the kingdom!"*

Seeing that his days were numbered, King Charles I made an attempt to have five members of Parliament arrested in 1642 — among them was John Pym. Unfortunately for the King, he failed. Hostility grew between Parliament and Charles I, and a civil war started in late 1642. Pym became an essential figure in helping to keep the Parliamentary Army financed and organized. His influence also helped convince the Scottish army to come to the aid of Parliament. Inevitably, King Charles I was defeated.

While the monarch was later be reinstated, the victory for Parliament resulted in permanent changes. The idea of "Divine Right," where a King is destined by God to rule completely and unquestionably over his subjects, existed no more in England.

The French Revolution

"Then let them eat cake..."
Marie Antoinette

Despite the fact that this is one of the most recognizable quotes in history, the person to whom it has been credited probably never said it. Supposedly, when Marie Antoinette, wife of the French King Louis XVI, was told that the peasants of France had no bread, she replied, **"Then let them eat cake."** The legend describes her complete ignorance and apathy towards the problems of the time.

Marie Antoinette

Though Marie Antoinette never did make that remark, the story behind it does have a hint of truth. During the latter half of the 1700's, the people of France were experiencing a time of hardship and poverty, and they were growing tired of the monarchy. As the wife of the king, Marie Antoinette was oblivious to this. She lived a life of extravagance—wearing elegant clothes, throwing fancy parties, and living in a lavish palace. Because she was surrounded by luxury, the people of France often blamed her, though unjustifiably, for the economic problems of the time.

In any case, Marie Antoinette's privileged lifestyle would come to an end. In 1789, the people of France revolted against the monarchy and started the ten year long French Revolution. Both Louis XVI and Marie Antoinette were captured—on October 16, 1793, she was put to death by the guillotine.

And, she wasn't the only one. The order "off with their heads" was being thrown around like confetti during the revolution—and there was no side that was safe.

French astronomer and politician Jean-Sylvian Bailly was one such victim. But, he knew how to stay calm under pressure. In 1793, Bailly had been falsely accused of conspiring with King Louis XVI. He was arrested and sentenced to the guillotine that same year. On his last night alive, he calmly told his nephew, **"It's time for me to enjoy another pinch of snuff. Tomorrow it will be impossible—my hands will be bound!"**

Another unlucky victim was Revolutionary leader Georges Jacques Danton. Danton had knowingly placed himself in danger by condemning the state's policy of crushing revolts by using excessive violence—a policy appropriately known as the Reign of Terror. Taking a solid stand, he declared, **"I shall break that damned guillotine or I shall fall under it."** Danton remained true to his word, though he probably didn't get the choice he wanted—he was executed for his unpopular views on April 5, 1794. Accepting his fate, he told the executioner, **"Show my head to the people—it is worth showing."** Danton was certain that he gave his life to help the citizens of France.

Before his demise, Danton was a member of the Committee of Public Safety, a leading body during the French Revolution. However, his distaste for the excessive violence clashed with the views of the Committee's leader, Maximilien Robespierre. Fearing that this would threaten the cause of the Revolution, Robespierre ordered the execution of Danton along with several other leading officials.

Eventually Robespierre would find himself the target of a revolt, and would lose his head at the guillotine later that year.

The tremendous turmoil of the time was pretty much summed up by political clergyman Emmanuel Sieyes. Sieyes had published controversial pamphlets before the revolution and served on a few key councils during the 1790's that would help determine its outcome; but, for the most part, the minister managed to stay out of the spotlight. At a time when people were literally losing their heads on a daily basis, his decision to remain cautious would yield one positive result—**"I survived!"** That's about all you could do.

Napoleon—Attempting to conquer the rugged terrain of Russia

"This is the beginning of the end!"
Charles Maurice de Talleyrand (1812)

French diplomat Charles Maurice de Talleyrand could see through the thick smoke—and he didn't like what he saw. Talleyrand made his famed prediction after Napoleon led his army into the Battle of Bordino on September 7, 1812. The confrontation was the first in Napoleon's invasion of Russia. Despite ending with the retreat of the Russian army, Talleyrand felt that Napoleon's army was in for tough times. His prophecy, *"This is the beginning of the end,"* would ultimately prove correct.

As Napoleon's former foreign minister, Talleyrand had resigned in opposition to the series of Napoleonic Wars that the Emperor had launched. Those were child's play, however, compared to the decision to invade Russia. The French army moved into the vast country in June 1812, with the first major battle not occurring until September. The Russians had established a purely defensive strategy, hoping to exhaust Napoleon's powerful army. It worked. By the time the Battle of

Bordino was fought, supply lines for the French were already stretched, and the army had been reduced by more than half.

Even though the French army defeated the Russians at Bordino, they paid the price. When the tired army finally arrived in Moscow, the city had already been deserted and stripped of supplies. To make matters worse, a harsh winter hit his men when Napoleon tried to march them out of Russia. With only a small percentage of the soldiers surviving, the disastrous campaign would ultimately ensure the Emperor's downfall.

"Soldiers of my Old Guard: I bid you farewell."
Napoleon Bonaparte (1814)

When French Emperor Napoleon Bonaparte failed in his invasion of Russia, he was forced to say farewell to the army and the people who had supported him for so long. Gaining power after the turmoil of the French Revolution, Napoleon had ruled France and the surrounding countries for over twenty years. Yet, on April 20, 1814, it was time to step down. He delivered a short speech to his remaining officers, reciting the stoic line, *"Soldiers of my Old Guard: I bid you farewell."* After the address, Napoleon was exiled to a small island off the coast of Italy.

But it was all for show. After leading France in a number of Napoleonic Wars, Napoleon wasn't going to be so easily cast away. Less than a year after his exile, he escaped back into France. Gathering about 1,000 members of his old army, Napoleon marched into Paris, recaptured the city, and once again became the Emperor.

His comeback was short-lived. On June 18, 1815, Napoleon was defeated once and for all at the Battle of Waterloo. While many of the people in France urged him to fight on, he had lost the support of the government, and was forced to flee the country. Soon after, he surrendered himself to the British.

"I have had them all shot!"
Ramon Narvaez   (1868)

    The priest of Ramon Narvaez had a simple request—he wanted the Spanish General to forgive his enemies. Known as the "strong man" of Spain, Narvaez replied, *"I do not have to forgive my enemies. I have had them all shot!"*

    Narvaez earned his intimidating reputation during the 1830's, fighting the royalist faction known as the Carlists. His loyalty was to Maria Christina, the acting regent for the very young Isabella II. But, the first time around, Narvaez failed them both, and the Carlist army forced Maria Christina and Isabella II into exile. That didn't last long, however. Narvaez, out for vengeance, organized another attack. This time, fighting against General Baldomero Espartero in 1843, he was successful, and Isabella II returned to the thrown.

    Because of his military success, Narvaez was appointed as a premier under Isabella II, and he used his authoritarian approach to help her rule. She needed it. Isabella II constantly had to deal with civil strife, and she even attempted to limit the independence of her people by abolishing the constitution. With Narvaez by her side, she was able to deal with the frustrated citizens. But, with his death in 1868, it wasn't long before the provoked people removed her from the thrown.

"It's better to die on your feet than to live on your knees!"
Emiliano Zapata   (1910's)

    Emliliano Zapata used this rallying cry to trigger thousands of peasants to fight during the Mexican Revolution. The lower class of Mexico was fed up with the living conditions under the dictator Porfirio Diaz. By the early 1900's, Diaz had already ruled the nation for nearly three decades. He and his few acquaintances were living a life of luxury, while almost the entire population of Mexico lived in poverty. The vast majority of the land was owned by just a few "bosses," and these bosses treated the workers basically as slaves. Even the lower class citizens who owned a little bit of land could have it confiscated without notice and given to their richer neighbors.

In 1910, Emiliano Zapata and Francisco Madero joined forces to overthrow Diaz. Zapata was born into poverty, and he was still an illiterate farmer when began to gather the peasants' support for a revolution. He rallied his troops with the cry, *"Land and Liberty!"* And, whenever there was any hesitation among his men, he reminded them, *"It's better to die on your feet than to live on your knees!"*

Porfirio Diaz was eventually forced to flee the country in 1911, and Madero took power. But, there was no immediate change, so Zapata and his followers soon found themselves opposing Madero. This caused turmoil in Mexico that continued for several years, ending with Emiliano Zapata's assassination in 1919. However, he continued to live on as a legend among the working class.

"Take a step forward lads..."
Robert Childers   (1922)

It's unusual to give advice to the firing squad that is preparing to put you to death. Irish revolutionary Robert Erskine Childers did just that, though, proving that he wasn't afraid of what was to happen in the next few moments. Showing no signs of nerves, Childers took the time to shake hands with his executors. When he assumed his position at the firing post, he snarled, *"Take a step forward lads — it'll be easier that way."* Seconds later, the gunmen ended Childer's life.

Childers had dedicated himself to the cause of creating a complete republican status for Ireland. But when an Irish Free State was created in 1922, he was enraged by the conditions of the treaty. He quickly became a member of the Irish Republican Army, and a civil war broke out in Ireland against the Free State government. In November 1922, Childers was arrested for treason, and he was sentenced to execution later that month. Since the accusation of treason was a little far-fetched, Childers was officially charged with carrying a small pistol with him at the time of his arrest.

Childers' son, Hamilton Childers, would ultimately become president of Ireland in 1973.

"God and history will remember your judgment!"
Haile Selassie I   (1936)

Haile Selassie I knew that he was doing something that was bigger than both he and his small country of Ethiopia. As the nation's last emperor, he delivered an appeal to the League of Nations in Geneva on June 30, 1936. Selassie explained to the delegates how important it was for them to provide Ethiopia with assistance in fighting the Italian army, who had invaded earlier that year. He warned that if the Italians, under fascist leader Benito Mussolini, weren't stopped, it would be the beginning of a reign of terror throughout the world.

In an impressive speech to the delegates, Selassie remarked, *"Should it happen that a strong government finds it may, with impunity, destroy a weak people, then the hour strikes for that weak people to appeal to the League of Nations to give its judgment in all freedom. God and history will remember your judgment!"* His request for aid was turned down. With his nation still under attack, he fled to England, and helped to organize a campaign to liberate Ethiopia. With the help of the English, his ill-equipped army defeated the Italians and he returned to power.

As emperor, Selassie did establish a constitution, a parliament, and a court system for his nation. But, he wasn't completely a man of the people. Ruling Ethiopia for over forty years, he made sure that he always had the majority of the power.

"The pope? How many divisions has he got?"
Joseph Stalin   (1935)

I think he missed the point. This is the question asked by Russian dictator Joseph Stalin after French Foreign Minister Pierre Laval suggested to him that he encourage Catholicism in Russia to gain the favor of the pope. With the world on the edge of war in 1935, Laval felt that the support of the papacy would help give the allies an edge over the ever-growing German army.

At the time, the pope was Pius XI, an outspoken critic of the communist government. Upon hearing about Stalin's sarcastic remark, he replied, *"Tell our brother Joseph that he will meet our divisions in Heaven!"* Though he may not have been on good terms with Stalin, Pius XI did support the allied cause. He strongly opposed the Nazi ideals of fascism and anti-Semitism.

In 1945, the powerful army of Russia helped to bring down the German forces. But Russia's problems weren't over. Stalin immediately developed a fanatic distrust for the Western world, leading to the Cold War. As the dictator from 1922 to 1953, his constant use of terror and violence to control his people earned Stalin the reputation as one of the cruelest leaders in history.

"I'm glad we've been bombed. I feel I can look the East End in the face."
Queen Elizabeth   (1940)

Demonstrating her ability to see the bright side of any situation, Queen Elizabeth made this statement after Buckingham palace was bombed by German planes in 1940. As the fighting of World War II intensified, "Queen Mum" and her husband, King George VI, often traveled across England to boost the morale of those in the war-torn cities. The sight of London's East End, where a constant barrage of bombing had left many people homeless, especially upset Queen Elizabeth. Despite the growing dangers of the war, the King and Queen felt that it was important not to live in fear, and therefore decided to remain at Buckingham Palace. Their poise helped to calm the nerves of the citizens in England.

However, as the Germans continued their blitz on England, they finally got a direct hit on Buckingham Palace. To make sure this wouldn't be a major setback for the morale of the people, Queen Elizabeth remarked, *"I'm glad we've been bombed. I feel I can look the East End in the face."* And, true to her word, she made herself more available than ever to those suffering from the terrors of the war. In addition to her visits to London's East End, she toured key sights like factories, schools, and hospitals. Her presence instilled confidence throughout England and the world. Queen Mum became a symbol for perseverance as the Allies succeeded in withstanding the Nazi attacks. Elizabeth remained Queen until 1952 when, after the death of King George VI, her daughter, Elizabeth II, took over.

The Wrong Choice

"I believe it is peace for our time..."
Neville Chamberlain   (1938)

This is the famous and drastically incorrect prediction of British Prime Minister Neville Chamberlain. He had just returned from the Munich Conference where he had dealt in negotiations with the infamous Nazi leader, Adolf Hitler. When he stepped off of the plane in England on September 30, 1938, Chamberlain believed that a peaceful resolution could be made between England and Germany, and any future wars could be avoided. He was wrong.

When Chamberlain returned to England after the meeting, he held in his hand a printed statement that he and Hitler had agreed upon. The paper stated the **"desire of our two peoples never to go to war with one another again."** Chamberlain read it to a crowd on the street, and then announced, **"I believe it is peace for our time. Go home and get a nice quiet sleep."**

British politician Winston Churchill was skeptical about this easy compromise. In fact, he was furious that Chamberlain had fallen into a trap—he had tried to take the easy way out. In Churchill's words, **"You were given the choice between war and dishonor. You chose dishonor, and you will have war."**

Winston Churchill

Winston Churchill was right—Hitler had no intention of honoring his word. He attacked Poland without cause a year after the Munich Conference, and quickly began on a mission to conquer all of Europe. World War II had begun, and Britain had no choice but to stand up and fight. Chamberlain's reputation took a drastic fall. After a rough first few months of the war, he resigned as Prime Minister in 1940.

Winston Churchill took over the position of Prime Minister after Chamberlain's resignation. He did a superb job of leading the British to an allied victory, and is regarded by many as the most influential British leader of the twentieth century.

As one of the great inspirational leaders of World War II, here is a little sample of what Winston Churchill had to say soon after becoming Prime Minister:

- "Arm yourselves, and be ye men of valour, and be in readiness for the conflict; for it is better for us to perish in battle than to look upon the outrage of our nation and our altar."
  —*First broadcast as Prime Minister. May, 1940*
- "I would say to the House, as I said to those who have joined this government: I have nothing to offer but blood, toil, tears and sweat."
  —*Speaking to the House of Commons. May, 1940*
- "Let us therefore brace ourselves to our duties, and so bear ourselves that if the British Empire and Commonwealth last for a thousand years, men will still say, This was their finest hour."
  —*After the fall of France. June, 1940*
- "Never give in--never, never, never, never, in nothing great or small, large or petty, never give in except to convictions of honour and good sense. Never yield to force; never yield to the apparently overwhelming might of the enemy."
  —*Speaking to students at his old school. October, 1941*
- "When I warned them that Britain would fight on alone, whatever they did, their Generals told their Prime Minister and his divided cabinet that in three weeks, England would have her neck wrung like a chicken - Some chicken! Some neck!"
  —*Speech to Canadian Parliament. December, 1941*
- "Never in the field of human conflict was so much owed by so many to so few."
  —*Speaking about the British Airforce. August, 1940*
- "We shall fight on the beaches. We shall fight on the landing grounds. We shall fight in the fields, and in the streets, we shall fight in the hills. We shall never surrender!"
  —*Speech prior to an early battle of the war. June, 1940*

"An iron curtain has descended across the continent!"
Winston Churchill   (1946)

On March 5, 1946, a crowd at Westminster College witnessed former British Prime Minister Winston Churchill deliver this legendary metaphor. His reference to an *"iron curtain"* became a symbol of the Cold War, describing the censorship and isolation policies that the Union of Soviet Socialist Republics (USSR) used to separate the people in eastern Europe from the rest of the world.

The night before the famous speech, Churchill traveled by train to Fulton, Missouri accompanied by President Harry Truman. The town of Fulton had a population of only 7,000 — over 40,000 came to hear him speak. The message of his address was that Russia, which had been a reliable ally to both Britain and the United States during World War II, was now a major post-war threat. Churchill declared, *"From Stettin in the Baltic to Trieste in the Adriatic, an iron curtain has descended across the Continent. Behind that line lie all the capitals of the ancient states of Central and Eastern Europe..."*

Eastern Europe remained locked behind the *"iron curtain"* until the collapse of communism almost fifty years later. Highlighted by the fall of the Berlin Wall in 1989, countries previously occupied by the USSR finally broke through and became united with the rest of the world.

"The living will envy the dead!"
Nikita Khrushchev   (1960's)

In the early 1960's, Nikita Khrushchev gave his scenario of what life would be like if the Soviet Union and the United States used their nuclear weapons to destroy each other. *"In the event of a nuclear war,"* he pointed out, *"the living will envy the dead!"*

Serving as Russian Prime Minister from 1958 to 1964, Khrushchev became a decision maker during the tense face-off between the Soviet Union and the United States that would last for decades. When striking the Japanese with a powerful atomic bomb ended World War II, a race began among the world powers to establish nuclear superiority. The end result was known as MAD, or Mutual Assured Destruction. Both the United States and the Soviet Union were so powerful that they could completely destroy the other. If either started to do so, the other would have enough response time to retaliate with equal force. Khrushchev knew that, in this scenario, everyone was a loser.

Fearing nuclear war, he adopted the policy of peaceful coexistence with the United States and other countries in the Western world. Khrushchev still believed that ultimately communism would prevail over capitalism, but it would do so by its own superiority and not through war.

> ### *"I became Prime Minister because that was how it was, in the same way that my milkman became an officer in command of a machine-gun squad in the '73 war..."*
> ### Golda Meir   (1974)

Golda Meir had a calling. After serving as the Israeli Prime Minister for five years, she resigned her duties in 1974, giving this explanation of how she had ended up where she was. She concluded the statement by saying, *"He didn't want the job, but somebody had to do it."*

Meir was born and raised in Milwaukee, Wisconsin, where she became active in the Zionist movement at an early age. The Zionist movement encouraged Jews from all over the world to settle in Palestine, a part of which would later become the Jewish state of Israel. Meir moved to Palestine herself when she was twenty-three years old, in 1921.

After being active in the development of the new nation, and serving in its government, she found herself as the Israeli Prime Minister in 1969. Her time as the premier was complicated by the constant struggle between the Israeli people and the people of the surrounding Arab nations. This tension would be the cause of a war in 1973 — the one in which her *"milkman became an officer in command of a machine-gun squad."* She received a great deal of criticism for Israel's lack of preparation for the war, and this forced her to resign her position a year later.

References and Acknowledgments

Everyone always asks the same question: **"Who or what, exactly, is the 'What Made Them Say That' Research Team?"** And, it's a good question. So good, in fact, that it requires a two-part answer. First, there is the small group of individuals (who, in the name of teamwork, prefer to remain nameless) that went out in search of the history's greatest quotations. They began where it seemed most obvious, by painstakingly sorting through the traditional, 1,000 page or more, dust-on-the-cover, quote books. And, they found several that proved to be exceptionally helpful:

Knowles, Elizabeth, ed. *The Oxford Dictionary of Quotations.* 5th edition. **New York: Oxford University Press, 2001.**

MacMillan Dictionary of Quotations. **New York: Macmillan Publishing Company, 1989.**

Platt, Suzy, ed. *Respectfully Quoted: A Dictionary of Quotations from the Library of Congress.* **Washington, DC: Congressional Quarterly Inc., 1992.**

But that wasn't enough! Even after the members of the Research Team sorted through these mammoth resources and picked out what they felt to be the best of the best, they still weren't satisfied. Frustrated, they dug deeper, looking for some smaller and more specific references. After some tedious searching, the Research Team found a few goldmines:

Baker, Daniel B., ed. *Political Quotations.* **Detroit: Gale Research, Inc., 1990.**

Flexner, Stuart Berg. *Listening to America: An Illustrated History of Words and Phrases from our Lively and Splendid Past.* **New York: Simon and Schuster, 1982.**

Morris, Mary and William. *Morris Dictionary of Word and Phrase Origins.* **New York: Harper & Row, Publishers, Inc., 1977.**

Prochnow, Herbert, ed. *The Complete Toastmaster.* **New York: Prentice-Hall, 1986.**

Safire, William, ed. *Lend Me Your Ears. Great Speeches in History.* **New York: W.W. Norton & Company, 1997.**

Warner, Carolyn, ed. *The Last Word. A Treasury of Women's Quotes.* **London: Prentice-Hall, 1992.**

Ecstatic, the **"What Made Them Say That?"** Research Team met together and agreed that what had been gathered was an outstanding, diverse, and highly interesting collection of the greatest things ever said. And, after a brief discussion, the members realized that what they had done was just the beginning. After all, the book that they were trying to create wasn't called, *"What did they say?"* That part was easy—now came the task of trying to find out, *"What made them say that?"*

To answer the question, *"What made them say that?"*, it is necessary to know much more than just the words that were spoken. For example, most people know that Franklin Roosevelt said, *"The only thing we have to fear is fear itself..."* But to determine exactly *what made him say that,* The Research Team had to find out what kind of a person FDR was, what was going on in the world around him when he was speaking, what was he thinking, and what consequences was he facing by saying what he said (check out page 188 for all these answers). There was no question about it—this was going to be the hard part. Having been schooled in their previous research of gathering quotations, the Research Team decided to once again start broad and work their way down to the specifics. So, they set out on the task of information collecting with some obvious tools:

Byers, Paula, ed. *Encyclopedia of World Biography.* **Detroit: Gale Research, Inc., 1998.**

Chambers, John Whiteclay II, ed. *American Military History.* **New York: Oxford University Press, 1999.**

Edwards, Paul, ed. *The Encyclopedia of Philosophy.* **New York: MacMillan Publishing Co., Inc., 1972.**

Hartt, Frederick. *Art: A History of Painting, Sculpture, Architecture.* **New York: Harry N. Abrams, Inc. 1976.**

Dictionary of American Biography. **New York: Charles Scribner's Sons, 1964.**

McGraw-Hill Encyclopedia of Science & Technology. **New York: McGraw-Hill Companies, 2002.**

The World Book Encyclopedias. **Chicago: World Book, Inc., 2002.**

But the Research Team didn't just rely on these standard tools for their research. To truly answer the question, *"What made them say that?"*, it becomes necessary to look beyond facts and figures. So, once again, the team dug deeper, and came up with some interesting finds (That's right, they even used *World History for Dummies*):

Bowers and Gottlieb. *1,000 Years, 1,000 People. Ranking the Men and Women Who Shaped the Millennium.* New York: Kodansha America, Inc., 1998.

Haugen, Peter. *World History for Dummies.* New York: IDG Books Worldwide, 2001.

Kane, Joseph Nathan, ed. *Facts About the Presidents.* 5th edition. New York: The H.W. Wilson Company, 1989.

Ploski, Harry A. and James Williams, eds. *The Negro Almanac: A Reference Work on the African American.* 5th edition. Detroit: Gale Research, Inc., 1989.

Nelson, Rebecca, ed. *The Handy History Answer Book.* Canton: Visible Ink Press, 1999.

After all of the research was complete, the original members of the **"What Made Them Say That?"** Research Team realized that they had only skimmed the surface. Why? Because everyday someone would come up to them with some fascinating piece of history that had somehow managed to be overlooked. At the office, someone would say, *"Did you know that the expression, 'Your name will be mudd,' is actually a reference to Dr. Samuel Mudd, a man who helped John Wilkes Booth after the Lincoln assasination?"* To this, the well-schooled members of the Research Team would respond, *"That's crazy!"* After a few hours of research, they learned that, while it may be crazy, it was also true (it's all on page 10).

Even as the book was getting into its final stages, the Research Team was always on the look out. While entertaining family for dinner one night, one of the members was told an anecdote about the legendary Davy Crockett. *"And then,"* the story teller exclaimed, *"Crockett told them, 'You can go to hell— I'm going to Texas!'* (page 174)" The next day, as the Research Team assembled for their task, the newly enlightened member shouted, *"We've got to put this in there!"* Once again, after just a little bit of research, it became all too obvious that another great moment of history had almost slipped through the cracks.

It happened in other ways, too. Occasionally, an acquaintance who was excited about the **"What Made Them Say That?"** concept would ask, *"Who exactly was the Dr. Livingston in the famous saying, 'Dr. Livingston, I presume.'"* The Research Team members would then immediately realize that they had forgotten to include one of the greatest and most famous quotations in history. Less than two hours later, that problem was fixed (see page 142). Or, when the Research Team asked a colleague to review the book for some constructive criticism, the reader would often get a puzzled look and say, *"Hey, you forgot to put in a quotation by Yogi Berra!"* Again, it was back to the laboratory (check out page 36).

In the end, it turns out that the **"What Made Them Say That?"** Research Team is far larger than the few members that originally began the task. It also includes all of those individuals who contributed their profound knowledge of history's key moments. And, of course, it includes every person who said, *"I've got a great one for you to put into your book..."*

The **"What Made Them Say That?"** Research Team (the originals and the slew of honorary members) is certain that it has put together an interesting collection of the greatest quotations in history. And, of course, the stories behind them. But, there is still more out there. From the beginning, it has always seemed that when one great remark was discovered, ten more great ones were waiting right around the corner. So, the Research Team hopes that there is no offense taken if there was a completely obvious quotation that was completely missed. It will be included in the next one (read page 286)!

# INDEX

A

Abolitionists
   King, Jr., Martin Luther   158
   Phillips, Wendell 153
   Truth, Sojourner 154
   Tubman, Harriet 152
Abortion 102
Adams, John 171
Adams, Samuel 206
Aesculapius (Greek God of
   Medicine) 68
Aesthetic Movement 50
Africa 142, 254
Agassiz, Louis Rodolphe 132
Agnosticism 95, 97, 98
Airplanes 8, 145
Aitken, Max 243
Alamo 174
Alcoholics Anonymous 99
Aldrin, Buzz 146
Alexander V, Antipope 88
Ali, Muhammad 28
Alice's Adventures in Wonderland
   12
Allen, Woody 63
America .... Chapters 10, 11
American Revolution 164, 167,
   204, 206
American Society of Newspaper
   Editors 113
Andrews, Samuel 106
Anthony, Susan B 156
Antioch College 71
Antoinette, Marie 262
Apollo 11 146
Apollo 13 148
Archimedes 124
Armstrong, Neil 146
Arts .... Chapter 3
Astor, John Jacob 108
Athens 232
Austin, Warren 223
Avery, Oswald 127

B

Babylonia 9, 12
Bacon 13
Bailly, Jean-Sylvian 263
Baker's Dozen 9
Barkley, Alben 99
Barnum, P.T. 48
Baruch, Bernard 112
Battery, storage 130
Bay of Pigs invasion 197
Becquerel, Antoine 132
Bee, Bernard 216
Bell, Alexander Graham 176, 184
Bell, "saved by the" 22
Bellamy, Francis 192
Bennett, Justice Gervase 90
Berlin Wall 200
Berra, Yogi 36
Bible
   Belshazzar, King 22
   Daniel, the Prophet 22
   "eye for an eye" 13
   telegraph, first message 176
   translation of 46, 89
Black Chamber 186
Blackbeard 6
Blacksmith 15
Blake, Eubie 65
Bohr, Niels Henrik David 133
Boise, Penrose 96
Boleyn, Anne 236, 238
Bonaparte, Napoleon .. *See* Napoleon
Boone, Daniel 144
Booth, John Wilkes 10
Bordino, Battle of 264
Borlaug, Norman 254
Boston Tea Party 206
Bouhours, Dominique 46
Bradford, Sarah H. 152
Brady, James 183
Britain 83, 204, 245, 246, 260
   See also England
Brooks, Phillips 97

Browning, Robert 47
Bruno, Giordano 70
Bryan, William Jennings 98
Bubonic Plague 18
Buck, passing the 191
Bucket (in slaughtering a pig) 21
Buckingham Palace 269
Bull Run, Battle of 216
Bunker Hill, Battle of 205
Burns, George 64
Bush, George W 201
Business .... Chapter 6
Butler Act .... *See* Scopes Trial
Byron, Lord 46

C

Cabot Lodge, Henry 247
Caesar, Julius 258
Calhoun, John 172
California Institute of Technology
 139
Canada 30, 252
Candle, "not fit to hold" 21
Cannon, Joseph 180
Capone, Al 186
Cardiff Giant 48
Carey, William 91
Carillo, Mary 41
Carlyle, Thomas 74
Carnegie, Andrew 107
Carroll, Lewis 12
Carter, Jimmy 224
Carthage 234
Castro, Fidel 197, 228
Catiline, Lucius 234
Cato the Elder 234
Chagall, Marc 50
Challenger, space shuttle 199
Chamberlain, Neville 270
Chamberlain, Wilt 33
Charles I, King 260
Charles II, King 236
Charles V, Roman Emperor 86, 87
Chavez, Cesar 160
Childers, Robert Erskine 267
China 253
Christina, Maria 266
Church of Jesus Christ of Latter-day
 Saints .... *See* Mormons

Churchill, Winston 270, 272
Cicero, Marcus Tullius 234
Civil War 92, 153, 155, 210, 212,
 213, 214, 216, 217, 218
Clarendon, Lord Lieutenant 242
Clark Air Base 255
Clay, Henry 172
Clemens, Samuel ... *See* Twain, Mark
Colbert, Jean-Babtiste 240
Cold War 58, 79, 200, 247, 249, 272
Collins, Michael 146
Comanche Indian tribe 179
Communism 112, 195, 248, 253
Computers 114
Conant, James Bryant 78
Conn, Billy 34
Constitution 164, 166, 168
Cook, Dan 38
Coolidge, Calvin 80, 113
Copernicus, Nicholas 120
Corbett, James 29
Corrigan, Douglas 145
Coughlin, Charles 189
Craig, Jim 39
Crazy Horse 179
Crick, Francis 127, 138
Crocker, Charles 175
Crockett, Davy 174
Cromwell, Oliver 260
Crusades 258
Cuban Missile Crisis 197
Custer, George 179
Czolgosz, Leon 182

D

Dali, Salvador 62
Dana, John Cotton 75
Danton, Georges Jacques 263
Darrow, Clarence 98
Darwin, Charles 16, 128, 133
Davis, Jefferson 212
Decatur, Stephen 210
Declaration of Independence ......
 .... 152, 164, 167, 171
Dederich, Charles 102
DeForest, Lee 115
Dempsey, Jack 26
Diaz, Porfirio 266
Diet of Worms 86

Disraeli, Benjamin 155, 156
Divine Right 260
DNA 127, 138
Dogs 170
Dominoes 226
Duell, Charles H. 128
Durocher, Leo 34

E

Economics .... Chapter 6
Eden, Anthony 247
Edinburgh University 74
Edison, Thomas 15, 125, 129, 130
Edwards, Jonathan 90
Egypt 20, 246
Einstein, Albert 134, 136
Eisenhower, Dwight 194, 226
Electricity 125
Elizabeth I, Queen 142, 236, 238
Elizabeth, Queen *(Queen Mum)*..269
Emmet, Robert 259
Energy Crisis 224
England...22, 155, 156, 236, 238, 270.
    See also Britain
English Civil War 260
English Renaissance 239
English Revolution 261
Entertainment .... Chapter 3
Equal Rights .... Chapter 9
Eruzione, Mike 39
Espartero, Baldomero 266
Esterhazy, Prince 45
Ethiopia 268
Euclid 121
Everett, Edward 218
Evolution 16, 128, 133
Exploration .... Chapter 8

F

Familiar Expressions .... Chapter 1
Faraday, Michael 125
Farouk I 246
Farragut, David 216
Faulkner, William 58
Federal Express Corporation 117
Fermi, Enrico 136
Fermi-Dirac statistics 139
Feynman, Richard 139

Fields, W.C. 95
Fisher, Irving 114
Fitzsimmons, Bob 29
Flying Colors (flags) 8
Ford, Gerald 198, 224
Ford, Henry 109, 129
Forrest, Nathaniel Bedford 217
Fourteen Points, Woodrow Wilson's
    221
Fox, George 90
France 237, 240, 262, 265
Frankfurter, Felix 187
Franklin, Benjamin .. 72, 152, 165, 166
    Poor Richard's Almanac 73
Franklin, James 72
Freaks, in P.T. Barnum's circus 49
Frederick II, King 241
French Revolution 262
Freud, Sigmund 76
Friedman, Milton 117
Fuller, Buckminster 138

G

Gagarin, Yury 147
Galilei, Galileo 120
Gandhi, Mahatma 244
Gauss, Carl Friedrich 124
Geodesic dome 138
Geometry 121
George III, King 152, 167
George VI, King 269
George, David Lloyd 245
Gettysburg Address 218
Gipp, George 32
Gladstone, William 155
Gold Rush 174
Golden Speech, Queen Elizabeth's
    239
Goldwyn, Samuel 60
Goldwynism.. See Goldwyn, Samuel
Gorbachev, Mikhail 200, 248
Grant, Ulysses S. 219
Great Awakening, The 90
Great Depression...30, 112, 114, 116,
    188, 189
Great Dunmow 13
Great Salt Lake 96
Great Wall of China 175

281—Index

Greatest Show on Earth, The..........
.....................*See* Barnum, P.T.
Greek philosophy..............................68
Greeley, Horace..............................174
Griswold, Alfred Whitney..............79
Gulf War.........*See* Persian Gulf War
Gustav V, King.................................26
Gwyn, Nell.....................................236

H

Hail to the Chief............................197
Haise, Fred....................................148
Hale, Sarah Josepha......................129
Hammurabi, King.........................9, 12
Hancock, John................ 152, 167, 207
Hand-shake.....................................14
Hannum, David..............................48
Harding, Chester...........................144
Harold, Childe................................46
Harvard University........ 78, 109, 226
Hatchet...14
Haydn, Franz Joseph......................45
Hayes, Rutherford B.....................177
Hearst, William Randolph...........220
Heatter, Gabriel..............................59
Heisenberg, Werner.....................134
Henry IV, King..............................237
Henry VIII, King............. 89, 236, 238
Henry, Patrick...............................204
Hewitt, Foster.................................30
Hiero II..124
Hill, Joe..157
Hinckley, John..............................183
History, American.........Chapter 10
History, World.............Chapter 12
Hippocrates..................................122
Hippocratic Oath.........................122
Hitler, Adolf............................34, 270
Holmes, Oliver Wendell..............213
Hoover, Herbert.............. 30, 116, 168
Horse, gift..19
Howard, General Oliver..............178
Hunt, John.....................................143
Huss, John.......................................88
Hussein, Saddam..........................229
Huxley, Thomas............................128

I

I am an American speech............. 190
I Have a Dream speech................ 158
Ickes, Harold................................. 190
India.......................91, 102, 244, 252
Industry
  automobile..............................109
  fur...108
  oil..106
  railroad....................................110
  steel...................................107, 111
Ingersoll, Robert............................. 97
International Style (architecture)..54
Iran-Contra affair......................... 228
Iraq... 229
Iraq, War in................................... 229
Ireland............................ 242, 259, 267
Irish Civil War.............................. 267
Iron Curtain.................................. 272
Iron, striking................................... 15
Irvine, Andrew............................. 143
Isabella II....................................... 266
Israel.. 273

J

Jackson, "Stonewall"..................... 216
Jackson, Andrew........... 172, 174, 209
James I, King................................ 142
Jazz Singer, The.............................. 54
Jefferson, Thomas.................. 171, 250
Jeffries, Jim..................................... 29
Jesuits.. 46
Jimmy V Foundation..................... 40
Johnson, Lyndon................... 168, 194
Jolson, Al... 54
Jones, Jesse.................................... 116
Joseph II, Roman Emperor............ 44
Joseph, Chief................................. 178
Jowett, Benjamin............................ 94

K

Kean College................................... 75
Keble, John...................................... 94
Keller, Helen................................. 184
Kennedy, John F. ...168, 194, 196, 250
Keroualle, Louise de..................... 236
Key, Francis Scott......................... 192
Khomeini Ayatollah Ruhollah....254

Khrushchev, Nikita 249, 272
Kidd, Captain 6
King, Jr., Martin Luther 158
Kipling, Rudyard 243
Kissinger, Henry 227
Korean War 8
Kuwait 229

L

La Guardia, Fiorello 190
Laval, Pierre 268
Lawrence, James 208
Lee, Robert E. 214
Lille, University of 126
Lincoln, Abraham 10, 92, 212, 218
Lindberg, Charles 145
Livingston, Dr. David 142
Lombardi, Vince 35
London 108
London Society of Poetry 47
Longstreet, James 214
Louis XIV, King 240
Louis XVI, King 262
Louis, Joe 34
Lovejoy, Elijah Parish 153
Lovell, Jim 148
Luther, Martin 86
Lycurgus 232

M

Macmillan, Harold 246
Mad Hatter 12
Madero, Francisco 267
Madison Square Garden 51
Madison, James 164, 165
Mallory, George 143
Manhattan Project 136
Mann, Horace 71
March to the Sea 215
Marcy, William 209
Marshall, Chaplain Peter 100
Marshall, Chief Justice John 170
Marshall, George 226
Marshall, Thomas 180
Marx Brothers 56
Marx, Groucho 56
Mary Had a Little Lamb 15, 129
Mather, Cotton 72
McAuliffe, Christa 199

McCarthy, Joseph 194
McKinley, William 128, 182
Meir, Golda 273
Mexican Revolution 266
Mexico 266
Michaels, Al 38
Mill, John Stuart 74
Miranda Warnings 161
Miranda, Ernesto .... *See* Miranda
  Warnings
Mobile, Battle of 216
Monica, mother of Saint Augustine
  7
Monkey 16
Montana, Joe 39
Morgan, Henry 6
Morgan, J.P. 111
Mormons 96
Morse Code 176
Morse, Samuel .... *See* Morse Code
Mother Goose 18
Mother Teresa 102
Motta, Dick 38
Mount Everest 143
Mount Pinatubo 255
Mozart, Wolfgang Amadeus 44
Muckraking Movement (journalism)
  112
Mudd, Dr. Samuel 10
Munich Conference 270
Murrow, Edward R. 135
Muskie, Edmund 195
Mussolini, Benito 268
Mutual Assured Destruction (MAD)
  273

N

Naguib, Muhammed 246
Napoleon 264, 265
Napoleonic Wars 265
Narvaez, Ramon 266
NASA 199
National forests 180
National War College 191
Natural family planning 102
Nesbitt, Stephen 199
New College of Oxford 181
New Deal 30, 188
New Harmony 209

Newman, Cardinal John Henry.....94
Nez Pérce Indian tribe...................178
Nicaragua 228
Niebuhr, Reinhold 99
Nixon, Richard 198, 224, 227
Nobel Prize 58, 250
North Carolina State University....40
North, Oliver 228
Notre Dame..32
Nuclear energy 133, 136
Nullification....................................172

O

O'Connell, Daniel 242
Objectivism 82
Olson, Ken.......................................115
Olympic Games.........................26, 38
Operation Desert Storm..*See* Persian Gulf War
Oppenheimer, Robert....................136
Organ (music)...................................17
Orwell, George 78
Otis, James.......................................204
Overpopulation debate 253
Owen, Robert..................................209
Oxford Movement 94
Oxford University............................94

P

Paige, Satchel 31
Papyrus plant 20
Parker, Cynthia Ann......................179
Pasteur, Louis 126
Patent Office 128
Patton, George S.............................222
Pearl Harbor 222
Perpetua, Vivia...............................235
Perry, Oliver Hazard.....................208
Persian Gulf War............................229
Petit, Phillippe 148
Phillips, Wendell............................153
Philosophy .... Chapter 4
Phonograph 15, 129
Pierce, Franklin...............................168
Pints and Quarts.................................7
Pirates 6
Pius XI, Pope...................................268
Pledge of Allegiance......................192
Polio, vaccine..................................135

Polygamy 96
Ponce de Leon, Luis 89
Prescott, William 205
Presidential Oath........................... 168
Prussia... 241
Psychoanalysis................................. 77
Ptolemy I, King of Egypt.............. 121
Puritans... 90
Putnam, Israel 205
Pym, John 261

Q

Quakers... 90
Quanah, Chief Parker 179
Quantum Theory........................... 134

R

Radiation... 132
Radio broadcasts 30, 55, 59, 189
Ragtime music 65
Railroads.................................... 8, 175
Raleigh, Sir Walter 142
Rand, Ayn... 82
Rankin, Jeannette........................... 220
Rayburn, Sam................................. 194
Reagan, Nancy 26
Reagan, Ronald.. 26, 32, 183, 200, 228
Religion .... Chapter 5
   Catholicism…......…....86, 237, 268
   Christianity…..88, 89, 91, 235, 258
   Church of England……..….......94
   Mormonism….......….............…96
   Muslim…......…..........….254, 258
   Protestantism…......….........86, 237
   Puritans…......…..........….......…90
   Quakers…......…........…......…..90
   Religious Society of Friends…..90
   War and Religion   92
Remington, Frederick 220
Ring Around the Rosy.................... 18
Roaring Twenties 81, 113, 114
Robespierre, Maximilien.............. 263
Rockefeller, John D....................... 106
Rockne, Knute.................................. 32
Rogers, Will 57
Rohe, Ludwig Mies van der 54
Roman Empire 234, 235, 258
Roman Inquisition......................... 70
Romans 7

Roosevelt, Franklin...30, 112, 136, 168, 188, 222
Roosevelt, Theodore 77, 182
Rushdie, Salman 254
Russell, Bill 33
Russia 264, 268
Ruth, Babe 30
Rutherford, Ernest 132
Ryland, Sr., Pastor John 91

S

Sacco, Nicola 185
Saint Ambrose 7
Saint Andrews, University of......... 74
Saint Augustine 7
Saint Francis of Assisi 69
Salamanca, University of 89
Salk, Jonas 135
Sanderson, James 197
Satanic Verses, The....*See* Rushdie, Salman
Schmeling, Max 34
Schrank, John 183
Schroeder, Patricia 160
Schurz, Carl 210
Schwab, Charles 107
Schwarzkopf, Norman 228
Science .... Chapter 7
   astronomy 120
   chemistry 126
   genetics 127, 132, 138
   hydrostatics 124
   nuclear physics..132, 133, 136, 139
   physics 125, 134
Scopes Trial 98
Scopes, John T .... *See* Scopes Trial
Selassie I, Haile 268
Selfridge, Harry Gordon 108
September 11th 201
Serenity Prayer 99
Severus, Septimus 235
Shakespeare, William 17, 239
Shaw, George Bernard 58
Sherman, William 215
Sieyes, Emmanuel 263
Sing Sing Prison 109
Singh, Dr. Karan 252
Smith, Frederick 116
Smith, Joseph 96

Smoot, Reid 96
Socrates 68
Soule, John 175
Soviet Union 200, 247, 272
Space exploration 146
Space exploration 148
Spain 266
Spanish Armada 238
Spanish Inquisition 89
Spanish-American War 220
Sparta 232
Spiro, Agnew 224
Spooner, Reverend William 181
Spoonerism 181
Sports .... Chapter 2
   baseball 30, 31, 34, 36
   basketball 33, 38, 40
   boxing 26, 28, 34
   decathlon 26
   football 32, 35, 39
   hockey 30, 38
   pentathlon 26
   tennis 27, 41
   track and field 26
   wrestling 14
Stalin, Joseph 248, 268
Stamp Act 204
Stanley, Sir Henry Morton 142
Star-Spangled Banner 193
Steffens, Lincoln 112
Stimson, Henry 186
Stowe, Harriet Beecher 212
Strenuous Life speech 77
Stuart, Mary 238
Suffrage, women's
   Anthony, Susan B. 156
   Schroeder, Patricia 160
   Truth, Sojourner 154
Sullivan, Anne 184
Sullivan, John L. 28
Super Bowl (football) 39
Superstition 133
Surrealist Movement (painting) 62
Swigert, Jack 148
Synanon 102

T

Talleyrand, Charles Maurice de.. 264
Teach, Edward 6

285—Index

Technology .... Chapter 7
Telegraph 176
Telephone 176
Teresa, Mother ...... *See* Mother Teresa
Texas 174
Thaw, Harry 51
Thorpe, Jim 26
Thrush 23
Tilden, Bill 27
Tracterianism 94
Trojan War 19
Trudeau, Pierre Elliott 252
Truman, Harry 191
Truth, Sojourner 154
Tubman, Harriet 152
Tunney, Gene 26
Twain, Mark 52
Twin Towers ..... *See* World Trade Center
Tyndale, William 88
Tzarapkin, Semyon 247

U

Uncertainty Principle 134
Uncle Don .... *See* Carney, Don
Uncle Tom's Cabin 212
Underground Railroad 153
Unions, worker 157, 160
United Nations 223
United States .... Chapters 10, 11
United States Military Academy at West Point 82
Urban II, Pope 258

V

Vail, Alfred 176
Valvano, Jim 40
Van Buren, Martin 209
Vanderbilt, Cornelius 110
Vanderbilt, William 110
Vanzetti, Bartolomeo 185
Vest, George 170
Vienna 45
Vietnam 198, 227
Volcanoes 18, 255
Voltaire 70

W

War of 1812 .... 193, 208, 210
War, America at .... Chapter 11
War, World at .... Chapter 13
Warhol, Andy 62
Warner, H.M. 115
Warner, Pop 27
Washington and Lee University ... 99
Washington, George 164, 166
Watergate scandal 198
Watson, James 127, 138
Watson, Thomas A. 176
Watson, Thomas J. 114
Watson, Thomas, Jr 115
Webster, Daniel 170
Welch, Joseph 194
Westminster College 272
White Man's Burden 243
White, Stanford 51
Wild Goose Chase 17
Wilde, Oscar 50
Wilson, Harold 83
Wilson, Woodrow 112, 221
Wittenburg, Germany 86
Wood, Charles 242
World Trade Center 148, 201
World War I 220, 221
World War II ... 59, 133, 137, 191, 222, 226, 269
Wright Brothers 129, 146
Wright, Frances 208
Wrong-Way Corrigan...*See* Corrigan, Douglas
Wycliffe, John 88

X

Xiaoping, Deng 253

Y

Yale University 79, 114, 116
Yancey, William 212
Young, Brigham 96

Z

Zapata, Emliliano 266
Zedong, Mao 253
Zionist Movement 273

Homecourt Publishers
Quick Order Form

Fax Orders:	(864) 232-7108. Just send this form.
Phone Orders:	1-800-648-8191. Toll free – have your credit card ready.
e-mail orders:	orders@homecourtpublishers.com
Postal Orders:	Homecourt Publishers 2435 East North St., Box #245 Greenville, SC 29615-1442

Please send me ____ copies of "What Made Them Say That?"
I understand that I may return any of them for a full refund. No questions asked.

Cost: $16.95 per book
   Deduct 10% from total if ordering 3 to 6 books.
   Deduct 25% from total if ordering over 6 books.
   Shipping: Add $4.50 for first book. $2.00 for each additional.
   (Please add 5.0% sales tax if shipped to South Carolina address)
   (extended discounts available for educators)

Name: _____
Address: _____
City: _____ State: ____ Zip: _____
Telephone: _____ e-mail: _____
Payment: ☐ Check: ☐ Credit Card:
                              ___Visa   ___MasterCard
Card Number: _____
Name on Card: _____ Exp. Date _____

I know, we forgot one...

If we missed one of history's great quotations and the exciting story behind it, please let us know. Just write to us with the quote and, of course, a brief description explaining *"what made them say that."* You can e-mail it, fax it, or send it to the above address. **If you are also ordering books, we'll discount you 30%.** Happy hunting!